Global Women Leaders

Global Women Leaders

Studies in Feminist Political Rhetoric

Edited by
Michele Lockhart and Kathleen Mollick

LEXINGTON BOOKS
Lanham • Boulder • New York • London

Published by Lexington Books
An imprint of The Rowman & Littlefield Publishing Group, Inc.
4501 Forbes Boulevard, Suite 200, Lanham, Maryland 20706
www.rowman.com

16 Carlisle Street, London W1D 3BT, United Kingdom

Copyright © 2014 by Lexington Books

All rights reserved. No part of this publication may be reproduced, stored in a retrieval system, or transmitted in any form or by any means, electronic, mechanical, photocopying, recording, or otherwise, without the prior permission of the publisher.

British Library Cataloguing in Publication Information Available
Library of Congress Cataloging-in-Publication Data Available

ISBN 978-0-7391-9342-6 (electronic)
ISBN 978-1-4985-0321-1 (pbk : alk, paper)

∞^{TM} The paper used in this publication meets the minimum requirements of American National Standard for Information Sciences—Permanence of Paper for Printed Library Materials, ANSI/NISO Z39.48-1992.

Printed in the United States of America

Contents

Introduction   vii
Janet M. Martin

PART I: THE ELIZABETHS: WOMEN AND LEADERSHIP IN THE UNITED KINGDOM

1   "The Heart of a King": Gender Components Affecting the Leadership and Political Rhetoric of Elizabeth I   3
Charlotte Evans

2   Queen Elizabeth II and Princess Diana: Saving the Monarchy   19
Kathleen Mollick

PART II: MAATHAI, OGOT, AND NGILU: WOMEN AND LEADERSHIP IN KENYA

3   Environmental Conservation, Peace, Democracy, and Development: A Case Study of Wangari Maathai's Speeches   41
Catherine Waithera Mwangi and Oscar Gakuo Mwangi

4   The "Extension of Self in Service": An Analysis of Female Kenyan Political Leaders   65
Joy Williams-Black

PART III: WHEN NATIONS UNITE: A GLOBAL COMMUNITY OF FEMALE LEADERS IN THE UNITED NATIONS

5 Women's Rhetorical Leadership within the United Nations 89
   Valerie M. Hennings and Laura Steckman

6 Samantha Power: Before and After "Hell" 109
   William Carney

PART IV: GLOBAL FIGURES: SOCIAL ISSUES AND SOCIAL MEDIA

7 Assessing the Rhetoric of Sheikha Moza: Mistress of *Ethos* 127
   Mohanalakshmi Rajakumar

8 Religiously Gendered: Online Political Discourse in the 2011 Egyptian Revolution 145
   Nicole Khoury

Bibliography 163

Index 177

About the Contributors 181

Introduction
Janet M. Martin

As we approach the twentieth anniversary of the 1995 United Nations Fourth World Conference on Women held in Beijing, Michele Lockhart and Kathleen Mollick have brought together a fascinating collection of chapters from scholars around the world for inclusion in the volume *Global Women Leaders: Studies in Feminist Political Rhetoric*. Among the speakers at that conference was First Lady Hillary Clinton. Her address to the conference members included a memorable line: "human rights are women's rights and women's rights are human rights."[1] The words were heard around the globe, and often quoted. At that time rights for women were limited—not only in Beijing, but in many countries around the world. Clinton's words put her on the global stage as an advocate of women's rights. Human rights became a part of a lexicon that transcended state boundaries. Yet the significance of that conference probably resonated more with women than men. And it was women political leaders that especially embraced the words spoken at that conference.[2]

Christopher Heurlin, Ph.D., an expert in Chinese politics, has noted the change in the sense of empowerment of women before and after the conference in Beijing. The conference brought members of non-governmental organizations (NGOs) to Beijing, introducing institutional structures in which women in Beijing could place themselves and their agenda in a broader, worldwide context. As a result, the conference had a large impact on the nascent NGO community in China—including on the Communist-controlled All China's Women's Federation (ACFW), a mass organization. In the run up to the conference, ACFW delegates joined a series of international meetings of NGOs and were surprised by the clout held by NGOs. The conference also led the ACFW to empower grassroots women's NGOs in China, as the ACFW held dozens of NGO workshops teaching the fundamentals of non-governmental organization to grassroots groups. The conference even led to transformations in the ACFW itself, marking the first time that the Chinese government referred to the mass organization as a "Non-governmental organization to elevate women's status."[3]

Global Women gives life to the rhetoric of women leaders. And *Global Women* helps explain why words are significant and effective, especially with women around the world. Language has been a means for women in many parts of the world to gain and maintain political authority, as well as to establish a universal policy agenda. The impact of the Fourth World Conference on Women has been magnified as speeches at the conference were recorded and have since been made available worldwide via YouTube. As a case in point, Hillary Clinton's address for diplomatic delegates has become known as the "Women's Rights Are Human Rights" speech. In an essay in the edited volume *Political Women: Language and Leadership*, Nancy Myers notes the scholarly attention given to Hillary's speech. A generally positive reception is given the speech by Western observers, yet the difference in the reception of the speech by non-Western women leaders illustrates the complexity in the delivery of a speech and its perception by targeted audiences.[4]

The chapters that follow all have a common theme: language matters and is empowering in and of itself. As efforts have been made over the past thirty years to remove gender bias in language, reflecting the power of language in placing limitations on women, their roles, goals, and aspirations, this volume is particularly enlightening in demonstrating the positive power of language. International political women have a voice, and have been using that voice in gaining political power and with it political authority. As Mary Tucker-McLaughlin and Kenneth Campbell have noted, in order for global change for women, the establishment and reinforcement of collective memory through speeches by women leaders as well as actions, journalistic accounts of that action, and scholarly analysis of the rhetoric and actions all must take place.[5] Hillary Clinton's 2008 run for the presidency in the United States illustrates the more complicated task of achieving political office, while her service for four years as secretary of state illustrates the power of her rhetoric (as well as her policy influence in a high-level foreign policy post). Maria Daxenbichler and Rochelle Gregory provide an excellent summary of the obstacles to Hillary's run as president in 2008.[6]

One commonality and contribution of this series of chapters is the study of women leaders working within the constraints of culture, religion, tradition, and history. The chapters serve a dual purpose, providing richness for those studying global women leaders and political authority, as well as for those studying language. Several chapters draw upon context for analysis of language as a tool for leadership.

The chapters are arranged first by regions of the world, with the first two chapters focusing on women and leadership in the United Kingdom, and the next two chapters looking at women who are leaders in Kenya and on the international stage. The third section has a focus on women leaders in the United Nations. Such an order emphasizes that women leaders are truly a global phenomenon. Finally, in the last section, two chapters look at the effect of modern communication in establishing women as global leaders, and how the use of modern communication broadens how the words of women can instantly reach both a local and international audience.

THE ELIZABETHS: WOMEN AND LEADERSHIP IN THE UNITED KINGDOM

The first two chapters focus on two monarchs of England who shared a name, Elizabeth. While the twenty-first century may be declared the "Century of Women," women have held leadership roles for centuries. The written speeches of Queen Elizabeth I allow for gender analysis of the rhetoric of women leaders dating back to the 1500s. One can see the challenges faced by future women leaders in the emphasis on motherhood or the absence thereof, in analyzing the first Elizabeth. In her analysis of Queen Elizabeth I in the chapter, "'The Heart of a King': Gender Components Affecting the Leadership and Political Rhetoric of Elizabeth I," Charlotte Evans confirms the transcendence of gender as an analytic construct of methodological significance.

In the past fifty years women as leaders and women as mothers have often been discussed as mutually exclusive roles. But the chapters on the two British monarchs illustrate that this debate goes back centuries, not decades. In fact, global women leaders have found a power in language which can reinforce power found through positions of authority. Evans illustrates this point in writing about the speech given by Elizabeth I as she addressed her troops the night before England faced the Spanish Armada in 1588. Each queen experienced a crisis of confidence, and each turned to rhetoric to reinforce their authority.

In a world so different in every way, the crisis Elizabeth II faced was properly resolved by carefully chosen words to honor the memory of a beloved Princess, Diana, the mother of a future King.

Elizabeth I and Elizabeth II both faced a challenge to the monarchy and responded with a speech to their subjects that affirmed their leadership and support for the monarchy itself. The personal lives of two monarchs separated in time by four centuries could not be more different. Elizabeth I remained single and childless, at times offering herself as mother and protector to her subjects. Elizabeth also invoked divine status for herself. In "Queen Elizabeth II and Princess Diana: Saving the Monarchy," Kathleen Mollick notes in her chapter, in contrast, Elizabeth II is a mother of four, grandmother, and great-grandmother. Yet gender influences how both women have handled crises, vastly different, yet similar in the survival of the monarchy. Elizabeth II has recently ensured that the monarchy will pass to the first-born child, regardless of gender, beginning with the rule of Prince William.

The importance of gender in an analysis of Elizabeth and Elizabeth II as political leaders, one choosing to rule as a virgin queen, yet also invoking divine status for herself and noting she was the daughter of a king, and the other queen embracing motherhood, comes through in subsequent chapters as well.

MAATHAI, OGOT, AND NGILU: WOMEN AND LEADERSHIP IN KENYA

In the next section, two chapters on global women leaders of Kenya again draw upon the multiple roles of women leaders, including that of mother. In the world and language of Maathai, Ogot, and Ngilu, an agenda inclusive of women is a given. The chapter illustrates the scope of women's political leadership. More importantly, the significance of time and place—that is, the country of origin, as a variable in gender analysis is vividly demonstrated in looking at global women leaders in Kenya.

In their chapter, "Environmental Conservation, Peace, Democracy, and Development: A Case Study of Wangari Maathai's Speeches," Catherine Waithera Mwangi and Oscar Gakuo Mwangi focus on the work and speech of the late Wangari Maathai. Maathai's work began locally, with a focus on environmental conservation. She went on to receive the Nobel Peace prize, which automatically conferred an international and global status on her work. Women in Kenya have not made in-roads into the male-dominated Parliament. But women have moved forward on an agenda with a focus on the work and speeches of the late Wangari Maathai.

Joy William-Black's chapter, "The 'Extension of Self in Service': An Analysis of Female Kenyan Political Leaders," introduces the concept of "the extension of self in service,"[7] a part of Kenyan culture which allows one to see the shared experiences of women defining leadership in part through service to others. Women's roles as mother, politician, minister, and business leader share a commonality in that women are extending themselves as mothers and wives in a nurturing role in a greater service to others. The lens of women themselves in a particular cultural setting broadens our understanding of political leadership and gender.

WHEN NATIONS UNITE: A GLOBAL COMMUNITY OF FEMALE LEADERS IN THE UNITED NATIONS

Valerie M. Hennings and Laura Steckman's study of "Women's Rhetorical Leadership within the United Nations," draws upon the context in which speeches are delivered—in this case, looking at speeches delivered before the General Assembly with a focus on the actions of women representatives through their speaking on issues regarding the United Nation (UN). In their analysis, the context of the speeches is important and constant across all cases. And the context provides a powerful venue for these speeches to be delivered. The content of the speeches is also important, and addressed in looking at the inclusion of provisions regarding the UN's Millennium Development Goals in addressing global poverty.

William Carney's chapter, "Samantha Power: Before and After 'Hell,'" looks at Samantha Power, U.S. ambassador to the United Nations, with Cabinet rank in the Obama administration. She has been navigating through the constraints of two institutions—the United Nations, and the administration of the presidency of Barack Obama. Power is one of the top foreign policy advisors of the president, institutionally, and by virtue of having worked for Obama in his Senate office and as a senior advisor in foreign policy in the 2008 presidential campaign. It is her persuasive writing skills on the most important of issues—human rights and genocide—which catapulted her to being one of the top foreign policy experts in the Obama administration, with a worldwide following, before achieving this structurally important position in the administration.

Power is unique among Cabinet members in a career path which included a career as an investigative journalist. Not only does Power demonstrate the power of language in establishing herself as a global leader with an ability to focus international attention on issues of human rights and genocide through her prize-winning writing, her activism and expertise on these issues coupled with her writing opened other forums for leadership.

Samantha Power's rhetoric led to her post as U.S. ambassador to the United Nations, as senator and candidate Barack Obama took note of her words. In fact, Samantha Power's powerful rhetoric is now limited, due to the position she holds. She is a part of an administration, and can't use the same rhetoric in her diplomatic post to bring attention to issues, so the authority she commands in office can restrain the power she had through her voice.

GLOBAL FIGURES: SOCIAL ISSUES AND SOCIAL MEDIA

The authors of the chapters in this section analyze public discourse of women political leaders, both through traditional media sources and social media.

Sheikha Moza Bint Nasser, wife of the former emir of the state of Qatar, and mother of the current emir, is the subject of a chapter by Mohanalakshmi Rajakumar entitled, "Assessing the Rhetoric of Sheikha Moza: Mistress of *Ethos*." Wife and motherhood again become important in an analysis of Sheikha Moza. Her global leadership is revealed as a balance between two worlds—she is a woman in a Muslim country restrained by religion, cultural, and gender norms, yet she has successfully established an international role, serving as the United Nation's Educational, Scientific and Cultural Organization's (UNESCO) Special Envoy for Basic and Higher Education as a well as an ambassador of the United Nations and a member of UN Groups. She is a role model in how women leaders through words and actions can navigate two very different worlds, achieving respect and an agenda shift in both worlds. Building on Islam's emphasis on education, Sheikha Moza's leadership at home and abroad has enabled a world class education to be brought to the women in Qatar, thus accommodating Islam's traditionalist values which place limits on advanced education for women. The attention and coverage given to Sheikha Moza both in Western media and Arab media affirms her leadership role on the global stage, as evident in her eldest daughter's ability to take on a similar role.

Asmaa Mahfouhz, one of the founders of the movement that led to the 2011 revolution in Egypt, is the focus of the final chapter, "Religiously Gendered: Online Political Discourse in the 2011 Egyptian Revolution," by Nicole Khoury. YouTube and video blogs illustrate the pervasiveness of social media and its ability to provide a non-Western context to analyze powerful rhetorical discourse. The increasing role of that discourse is defining leadership with such rapid advances in communications technology that the study of language, political authority, and leadership will continue to expand, as will the ability of women to increasingly use this technology to become global leaders. This is a study that draws upon the richness of context for an analysis of language as a tool for leadership.

In this edited collection one major contribution and commonality is the study of women leaders working within the constraints of culture, religion, tradition, history, and institutions. Rhetoric is bounded and shaped by these constraints, yet as is often the case with the global women leaders in this volume, words, language, and rhetoric have empowered these women to take on roles beyond these constraints to become global leaders. Leadership can require political office, but the power of words can yield the same authority as political office.

The chapters in *Global Women Leaders: Studies in Feminist Political Rhetoric* put such issues as education, development, the environment, human rights, and political office, at the forefront. The authors of the chapters that follow look at the power of language, and how it has transformed the political landscape around the world. The authors in *Global Women* all contribute to a "collective memory," which will make it easier for women to achieve high political office in the future. Hillary Clinton is poised to run for the top political office in the United States in 2016 with the backing of President Barack Obama who narrowly defeated her for the Democratic Party nomination in 2008. The party nomination in the United States by one of the top two parties—Democrats or Republicans—is a prerequisite for winning the presidency. Clinton not only has contributed to a "collective memory" needed for success at the top, but also will benefit from her role as a global woman leader and from the words, actions, and coverage of other global women featured in the scholarly analyses in this volume.

NOTES

1. Tyler, Patrick E., "Hillary Clinton, in China, Details Abuse of Women," *New York Times*, A-10, September 6, 1995, accessed April 30, 2014, www.nytimes.com/1995/09/06/world/hillary-clinton-in-China-details-abuse-of-women.

2. In 1998, when President Bill Clinton was in Beijing and was asked a question about human rights in the United States, he failed to make the connection between a landmark U.S. Supreme Court ruling on sexual harassment and the status of women's rights as human rights. For further discussion see Janet M. Martin *The Presidency and Women: Promise, Performance and Illusion* (College Station: Texas A & M University Press, 2003).

3. Based on several conversations with Chris Heurlin between 2012 and 2014, and email exchanges in May, 2014. For more detailed discussion see Qiusha Ma, *Non-Governmental Organizations in Contemporary China: Paving the Way to a Civil Society?* (London and New York: Routledge, 2006).

4. Nancy Myers, "Western Women's *Ethos* and a Response to Privilege: Advocacy in Hillary Rodham Clinton's 'Women's Rights Are Human Rights,'" in Michele Lockhart and Kathleen Mollick, eds. *Political Women: Language and Leadership* (Lanham: Lexington Books, 2013).

5. Mary Tucker-McLaughlin and Kenneth Campbell, "Media and Hillary Clinton's Political Leadership: A Model for Understanding Construction of Collective Memory," in Michele Lockhart and Kathleen Mollick, eds. *Political Women: Language and Leadership* (Lanham: Lexington Books, 2013).

6. See Maria Daxenbichler and Rochelle Gregory, "Electing the Commander in Chief: The Gender Regime and Hillary Clinton's 2008 Campaign Rhetoric," in Michele Lockhart and Kathleen Mollick, eds. *Political Women: Language and Leadership* (Lanham: Lexington Books, 2013).

7. The "extension of self in service" first appeared in Williams-Black's dissertation, "*The Expansion of Higher Education for Kenyans, with Special Emphasis on Women, 1959–1969*" (Ph.D. diss., University of Illinois Urbana-Champaign, 2008). However, Williams-Black was unable to explore the paradigm in greater detail since her research focused on study abroad. Williams-Black originally became aware of this term while completing dissertation fieldwork in Nairobi, Kenya 2004; Charity Ngilu discussed why she extended herself in service while running for president a second time, on Cheche News Program, "Interview with Charity Ngilu," September 5, 2012, accessed April 23, 2014, www.citizennews.co.ke/.

Part One

THE ELIZABETHS: WOMEN AND LEADERSHIP IN THE UNITED KINGDOM

Chapter One

"The Heart of a King"

Gender Components Affecting the Leadership and Political Rhetoric of Elizabeth I

Charlotte Evans

Despite a significant prejudice against political rulers during the early modern period, Elizabeth I successfully used her gender and, at the same time, transcended gender-based identity throughout her reign. To various degrees, this opinion has emerged in the body of scholarship pertaining to Elizabeth I's reign and the broader political and social culture of her day. The editor of *Elizabeth I: Collected Works*, Mary Beth Rose, argued that "Elizabeth I's gender constrained and paradoxically enabled her."[1] Perhaps more importantly, that Elizabeth I did nothing as obvious as "identify fervently and consistently with the roles of virgin and mother."[2] Just the opposite seems far closer to the truth.

As shall be argued here, Elizabeth I developed a leadership style and political rhetoric to overcome the constraints of her gender through several particular strategies. First, and especially during the early years of her reign, she addressed the constraints of her gender directly and found a means to contextualize her role as monarch to the more traditional and acceptable female roles of virgin and mother. Second, and more obviously toward the end of her reign, she used her position as a woman to wield political authority and to exercise power in foreign policy. Third, and most importantly, she found a means to transcend the limitations of a gender-based identity, defining and representing herself as an authority beyond gender itself.

In addition to discussing Elizabeth I's particular approach to leadership and rhetoric, this chapter will also examine the development of Elizabeth I's particular brand of leadership—the overarching strategy and style she developed to represent herself and her authority, as well as her tactics for wielding that considerable authority in a public sphere. In particular, the discussion will consider ways in which Elizabeth I's brand was anything but linear; how, in some instances, her political and rhetorical representations were reactionary, and, in others, too radical to be immediately acceptable.

"MONSTROUS REGIMENT": ELIZABETH ADDRESSES THE CONSTRAINTS OF GENDER

When Elizabeth I came to the throne in 1558, the immediate circumstances of her ascension were unfavorable.[3] The problem of gender was especially acute, in fact, because of the one historical and the two immediate examples of female monarchs in England. The only queen of England, excepting Elizabeth I herself, her half-sister Mary I, and their cousin, Lady Jane Grey, had an abortive reign in in the twelfth century.

Although there was no question of her legitimacy and no doctrine divisions of the church to contend with, as there were in Elizabeth I and Mary I's day, Matilda's ascension triggered civil war in England, popularly known as the Anarchy.[4] Matilda was the wife of the Holy Roman Emperor. She also had a male heir, the future Henry II. On two counts, she performed her duty and conformed to the standards for female royals.[5] In spite of this, though, Matilda faced opposition from the Church; so much so, in fact that her male cousin usurped the throne and forced her into exile. The resultant Anarchy, as it was popularly known, lasted from 1135 to 1153 and caused considerable political instability. The crown changed hands several times although Matilda had been the legitimate daughter and named heir of Henry I. This was because the nobility had divided loyalties—while many recognized the legitimacy of Matilda's claim, many others were reluctant to accept a woman as their principle leader. This destabilized the political power.[6]

Although the daily happenings for ordinary folk did not change all that much, instability at the top of the hierarchy did little to support the higher functioning of the nation. There was only a final resolution when Matilda's son, Henry II, reached maturity and was able to essentially force the usurper Stephen to accept him as his heir.

The abortive reign of Jane Grey and the five-year reign of Mary Tudor proved problematic as well. Jane Grey was queen for a full nine days, in the midst of political unrest and popular dissent tied to the problem of who should succeed Edward VI—his Catholic sister, Mary, or his Protestant cousin, Jane Grey. The popular depiction of Mary, in the end, was equally unsuccessful. She was eventually called "Bloody Mary" because of her religious policies and the many burnings of Protestants and most considered her reign a consummate failure. "Positive achievements there were none," said Tudor historian, G.R. Elton, in his comprehensive study of Tudor England,[7] insisting that even the evidence of financial and administrative recovery, following the power struggles from 1547 to 1552, was not attributable to Mary. As A.F. Pollard famously said, as well, "sterility was the conclusive note of Mary's reign,"[8] leaving no particularly positive feeling about female rulers at the time of Elizabeth I's ascension in 1552.

Although the accession of Mary I and Elizabeth I coincided with the emergence of the prominence of several other female rulers in Europe,[9] such women had to demonstrate virtues often entirely contrary to those ascribed to typical women.[10] Indeed, the increase in the number of female rulers in Europe created a conundrum alongside the increased complexity of theories of government and leadership.[11]

The Scottish theoretician, John Knox, published *First Blast of the Trumpet Against the Monstrous Regiment of Women* to make public his sentiments on the illegitimacy of female rule. Indeed, Knox's text offers copious examples of the negative depiction of female rulers. His language also expounds on the type of imagery applied to depict female rulers in the popular consciousness. Particularly striking, in fact, is the vision of the "monstrous empire of a cruel woman" and the conception that the counsel of women is "wicked," using the example of Eve and her so-called counsel to Adam that caused man's fall.[12]

As Cristy Beemer outlines in her study of "The Female Monarch," in which she largely compares the rhetorical strategies of Mary I and Elizabeth I, when Elizabeth I came to the throne in 1558, she did so as "a single woman in a traditionally male role,"[13] and needed to "establish iterations of power that [would provide] a strong image."[14] More immediately, perhaps, than at any other time in her reign, during the first years, Elizabeth I also needed to confront the constraints of her gender and the popular belief that women could not rule effectively—that being a ruler was outside the scope of female skill, perhaps.

Rose argues that Elizabeth I addressed the constraints of gender up until 1563.[15] Indeed, Rose's argument, very much supported by a textual review of Elizabeth I's public speeches, is that Elizabeth I basically established a context for her reign in the early years, from 1558 to about 1563, with powerful and frequent comparisons between her role as queen and the traditional female roles of virgin, mother, and even maiden.[16]

Elizabeth I's first speech before Parliament, delivered on February 10, 1559, offers perhaps the best and among the most famous examples of this developed and careful comparison.[17] Describing the duty of a female ruler, Elizabeth I acknowledged the petition she had received from Parliament about their desire for her to marry. She then moved on to declare that she appreciated their concern but, in effect, her first duty was to her people. She argued, in essence, that the role of a queen equated to that of a wife and mother, making it necessary for her to remain an actual virgin or maid so as to be faithful to her first charge.

In the opening of the speech delivered to Parliament, she expresses her displeasure that she had been petitioned to marry at all. She insisted that it was "not much pleasing"[18] that she had been petitioned to marry but that the sentiment—the desire to have her marry—at least, was "most acceptable."[19] Like a mother accepting the erring behaviors of a child, she chided the House of Commons in her response but also chose to interpret their actions and their petition, as a sign of their "goodwill."[20]

From this seemingly understanding and forgiving stance, Elizabeth I proceeds to stress not only the absoluteness of her authority but also the importance of her personal will. "I have been ever persuaded," she said, "that I was born by God to consider and, above all things, do those which appertain until His glory."[21] In other words, she understood better than her people, that she should remain single.

Elizabeth I stresses the absoluteness of her own authority in answer to the petition and on two counts. "I must commend you," she says, "that you have not appointed me a husband. For that were unworthy the majesty of an absolute princess, and the secretion of you that are born my subjects."[22] She thus stresses the nature of her relationship to her people, the nature of her "majesty" as "absolute."[23] She then immediately follows this declaration by inferring that God specifically ordains this position: "if God have ordained me to another course of life," she says, "I will promise you to do nothing to the prejudice of the commonwealth."[24]

Whatever the best intentions of her people and their understanding of what is in the nation's best interests, Elizabeth I had a better understanding of the best outcome by virtue of her position as queen. She also, as she specifically states in two points, had the benefit of understanding her queenly role as being that of a mother and a wife. Indeed, she argues that her decision to remain unmarried is an act of loyalty to her people as well as her adherence to God's will. "I have made choice of this kind of life, which is most free and agreeable for such human affairs as may tend to His service only"[25] she insists. "The public charge of the kingdom,"[26] however, changes the definition of duty for Elizabeth I. To contemplate marriage, while she has the duties of the kingdom to consider and while she is not inclined to marriage by God, is "an inconsiderate folly."[27]

Having laid this foundation and implied that an ordinary marriage, for her, would distract from higher duties, Elizabeth I applies the specific metaphor that equates her rule to a marriage. "To conclude," she says, "I am already bound unto a husband, which is the kingdom of England."[28] She adds, too, that her relationship to the people of England compares to a mother's relationship with her children. "Every one of you," she says, "and as many as are English, are my children and kinsfolk."[29]

As Rose suggests in her review of all Elizabeth I's public speeches, in this early speech, one of her first before Parliament, Elizabeth I uses language to carefully contextualize her position as queen and to build her authority in a manner that would, no doubt, have resonated with her audience. She speaks in the first person with obvious authority. She clearly expresses her opinion about her Parliament's actions and undercuts their authority by branding their act as misguided. She then builds her own image through her argument and through her word choices, labeling herself as a wife and mother, even as she establishes that her will is important than her counselors.

"A THING APPROPRIATE TO MY SEX": ELIZABETH USES GENDER TO WIELD AUTHORITY

Considering Elizabeth I's second speech to Parliament on the subject of her marriage, delivered January 28, 1563, in response to another petition for her to marry, she was quick to appreciate how to apply her gender to craft authority and take ownership of a political situation. Responding to a second address from Parliament, in her 1563 speech, Elizabeth I opens by declaring that she has understood the request from the Commons but nonetheless struggles with it. "The weight and greatness of this matter," she says, "might cause me, being a woman wanting both with and memory, some fear to speak and bashfulness besides, a thing appropriate to my sex."[30] Before, she sought to frame her authority according to the traditional female roles.[31] In this speech, she applies her gender as a tool. Her gender, her literally, "being a woman," provides a means for her to deflect or at least the potential for deflection.

Although she insists that she may, on the one hand, lack the capacity to understand because she is a woman, her second point is really to undercut this perspective entirely. If she were only a woman, the problem of her marriage would be overwhelming. As it is, "the princely seat and kingly throne" under her influence also empowers her. It may be "grievous . . . to your ears," she says, but "this so great a demand needeth both great and grave advice."[32] In other words, as she proceeds to reiterate, the matter is too weighty for her to think on and decide on in any reasonable amount of time. In part, this weightiness is also because of her "kingly throne" and the authority that bestows.

As she did in the 1559 speech to Parliament on the subject of her marriage, Elizabeth I then contextualizes her role as king. She acknowledges the reasoning for Parliament's request, their apparent lack of appreciation for her special position and their judgment that she does, perhaps, want "both wit and memory."[33] Whatever their estimation may have been, though, she quickly establishes her position as one chosen by God, her authority and inclinations thus divinely inspired.[34]

Elizabeth I also alludes to a life-threatening illness she had, at the time of the speech, quite recently overcome:

> Although God of late seemed to touch me rather like one that He chastised than one he punished, and though death possessed almost every joint of me, so as I wished then that the feeble threat of life . . . might . . . have quietly been cut off, yet desired I not then life . . . so much for my own safety, as for yours . . . I know now as well as I did before that I am mortal. I know also that I must seek to discharge myself of that great burden that God hath laid upon me; for of them to whom much is committed, much is required. Think not that I, that in other matters have had convenient care of you all, will in this matter touching the safety of myself and you all be careless.[35]

With subtlety, she stresses her importance and reaffirms her God-given status. Her argument, in effect, is that her survival was necessary or at least the best outcome for her people. Elizabeth I then extends this argument, undercutting Parliament's demands, with the declaration that she has a perhaps inherent mindfulness of her people. She has a care for them and knowledge of what is best, equal to the instincts of a mother toward the interests of her child. Rather, she chides her audience and warns that "I will discharge some restless heads in those brains the needless hammers beat with vain judgment that I should dislike their petition."[36] In no uncertain terms here, she emphasizes her intellectual superiority and her superior understanding of the political problems in question. She accepts the sentiment of the petition and that her subjects delivered it to her out of genuine concern for her well being as much as for theirs. She simultaneously rejects its foundation, however, because of her innate authority and her motherly position of superiority. She concludes her speech with an interesting summation and evocation of this: "And so I assure you all," she says, "that though after my death you may have many stepdames, yet shall you never have any a more mother than I unto you all."[37] In other words, she concludes her speech, forceful though it otherwise has been, with a reminder to her people that she is a mother figure. She is a mother above all else.

ELIZABETH'S LEADERSHIP STRATEGY AND HER TRANSCENDENCE OF GENDER

From 1563 onward, Elizabeth I rarely referred to her gender directly and even more rarely referred to herself in the role of wife or mother.[38] As Rose argues, in fact, Elizabeth I altogether avoided identifying with "roles of virgin and mother,"[39] probably because of the "given realities of the English Renaissance constructions of gender and sexuality."[40] Instead of allowing gender to define her, after Elizabeth I had contextualized her authority, especially in her public speeches between 1558 and 1563, she appears to have moved beyond the limits of gender—literally transcended it.

In her later use of language and imagery, Elizabeth I concentrated either on using her gender or on transcending it. In particular, she made an art of playing one European suitor against another and using a prospective husband as representative of potential alliance. When the Spaniards threatened English interests, Elizabeth I threatened an alliance with France, and sometimes even a lesser principality from what remained of the Holy Roman Empire.

Most are familiar, of course, with Elizabeth I in her self-created role as the Virgin Queen. In the late 1570s, Elizabeth I altered her appearance to present this quite dramatic visual to her court. Visual representation was not all that mattered to her position, though. There was more to it than that. The rhetoric she used to define her position was equally, if not more important, to her exercise of power and her definition of leadership. Her concept of the Virgin Queen clearly emerged from classic religious doctrine. Although the Church of England did not feature Mary, mother of Christ, as prominently as the Catholic Church, as a popular figure, she was still much revered in English popular culture. In an even wider political sphere, the image and rhetoric pertaining to this status also carried tremendous importance. A good portion of Europe was still Catholic. England's most immediate threat, the kingdom of Scotland, was predominantly Catholic. The choice to brand herself in the image of such a significant religious icon provided a very real reminder of her divine as well as her queenly status.

The guise of the Virgin Queen was not Elizabeth I's only application of blended religious and historical imagery, though. Before she developed that image of herself, she associated herself with a variety of other female figures from classical mythology primarily. In 1569, for instance, she had an allegorical painting commissioned to depict her triumphing over three goddesses and quite vivid representatives of female power. The three goddesses in the painting were Juno, Minerva, and Venus.[41] At the time of her coronation, she framed herself as being like various biblical figures, too. She presented herself as Deborah, who was not only a judge in Israel and a prophet, referred to as a mother in the Book of Judges. She also identified herself with Daniel, though, too, with particular reference to his escape from a den of lions, with lions often considered a symbol of monarchs or royalty.[42]

Having used political rhetoric to contextualize her position before 1563, from that point onward, Elizabeth I emphasized a divine status for herself by presenting of herself as divine, rather than specifically likening her role to that of an ordinary mother or virgin figure. Indeed, she presents herself in the image of the mother of God, a divine creature of peace, commanding respect and demanding loyalty. Even more specifically, and a testament to how carefully she cultivated her self-image and how well she related it to the broader cultural context of her day, a wealth of evidence demonstrates how she cultivated the image of herself as the "true Virgin" or the "Protestant substitute" for the Virgin Mary.[43] Although there are various problems with assuming that, as Virgin Queen, Elizabeth I simply replaced the Catholic cult focus, in large part, the key to the substitution was "the identification of secular power with sacredness."[44]

Elizabeth I built various personifications and worked to make visual and rhetorical connections that would reaffirm her authority and power; through various forms of propaganda, and later examples, such as miniatures of herself as Diana, Cynthia, or Phoebe.[45] She also built the connection through her personal appearance—the clothes she wore, the type of make-up, and the extravagant hairstyles, mostly wigs. She also built the connection through rhetoric—comparing her role as queen to the dual role of wife and mother. She was "married to England," as she famously said in 1559.[46] She was also mother to her people and charged to care for their welfare at the state level, just as an ordinary woman, by virtue of her gender, would care for the welfare of her children in the home, both nurturing and disciplining them as circumstances required.

On many occasions, too, Elizabeth I inverted the gender values of her day, the social parameters and expectations, to make her position and role as monarch that much more accessible to the consciousness of the ordinary citizen. To minimize the potential objections, however, most of these inversions were very subtle. They were not, for instance, imparted in political speeches so much as they were expressed through particular propaganda elements or public acts. For instance, Elizabeth I participated in a variety of rituals that were heavily traditional for queens. She would, for instance, wash the feet of poor women on Maundy Thursday and have women join her during the feast of St. George, with her ladies-in-waiting specifically participating in the Great Procession.[47] Traditionally practiced by the queen, Elizabeth I's participation in all of rituals helped to affirm that she could be both an actively, princely monarch, wielding political authority, and a functioning female monarch. She provided her people with a king and a queen, rendered in her self-image.

ELIZABETH'S RHETORIC AND HER TRANSCENDENCE OF GENDER

As historian Cristy Beemer argues, Elizabeth I "borrowed the *ethos* of traditional values by employing three traditional female roles and reclaiming them as images of power."[48] Later in her reign, and Rose argues that it is specifically beyond 1563, Elizabeth I tended to discard her gender almost entirely to construct a different rendering of her authority. Indeed, during one of her most famous later speeches—a speech delivered at Tilbury Camp in 1588 and known as the Armada Speech—Elizabeth I represented herself as a king in female form, descended from kings, and empowered to lead as a king, setting aside the problem of gender entirely in that instant, as a mere physical rendering of herself if it was anything at all.

The Tilbury Camp speech occurred at perhaps one of the most difficult moments of Elizabeth I's reign. It recognizes that the Spanish Armada, dispatched by Philip II, was upon England's doorstep. The troops assembled at Tilbury Camp represented England's military defense on land. If the Armada defeated the English fleet, the men Elizabeth I addressed on August 9, 1588, would have provided England's last defense. Her address to the troops intended to inspire patriotic feeling and loyalty, to establish why Elizabeth I was worth fighting and dying for.

Close analysis of the speech itself, as an example of Elizabethan use of language, reveals several elements that enhance this notion of Elizabeth I's self, her personal identity as fundamental to her leadership identity beyond gender conception, though. In the opening two lines of the speech, Elizabeth I makes much of her bond and her authority over others. The address to her "loving people" emphasizes her role as a figure of reference and even adoration. Then, she shifts to discuss the contrast between her perspective and her desire and those of her counselors. She places the "fear of treachery"[49] firmly within the mindset of her concerned advisors and thus, by default, removed from her own mind. Others have asked her to "take heed" of how she becomes involved with "armed multitudes,"[50] speaking, of course, before her army and riding on horseback before them, donned in armor herself.[51]

The shift to from the royal "we" occurs at the same time. Elizabeth I delivers assurances and promises to her people with the use of the first person, "I,"[52] declaring her faith and her love for her people in powerful and deliberate style. The imperative follows, with "Let tyrants fear,"[53] and Elizabeth I contextualizes her faith and her strengths, which include the individual strengths of herself, divinely empowered "under God", and the body of her "loyal" subjects.[54]

Within the first two lines, Elizabeth I blends a dual identity for herself. She is the manifestation of a monarch, with a cautious, judicious attitude, on the one hand, and an empowered and powerful individual, a commanding self, on the other. She contrasts her two political selves and uses them to portray the quality of her kingship. The language contrasts continue, setting treachery against safeguarding and cautious behavior, tyrants against the faithful and loyal subjects of a monarch.[55]

Another concept embedded in these initial lines is Elizabeth I's own confidence in her royal self. The advice given to her, she says, pertains as much to how she goes among "armed multitudes,"[56] a deliberate reference to the location and context in which she delivered the speech and the spectacle that she created in the actual performance of it. In the face of an "armed multitude," however, the commanding and confident self, "I," emerges to overwhelm.[57]

She declares her serious purpose for making the address. "I come amongst you,"[58] with perhaps an allusion to the notion of a divine figure descending among mortal people. Although she is powerful and commands the love of her people, although God empowers her and she has a body of faithful councilors who advise caution, she descends among her people, and those who may be more aggressive than most, prepared to sacrifice herself. The language of the speech also draws to the spectacle she created, as she rode in armor, on a white horse, before her army, surveying the troops, as it were. "I come amongst you, as you see, at this time,"[59] stresses not only the instant as a period in time but the location and the context of the location, the full context of perceived uncertainty, on the eve of battle.

Still, the most masterful imagery and rhetorical devices follow as the tension of the speech increases. The emphasis of her somber intent, she stresses that her visit was not for "recreation and disport,"[60] but for sacrifice. She intended it as a show of loyalty and courage, equal to that demonstrated by her subjects. She is "resolved" to make the ultimate sacrifice "in the midst and heat of the battle."[61] In a divine, largely religious, largely symbolic manner, she stresses that she will put her faith in not only God but also her people, "to live and die amongst you all."[62] Her three-fold sacrifice and loyalty—to "my God," "my kingdom," and my people"[63]—also rings of various powerful notions of her day. The Holy Trinity is an obvious point of comparison in terms of imagery and focus, an idea of the manifestation of something in three equal but distinct parts. The expression of Elizabeth I's loyalty is well done in this, too, as is her reference to laying down "my honour and my blood" and "even in the dust."[64] The construction itself and the language is an obvious reference to a classic notion of sacrifice and the sacrifice of life to defend honor. One might almost revert to Horace and his declaration, *dulce et decorum est pro patria mori*, because of the argument he offers about the glory of dying for one's country.[65] This seems precisely the concept and sentiment that Elizabeth I seeks to raise; it fits the context because she was addressing soldiers on the eve of battle.

Then, Elizabeth I truly reaches the peak of excellence within the speech, offering a series of images combined to present her as the ultimate Christian monarch:

> I may have the body of a weak and feeble woman, but I have the heart and stomach of a king and a King of England, too—and take foul scorn that Parma

or any prince of Europe should dare to invade my realm. To which rather than any dishonor shall grow by me, I myself will venture my royal blood; I myself will be your general, judge, and rewarder [sic] of your virtue in the field.[66]

With the body of a "weak and feeble woman,"[67] it is as if she embraces popular prejudice within her rhetoric. Just as she, using the royal "we,"[68] considered the advice of her counselors to be cautions and protect herself, she recognizes the perception of her feminine form, the perceived weakness yet she can also reject it. Her "heart and stomach" are those of a "king,"[69] with the further distinction of Englishness, to rouse feelings of nationalism.

The rhetoric then focuses on the threat in hand, the Spanish Armada that was fast approaching: "the foul scorn that Parma or Spain," in the face of which, Elizabeth I becomes, "general, judge, and rewarder of every one of your virtues in the field."[70] This declaration almost seems to draw on the numerous depictions of Elizabeth I to that point, the associations built with goddesses, with the Virgin Mary even, though to a lesser extent here, and even with biblical heroes like Daniel, to imply the sense of her potency and authority, her divinely inspired power to overcome such threats from Spain. It expresses the combined personal and political authority of the queen and the degree of her power, her determination, to see justice done.

The final portion of the speech deals with the matter of payment or "deserved rewards and crowns,"[71] with the further assurance that all shall be "duly paid"[72] to the soldiers who show loyalty and fight for England. And while Elizabeth I confirms her lieutenant in her stead, Elizabeth I also emphasizes what was perhaps her strongest weapon as a sixteenth century political leader—that she was born the daughter of a king and had become queen through divine will. Fundamentally, although she expressed it in many different ways, this was the inescapable point that she would always maintain as the source for her political and personal authority.

This was also the problem that Nicholas Heath, Archbishop of York, perhaps unknowingly struggled with, when he made his objections to Elizabeth becoming the Supreme Head of the Church of England. She was, he said, "a woman by birth and nature," thus establishing the basis for his objection to her leading the Church.[73] Undermining his argument, however, was his subsequent comment that she actually had two identities by virtue of her royal birth and her accession to the throne. Indeed, by the "appointment of God," he admitted, she was "our sovaraigne lord and ladie, our kinge and quene, our emperor and empresse."[74]

Joseph Robson Tanner, in his study of Tudor constitutional documents, went so far as to argue that the sixteenth century perception of political women was such that, by virtue of having political power at all, a female sovereign became male.[75] Politically, that is, a queen is a man, having the same rights as a male ruler. According to some interpretations of the 1554 Act Concerning Regal Power, a female ruler was politically male.[76]

Although the wording of the Act implies something more complex than a female ruler being physically male, however, it does at least state that a woman as queen has the same rights as a male monarch. The power of monarchy appears to extend beyond the traditional representations of power as only male, though, within the wording of this act: "The same all regal power, dignity, honour, authority, prerogative, preeminence, and jurisdictions doth appertain, and the right ought to appertain and belong unto her Highness."[77] Politically Elizabeth I is a man or perhaps she is a woman who is capable of taking on the rights of a man, embodying both king and queen together. This is even encapsulates in the language of the law.

Elizabeth I was not the only female ruler to use the title of "king" and to have others refer to her as such. She was not the only female ruler to be considered male in certain contexts either, although not all other examples of female "kings" are predominantly positive.[78] The example of Mary of Hungary, crowned as king, is far from a positive advertisement for female rule during the sixteenth century, since her reign involved quite violent attempts by her agnate to seize the throne from her.[79]

According to Lisa Hopkins, in fact, in her study of the writings of Elizabeth I and Mary, Queen of Scots, what developed into a rather mocking use of the term "King" was a "prominent and recurring feature of typical responses to the spectacle of a female in power."[80] Nevertheless, various assessors conclude that female rulers tended to consider themselves and be considered kings rather than queens. Mortimer Levine is another who suggests specifically that both Mary Tudor and Elizabeth I were "legally kings" or "male for the purpose of ruling," with Hopkins also suggesting that there was perhaps at least a partial "internalization" of this idea as well.[81] Indeed, Elizabeth I refers to herself as king in the Tilbury speech.[82]

Allowing for the obvious exercise in rhetorical devices, the sentiment of the speech, if taken as relatively genuine, might also allow that she internalized her kingship, too. There is a notable contrast in her approach to the title and use of authority comparing her to her cousin, Mary, Queen of Scots, who, to some extent, "acted at best as a kind of transmitter" for power, seeking to pass it on to a male relative—in Mary's case, a husband—as soon as possible.[83]

The duality of Elizabeth I's leadership and exercising of political authority certainly emerges from this blend of male and female qualities, characteristics, and deliberate representations. She was the "Virgin Queen" on the one hand, married to England on the other, and, when needing to demonstrate particular political muscle, she discarded her gender entirely and made herself a fundamentally masculine being and one whose affinity was to the by then longstanding tradition of the Renaissance monarch. Elizabeth not only managed gender and applied it to establish her leadership and political power, she expanded and used it as a means of self-branding, even self-aggrandizement.

The duality of Elizabeth I's gender role took on many other pageantry qualities. Her Tilbury speech was delivered in 1588, at one of the highest danger points of her career, the might of Spain on England's doorstep. It gives a sense of her as something of an adventurer, of even, perhaps, being in the midst of a pilgrimage or on the brink of uncertainty. Uncertainty and a sense of being in medias res, or in the midst of things, also seem to apply to Elizabeth I's persona within the speech. They establish a context, in a sense.

The sense of uncertainty and the sense of being in the midst of things apply for Elizabeth I as an individual, and as a queen. It even applies to her as a divine figure, in a limbo of uncertainty about the outcome of the war with Spain, the invasion attempt orchestrated by the Spanish. Discussing Spenser's *The Faerie Queene*, Hopkins considers the importance of this particular image for Elizabethans,[84] too, and the lasting impact it would have on her popular image.

CONCLUSION

Although she was a woman and hampered at least partly by the popular perception of gender and the perceived inferiority of women in political and leadership positions, Elizabeth I came to defined her own authority and to make herself a leader on the platform of divine authority. And this perception was the result of a process in itself. As a new queen, very directly confronted by gender expectations, she clarified her authority in that familiar gender sphere. As she gained leadership experience, however, and as time provided her some distinct separation from first impressions, she built allusions to popular stories and myths—crafting her status through direct reference to divine figures.

What the Tilbury Camp speech emphasizes, too, in terms of language, and what popular Elizabethan cults suggest, too, as they relate to the queen, is that Elizabeth not only moved past contextualizing her reign according to traditional female roles, as Rose and Beemer have suggested.[85] She, in fact, moves beyond even the use of her gender to the point of transcendence through creation of a divine status. Indeed, the image that Elizabeth cultivated, which she reinforced through language, is that she herself is a being beyond gender definitions. As a prince and a divinely ordained ruler, she transcends gender entirely, to the point that it is hardly relevant at all. Her body, as she refers to it in the Tilbury speech, is merely a shell of herself, not representative at all of the power that she wields.

In effect, she first utilized the paradox of her position and then to overcome it. As she gained in confidence, she moved beyond these constraints, affirming a distinct political identity that used her gender for maximum effect.

NOTES

1. Mary Beth Rose, "The Gendering of Authority in the Public Speeches of Elizabeth I," *Convention Miscellany*, 115 (1999), 1079.
2. Rose, "The Gendering of Authority," 1079.
3. Elton discusses the "immediate problem confronting the government," which was the problem of religion. Also troublesome was England's foreign relations. Technically, they were still at war with France. For more, see: G.R. Elton, *Tudor England* (London: The Folio Society, 1997), 261.
4. J. Panton. "Matilda," *Historical Dictionary of the British Monarchy* (Scarecrow Press, 2011), 340–42.
5. Ibid, 340–42.
6. Ibid, 340–42.
7. G.R. Elton, *Tudor England* (The Folio Society, 1997), 211.
8. A.F. Pollard, *The Political History of England: From the Accession of Edward VI to the Death of Elizabeth (1547–1603)* (London: Longmans, Green and Co, 1910) 172.
9. Examples from the period include Juana of Castile, Anne of Brittany, Catherine de Medici, Mary Tudor, Mary of Guise, Mary Queen of Scots, Jeanne d'Albret in Navarre, Margaret of Austria, Mary of Hungary, Margaret of Parma, and Archduchess Isabella of the Netherlands.
10. H.G. Koenigsberger, George L. Mosse, and G.Q. Bowler, *Europe in the Sixteenth Century* (Essex: Pearson Education Limited, 1989), 73.
11. Lisa Hopkins, *Writing Renaissance Queens: Texts by and about Elizabeth and Mary, Queen of Scots,* (University of Delaware Press, 2002), 29.
12. John Knox, "the First Blast of the Trumpet Against the Monstrous Regiment of Women 1558," *Selected Writings of John Knox: Public Epistles, Treatise, and Expositions to the Year 1559* (Dallas, TX: Presbyterian Heritage Publications, 1995). Accessed April 2, 2014. www.swrb.com/newslett/actualNLs/firblast.htm
13. Cristy Beemer, "The Female Monarchy: A Rhetorical Strategy of Early Modern Role," *Rhetorical Review* 30 (2011), 258.
14. Beemer, "The Female Monarchy," 258.
15. Rose, "The Gendering of Authority," 1077.
16. Ibid, 1078.
17. Leah S. Marcus, Janel Mueller, and Mary Beth Rose, eds, *Elizabeth I: Collected Works* (Chicago: University of Chicago, 2002) Kindle Edition, 1097.
18. Marcus, Mueller, and Rose, *Elizabeth I: Collected Works*, 1141.
19. Ibid, 1141.
20. Ibid, 1141.

21. Ibid, 1141.
22. Ibid, 1154.
23. Ibid, 1147.
24. Ibid, 1147
25. Ibid, 1147.
26. Ibid, 1147.
27. Ibid, 1147.
28. Ibid, 1147.
29. Ibid, 1147.
30. Ibid, 1351.
31. Rose and Beemer recognize this interpretation of Elizabeth's early speeches, including the speech to Parliament delivered in 1559.
32. Marcus, Mueller, and Rose, *Elizabeth I: Collected Works*, 1351.
33. Ibid, 1345.
34. Ibid, 1345.
35. Ibid, 1355–67.
36. Ibid, 1367.
37. Ibid, 1379.
38. Rose, "The Gendering of Authority," 1078–79.
39. Ibid.
40. Ibid.
41. Susan Doran, "Elizabeth I: Gender, Power, & Politics," *History Today* 53 (May 2003).
42. Ibid.
43. Helen Hackett, "Rediscovering Shock: Elizabeth I and the Cult of the Virgin Mary." *Critical Quarterly* 35 (September 1993).
44. Hackett, "Rediscovering Shock," 39.
45. Doran, "Elizabeth I: Gender, Power, & Politics," 34.
46. Marcus, Mueller, and Rose, *Elizabeth I: Collected Works* 1147.
47. Doran, "Elizabeth I: Gender, Power, & Politics," 29.
48. Cristy Bemer, "The Female Monarchy: A Rhetorical Strategy of Early Modern Role," *Rhetorical Review* 30 (2011): 259.
49. Marcus, Mueller, and Rose, *Elizabeth I: Collected Works*, 5500.
50. Ibid, 5500.
51. Janet M. Green, "'I Myself'": Queen Elizabeth I's Oration at Tilbury Camp," *The Sixteenth Century Journal*, 28 (1997), 421–45.
52. Marcus, Mueller, and Rose, *Elizabeth I: Collected Works*, 5500.
53. Ibid, 5500.
54. Ibid, 5500.
55. Green, "'I myself,'" *The Sixteenth Century Journal*, 421–25.
56. Marcus, Mueller, and Rose, *Elizabeth I: Collected Works*, 5500.
57. Ibid, 5500.
58. Ibid, 5500.
59. Ibid, 5500.
60. Ibid, 5500.

61. Ibid, 5500.
62. Ibid, 5500.
63. Ibid, 5500–11.
64. Ibid, 5500–11.
65. Translated as, it is sweet and right to die for one's country.' See Horace's *Odes*, III.2.13).
66. Marcus, Mueller, and Rose, *Elizabeth I: Collected Works*, 5511.
67. Ibid, 5511.
68. Ibid, 5511.
69. Ibid, 5511.
70. Ibid, 5500–11.
71. Ibid, 5511.
72. Ibid, 5511.
73. Constantius Archiopmlus, *Memories of the Reformation of England in Two Parts*. (London: Keating and Brown, 1826), accessed February 2, 2014, archive.org/stream/memoirsofreforma00hatt#page/n7/mode/2up.
74. John Strype, *Annals of the Reformation and establishment of religion and other various occurrences in the Church of England*, (John Wyat, 1709) 7.
75. Joseph Robson. *Tudor Constitutional Documents, A.D. 1485–1603*. CUP Archives, 1948.
76. This act afforded a queen the same rights as a king.
77. Joseph Robson Tanner, *Tudor Constitutional Documents, A.D. 1485–1603*. (CUP Archives, 1948), 123.
78. For historical instances of women using the term "king," see also Anne Pyburn, *Ungendering Civilization* (New York: Routeledge, 2004), 128; Tadeusz Gromada, and Oskar Halecki, *Jadwiga of Anjou and the rise of East Central Europe*, (Social Science Monographs, 1991), 98.
79. Gromada, and Halecki, *Jadwiga of Anjou and the rise of East Central Europe*, 98.
80. Hopkins, *Writing Renaissance Queens: Texts by and about Elizabeth and Mary, Queen of Scots*, 30.
81. Mortimer Levine, "The Place of Women in Tudor Government," in *Tudor Rule and Revolution*, edited by Delloyd J. Guth and John W. McKenna, (New York: Cambridge University Press, 1982), 110.
82. Susan Bassnett, *Elizabeth I: A Feminist Perspective* (Oxford: Berg, 1988), 8 and 76–78. For further comment on uses of the term, see Leah Marcus, *Puzzling Shakespeare: Local Reading and its Discontents* (Berkeley: University of California Press, 1988), 56–57.
83. Hopkins, *Writing Renaissance Queens: Texts by and about Elizabeth and Mary, Queen of Scots*, 30.
84. Hopkins, *Writing Renaissance Queens*, 43.

Chapter Two

Queen Elizabeth II and Princess Diana
Saving the Monarchy
Kathleen Mollick

In his biography of Queen Elizabeth II, Robert Lacey noted that, had she been able to choose her own destiny, Elizabeth Windsor would have been a countrywoman, living a quiet yet busy life with her family and her dogs.[1] Since inheriting the throne in 1952, however, Elizabeth II has been a figure of interest not just for her longevity, but because of her ability to weather the kinds of political and social change that has sometimes threatened the stability of the monarchy that has united Britain across the centuries. She is the longest living British monarch,[2] and if she is still on the throne by the fall of 2015, she will have eclipsed her great-great grandmother, Queen Victoria, as the longest reigning British monarch.[3] She is also part of a select group of British queens that are still regarded with interest by historians and the people who read books about them and watch the films and mini-series based on their lives. Elizabeth II has commanded a solid body of scholarship of her life, due in part to her active presence as a woman political figure on the global stage.

With a reign as long as hers, Elizabeth II has experienced the defeats and triumphs common in any long-held political position,[4] but the one that has potentially garnered the most attention is her misreading of the public's reaction to the death of Princess Diana. What this chapter will investigate is how Elizabeth II's reign has been marked from the beginning by the power of speech as it defines the monarch's symbolic role within Britain, as well as how the country is perceived on the global stage, and how these elements played a significant role in shaping her ability to mold her own public image and react to crises. This chapter will provide a rhetorical analysis of the speech that Elizabeth II gave to her subjects before the funeral of Princess Diana, and will demonstrate how her ability to learn from past missteps in her communication with her subjects. Examples of emotional and ethical appeals, and examples of her ability to use what Kenneth Burke defines as identification, will illustrate what made the speech important not only in the short term, but also how this speech paved the way, in the long term, for Elizabeth II to strengthen her position as monarch and the British monarchy overall.

COMMUNICATION AND THE MONARCHY: GEORGE V TO GEORGE VI

In order to understand the effect that Elizabeth II's refusal to comment on Princess Diana's death had on the British public's perception of her ability to rule in the days following Diana's fatal car accident in Paris, it is important to understand how the queen's absence of comment was seen by her subjects as an act of a monarch no longer in touch with public sentiment. For the British monarchy in the twentieth century, the ability to communicate directly to its people has been a strong component of its ability to survive the political strife of World War I and the loss of empire after World War II. For Elizabeth II, her childhood was heavily influenced by the period from George V's reign, which had started in 1910, and ending with the reign of George VI in 1936.[5] George V's decision to embrace radio as a means of communicating with his subjects, the role of film, radio, and newspapers in covering the ascension to the throne of Edward VIII and his subsequent abdication in 1936, and George VI's succession to the throne as he dealt with a stammer all provided the foundation on which the queen communicated with her subjects.

Much like his father, Edward VII, George V came to the throne after several years of playing a king-in-waiting. One of his contributions to the modern monarchy was his decision to address his subjects on the radio. He was the first monarch to address his subjects on Christmas Day, a tradition that continues to this day.[6] George V "did not write his own speeches, yet they were always in character; yet they seemed to be a natural emanation from and expression of the man."[7] As effective as he was in speaking on the radio, his eldest son, Edward, the Prince of Wales,[8] was immensely popular because of his handsome looks and charming way of speaking, making him a popular media figure in newsreels, newspapers, and magazines.[9] Blond-haired, blue-eyed, and a socially outgoing person, the young and athletic Edward was a physically and emotionally appealing young man which made him a popular figure among his future subjects. His appeal was communicated not only through his official duties in Britain, but also through his social popularity. This level of attraction often worked in his favor, and when he gained the throne after his father's death in 1936, it seemed as though he might go on to become a well-known and well-loved monarch. But his affair with American divorcee Wallis Warfield Simpson proved an insurmountable obstacle for him. As head of the Church of England, he could not marry a divorced woman, unless he entered into a morganatic marriage.[10] In that situation, however, his wife would be unable to be queen, and Edward VIII wanted Wallis Simpson at his side.[11] No solution to the problem could be found that would please the king as well as the government.

Edward VIII had hoped that he would be able to harness public opinion in his favor, and that he could push the British religious and political establishment to accept his choice of a wife. But the establishment prevailed, even in light of the fact that his brother, and next in line to the throne, Prince Albert,[12] struggled with a stammer that frequently made communicating with others difficult. Although there were concerns about Prince Albert's ability to communicate effectively in public, the concerns were not strong enough to give in to Edward VIII's insistence that he be given permission by the government to marry Mrs. Simpson. For the first and only time in British history, a king abdicated his throne, and the repercussions of that act still haunt the royal family. When King George VI ascended the throne, Princess Elizabeth's life moved her from the shadows of her relatively private life as a child princess to a more visible on the world stage, as the next in line to the British throne at the age of ten.[13] The forces of duty, divorce, and communication made themselves known to her at a very early age, and would ultimately revisit her again when Princess Diana died.

NATIONAL TRANSITION: FROM ABDICATION TO WAR

When Edward VIII abdicated, he gave a public address in which he stated why he was taking that action and to offer his allegiance to his younger brother. The act of abdication had not occurred before in British history, and so there was no precedent for the kind of speech that needed to be given. The speech therefore had to provide two rationales: why the king was giving up his throne, and his duty to his country, in order to marry an American divorcee, and then provide assurances to those who felt as though the British government was pushing him off the throne and thus might choose not to accept the ascent of George VI to the throne. The most memorable line of the speech, and the one that generated the greatest public sympathy, was his vow that "I cannot accept the burden to carry the terrible responsibility of being your king without the help and the support of the woman I love."[14] This sentence encapsulates the crisis the former king had reached; the burdens of the office he had been born to were too overwhelming for him without Wallis Simpson, and if he couldn't be married to her and have her acknowledged as his wife, then he could not continue as king. For those of his subjects who felt he was pressured to step down, he stated, "And I want you to know that the decision I have made is mine and mine alone. This was a thing I had to judge entirely by myself."[15] He went on to acknowledge the support he had received from the prime minister and his family,[16] thus letting his audience know that he had ultimately decided to step down on his own. He had rhetorically set the stage for his own departure, and preparing his subjects for their next king.

When George VI ascended the throne, Europe was heading into war, and so on top of the pressures his brother had found unbearable as king, George VI had the burden of trying to ascertain where Hitler's actions would take the rest of the world. Within a year of war being declared in 1939, the possibility of German air raids over London became reality in 1940. And despite the concerns over the king's stammer when he spoke in front of a microphone, the war unintentionally brought out the king's strength: establishing himself as a fitting monarch for his country in a time of crisis. By 1940, with Queen Juliana of the Netherlands living with her family abroad after the German occupation, as well as many British children being sent out of the country in case of a German invasion, many of the king's subjects wondered if he might leave, or send his daughters to the United States. In one of her most memorable public statements during the war, when asked if her daughters would be evacuated, Queen Elizabeth replied, "The children won't leave without me; I won't leave without the King; and the King will never leave."[17] The photographs of the king and queen visiting bombed sections of London, as well as Buckingham Palace when it was bombed during the Blitz, were widely published, and their remarks to the people who came to see them as they walked around other parts of London that had been bombed became an integral part of their appeal. Queen Elizabeth's remark that she was glad the Palace had been hit because "I can look the East End in the face"[18] only strengthened their bond with their subjects. On another occasion, an unidentified person called out, "'Thank God for a good King!'"[19] and the king responded, "'Thank God for a good people!'"[20] Any questions about the fitness of King George VI to take his place had been put to rest with his high visibility and hard work during the war.

Against this backdrop of war, and as her parents' popularity as monarch and consort was solidified, Princess Elizabeth began to develop her own voice as a future monarch. In October 1940, she made a speech on the BBC radio program *The Children's Hour*, which was broadcast around the world for those children who had been sent from Britain for their safety.[21] The speech, which was approximately five minutes long, was specifically tailored to give encouragement to children living in different parts of the Commonwealth.[22] She began the speech by assuring her listeners that she and her sister, Princess Margaret, know what they are experiencing in living far from their families, because she and her sister have also been separated from their parents in the past.[23] She tells them that not only will they not be forgotten by their friends back in England, but that they must also know that the children there are doing well, too, sharing in the war effort as best as they can.[24] At the end, she said with cheerful exuberance, "Remember that when peace comes, it will be for us, the children of today, to make tomorrow a better and happier world."[25] In this radio broadcast, the first she ever gave, Princess Elizabeth introduces herself as a caring young woman, concerned with the well-being of other children living far from home in trying circumstances. She empathizes with their situation, and lets them know she has an idea of what the emotions they're going through.

As the war continued, and the princess grew older, she wanted to play a more visible role in the war effort. In 1944, Princess Elizabeth persuaded her father to let her to join the Auxiliary Territorial Service, where she served as a second subaltern and became a mechanic.[26] Her public presence through her public speaking and public actions added to her stature as a member of the royal family, and as the heiress presumptive to the throne. These actions were conducted under the watchful eye of her father, who tried to prepare his daughter as best as he could for the tremendous job that she would inherit in the future. George VI referred to the royal family as "the Firm"[27] and treated his daughter as the rising junior partner. This combination of a clear projection of a solid family life and a dedication to royal responsibility highlighted what British biographer Dorothy Laird said about the role of the monarchy in British life: "The Monarchy links us to our past, and in doing so gives our troubles perspective and our efforts a future. We feel linked to our history."[28] Laird also went on to note that "The Queen is strongly linked to the family symbol. Indeed, so much has a happy family life become identified with the British Royal Family that it is doubtful whether a Sovereign could sustain his sovereignty were this shattered . . . ."[29] When Laird wrote this passage in 1959, the short duration of Edward VIII's reign and the high affection in which George VI and his family were held would have seemed to support this point as Elizabeth II completed her fifth year on the throne with her husband and two children. Nearly 50 years later, in 2007, this belief was echoed by another British historian when he noted that, "With the exception of Edward VIII, modern British monarchs have been careful to respect the great royal paradox, namely that we want our monarchs to be just like 'us' but also completely different from 'us.'"[30] But at the same time this sentiment was expressed, another event took place that set in motion the other important aspect of the public communication of her early years on the throne.

LORD ALTRINCHAM AND HIS INFLUENCE

Upon her father's death in 1952, Elizabeth II became the queen of a British empire in decline, due in part to the slow recovery from the war and to a changing world in which colonies of the empire wanted to chart their own destiny. But with the advent of her reign, there was a sense that perhaps Britain would embark on a new Elizabethan era.[31]

By 1957, however, the criticism of her tenure on the throne was being heard. The most powerful criticism came from the editor of "an obscure publication called *National and English Review*": John Grigg, Second Baron Altrincham.[32] His criticism of the queen focused on the way in which she spoke. He believed that whether she was aware of it or not, the persona that she was creating of herself through her speeches was that of an out-of-touch ruler. Altrincham believed that her speeches created the impression of "'a priggish schoolgirl,' preventing her from coming into her own 'as an independent and distinctive character.'"[33] He also criticized how she read her speeches, noting that "Like her mother, she appears to be unable to string even a few sentences together without a written text. . . . Even if the Queen feels compelled to read all her speeches . . . she must at least improve her method of reading them."[34] The content of her speeches up until that point did seem rather simplistic. In her Christmas Message of 1953, there is one interesting passage in which she addresses the idea that hers will be a new Elizabethan era. In an incredibly frank way, she says, "Some people have expressed the hope that my reign may mark a new Elizabethan age. Frankly I do not feel like myself at all like my great Tudor forbear, who was neither blessed by a husband nor children, who ruled as a despot and was never able to leave her native shores."[35] While her assessment of the differences between the first Elizabeth and herself were true, particularly in terms of the power each wielded as monarchs, the language is very stark. But the language is then tempered by her statement that the similarity shared by both eras was the spirit adventure embraced by their subjects.[36] There is always a sense that the queen's speech must be calming and emphasize the unity of the nation and the Commonwealth. The language is weakened, however, by the queen's delivery; it's not that far removed from the deliberate pacing of the speech she gave in 1940.

Altrincham also believed that not only her speechmaking, but her overall view of the tone of the royal court should change as well to generate a more modern *ethos*.[37] He thought that when the time came that she "'lost the bloom of youth,' her reputation would depend primarily on her personality. 'She will have to say things which people can remember, and do things which will make people sit up and take notice.'"[38] Perhaps Altrincham was thinking of the queen's passive role in her sister Margaret's decision not to marry Group Captain Peter Townsend. In a situation that harkened back to the abdication scandal, Margaret had fallen in love with her father's equerry, Peter Townsend, who was also divorced. Their relationship, which was made public in 1953, was problematic because the queen's two children were both under the age of ten; if the queen died suddenly, then Margaret would rule until her nephew, Charles, turned eighteen. Margaret needed her sister's permission to marry Townsend, but as Defender of the Faith, the queen was under great pressure to not allow her sister to marry a divorced man. After a separation of two years, in which Townsend lived in Belgium, he returned to Britain, but in 1955, Margaret decided she wasn't certain that she wanted to marry him, and so they parted permanently.[39] Public opinion on this issue was sharply divided among those who thought the queen acted properly for counselling her sister to wait before marrying a divorced man, and among those who thought the idea of immediate members of the royal family not marrying divorced persons was outdated. Some thought the queen should have taken a more active role in supporting her sister's choice, since the likelihood of Margaret ever ascending the throne was very unlikely.

Altrincham's criticism drew a heavily negative response from the public once it was publicized. The *Daily Mail* conducted a poll that "showed that although a majority (fifty-two percent) of people disagreed with Lord Altrincham's criticism in general terms, on particular points he had public support. Fifty-five percent [of those polled] wanted the Court circle widened . . . and there was little suggestion that examining the conduct of the reigning Monarch was itself illegitimate."[40] Others agreed with the poll taken by the *Daily Mail*, believing that the criticism was "on the mark."[41] Among those who felt Altrincham's criticism was justified was the queen's husband, Prince Philip. Long frustrated by the way in which his suggestions were turned aside by the courtiers in the Palace, he joined forces with the queen's assistant private secretary, Martin Charteris, to start implementing changes necessary to keep the monarchy relevant.[42] The steps that were taken did not unduly upset the status quo, but they signaled that the criticism had been taken seriously. One example was the fact that the traditional "presentation parties" held for young debutants at court would be "replaced by more garden parties, so that larger numbers of people could be invited to Buckingham Palace."[43] Ultimately, Altrincham's criticism served as "the trigger . . . which enabled the image of royalty, frozen for so long, to advance."[44] Over the next several decades, the queen would face opportunities to show this advancement, opportunities that would show her subjects that she was capable of making changes to meet changing times. Some of these changes would be successful, but others would show her fallibility in that she would not push for change. In the case of Princess Diana's death, there were two events that took place relatively early in the queen's reign that showed these two aspects of her ability to lead, both of which would come together later in the events that would lead to the queen giving a broadcast to the nation in order to keep the monarchy intact into the twenty-first century.

BENDING PROTOCOL

Winston Churchill's Death

When Winston Churchill died on January 30, 1965, his death did not just mark the passing of a former British prime minister. Churchill's remarkable political career was comprised of periods of great political success as well as stinging defeat. Churchill had been involved with the events of Edward VIII's abdication, but had developed a close relationship to George VI during World War II. The king's death was so devastating to Churchill that he broke down in tears and struggled to write a speech to mark the occasion.[45]

For his funeral, Queen Elizabeth II relaxed the strict demands of royal protocol that demanded that her presence outweigh anyone else's. Churchill's daughter, Mary Soames, recalled how "the Queen 'awaited the arrival of her greatest subject.' Elizabeth II also told the Churchill family 'we were not to curtsy or bow as we passed her, because it would have held everything up.'"[46] Further change to royal protocol occurred after the service when "the Queen again broke precedent and left after the Churchill family had followed the coffin . . . [and] the Queen hosted a buffet luncheon at Buckingham Palace for all the chief mourners and foreign dignitaries."[47] Her decision to bend protocol for Churchill's funeral showed that she was willing to change in the face of honoring an important public individual who was not a member of the royal family. This is important to remember in the circumstances surrounding Princess Diana's death; although she was no longer a member of the royal family, she was an incredibly popular figure both nationally and internationally. A precedent had been set with Churchill at the queen's direction, so it would have made sense for the queen to set a similar standard for Princess Diana.

The Aberfan Disaster

The Aberfan disaster highlighted the Queen's fallibility as a leader, and that her public actions could undermine her *ethos* as a leader. Aberfan was a quiet Welsh town that was devastated when a landslide "killed 115 children and 28 adults . . . despite urgings from her advisers, the Queen resisted visiting the scene."[48] She didn't go because her presence, she thought would hamper rescue operations.[49] Once the last of the bodies were recovered, one week after the disaster, Elizabeth II came to visit Aberfan "and spent more than two hours talking to relatives of the deceased, walking up the mound covering the school, and laying a wreath in the cemetery where eighty-one children had been buried in rows."[50] According to one royal biographer, "A compelling circumstance pulled her out of her bubble into direct and spontaneous contact with her subjects, who showed their appreciation."[51] Yet her slow response to the disaster at Aberfan wasn't so easily overlooked, despite her insistence that her presence would slow down the search for survivors. As the events of Aberfan faded from public memory, the memory of "her tardy reaction to the crisis showed an unyielding side to her nature that would cause problems in the years to come."[52] This is the fine line that the queen must walk in her role as monarch. So many of the practices of the British monarchy are based on tradition and observances of ceremonial tradition, and yet refusing to yield to change, as was demonstrated by reaction within Buckingham Palace to Lord Altrincham's criticism, can weaken its effectiveness substantially.

What the Churchill funeral and the Aberfan disaster show is the way in which Elizabeth II could use the fundamental symbols of her reign, such as duty, family, and adaptability, to keep herself steady and flexible during the changing times her nation faced. This steadiness and adaptability meant that the monarchy could endure along with the changes in the way the British people faced changes in the economic, political, and spiritual makeup of the times. But what the Abersfan disaster underscored was the queen's fallibility in judgment. Despite her desire to not hinder recovery operations at the site of the disaster, she miscalculated how the public would respond to her hesitation in coming to Aberfan immediately. All of these aspects of her nearly forty-five-year reign came to a head with Princess Diana's untimely death in a car crash in Paris in August of 1997.

THE DEATH OF PRINCESS DIANA

Queen Elizabeth II's children grew to maturity during the 1970s; Princess Anne married first in 1973, with her brother Charles following in 1981. During that period, the monarchy showed a stable conventional royal family, with the public wanting more and more information about their lives.[53] To some extent, the queen also bowed to this pressure by allowing her family to be filmed for a documentary entitled *Royal Family*.[54] Although cautioned that filming her family might be too open, Elizabeth II decided that it was the right decision to make. Once the film was released to generally favorable reviews, the queen's family became as popular a media focus as other celebrities. By

1980, when Prince Charles began his courtship of Lady Diana Spencer, this media attention would be crystallized in its pursuit of her as her relationship with him became more important. The media frenzy focusing on their courtship would reach a crescendo with their marriage, but as time passed, it became clear that the media fascination with the royals, and Diana in particular, seemed to have no end. There wouldn't be a single climax to the attention, but an endless series of peaks and valleys. The media attention would then upend the queen's mission to sustain the public view of the royals as serving as solid upholders of British middle-class values while selflessly serving their country as duty demanded.

THE QUEEN'S SPEECH: A TRIBUTE TO PRINCESS DIANA

Throughout the remarks that were given by Elizabeth II before the public funeral for Diana, Princess of Wales, there are clearly stated appeals to what Aristotle defined as *logos*, *ethos*, and *pathos*. In *Rhetoric*, Aristotle stated that the rhetor uses three particular appeals to an audience: the rhetor's character must be communicated clearly to the audience, as well as the ability to appeal to the audience's emotions and their intellect.[55] While the organization of the speech is meant to convey the queen's official position on the death of Princess Diana, the appeals to *pathos* and *ethos* are the strongest parts of the speech, and the ones her audience would be most likely to respond to most strongly. In addition to the Aristotelian appeals notable in the speech, identification is also evident. As Burke defined it, two individuals may be joined together in part by a shared interest in something, and "In being identified with B, A is 'substantially one' with a person other than himself. Yet at the same time he remains unique, an individual locus of motives. Thus, he is both joined and separate, at once a distinct substance and consubstantial with another."[56] This kind of identification is crucial to the longevity of a monarchy; people must feel a connection to the monarch, and that the monarch who leads them is worth following because she represents and supports what is best about the nation she leads. The queen's speech was political in nature because its exigence came from her perceived indifference to the death of Diana, based on the queen's decision not to return with her family to Buckingham Palace and her decision not to comment on Diana's death until public pressure came to bear.

There are five significant sections of this relatively short address by the queen. The first section of the speech can be viewed as the queen addressing the exigency that has arisen and speaking about the death from a general perspective, which then leads to her own perspective on the event. The second part of the queen's remarks then addresses the grief of her audience, which is then followed by a section on addressing the grief of the audience and the queen acting as matriarch of her family in acknowledging the condolences received by her family. Then the next section of the speech addresses the other victims of the crash, and the speech ends with a benediction of sorts, as the queen prepares her audience for the funeral the following day.

The Statement of Exigency and Its Appeals

The first sentence of the queen's remarks to her audience clearly indicates the exigency of her speech, as well as setting the stage for the first of many appeals, both to the *pathos* of the exigency, and an appeal to establishing a bond of identification between the queen and her audience. The queen addresses the cause for her remarks immediately, stating, "Since last Sunday's dreadful news we have seen, throughout Britain and the world, an overwhelming expression of sadness at Diana's death."[57] As she acknowledged her audience, the queen also included herself, demonstrating that she included herself among the grief-stricken. This was a particularly important point considering the strong criticism that had flourished as the queen's response to the princess's death appeared muted and then non-existent. In her use of "we," the queen not only makes an appeal to the emotion of her audience by implying that she shares their emotional reaction to the death of Diana, but she also seeks to build a sense of identification with them, stating that their grief over the loss of the princess is an emotion shared between the monarch, her subjects, and a wider global audience.

In a nod to the more open forms of grieving that she had been accused of not showing, the queen makes an indirect acknowledgement of the criticism levelled against her for being indifferent to the global mourning surrounding Diana, while also offering a rationale for why her behavior might appear to be indifferent. After recognizing the outpouring of emotion over Diana's death, the queen notes that "We have all been trying in our different ways to cope. It is not easy to express a sense of loss, since the initial shock is often succeeded by a mixture of other feelings: disbelief, incomprehension, anger—and concern for those who remain."[58] This statement not only informally identifies the different stages of grief that are culturally held to be common in Western society, but she also is providing a framework for her audience to understand her own actions over the last few days in regard to Diana's death. She appears to remind her audience that there are many different ways to show mourning, and that she was mourning in her own way. The queen makes an attempt at identifying with older members of her audience who, like her, may be more circumspect in expressing their grief, as well as reminding those who are more vocal in their grief that not everyone mourns in the same way. Despite these different approaches, however, the queen notes that everyone has felt sorrow over the death of Diana, and in that way, everyone shares the same sorrow, even if it is expressed in different ways.

The queen uses this common feeling to introduce her own emotions on the death of Princess Diana. She mentions the commonality of grief before seguing into her own statement of her feelings. She states that, "We have all felt these emotions in these last few days. So what I say to you now, as your Queen and as a grandmother, I say from my heart."[59] In this passage of the speech, the queen seems keen to reassure her audience that she has, in fact, had an emotional reaction to Diana's death, and she appeals to their emotion by invoking her role as the monarch and her role as a grandmother, particularly to the sons of the woman who has just died. She goes further by clarifying that her next remarks ("So what I say to you now . . . I say from my heart") will come from an emotional position, rather than one of court etiquette and historical precedent, the basis by which she had made her decisions during the last several days. She is also invoking her *ethos* as a monarch in this passage, taking on the role of what Karlyn Kohrs Campbell and Kathleen Hall Jamieson describe in the context of American presidential rhetoric as a national pastor, delivering what they call the "national eulogy" which "links the present to the future with a central line of argument: that those who died exemplify the best of a nation that will survive this moment because its ideals cannot be undermined by events such as those that took their lives."[60] Her *ethos* as a monarch and as a grandmother not only seeks to remind her audience of the crucial role she plays in giving this address, and in having the public and personal authority to speak, but she is also establishing a sense of identification between herself and her audience. Many of the people in her audience may not know what it is to be a monarch, but if she is their queen, then they know she has the public authority to speak; many of the people in her audience, however, know what it is to be a grandmother, and so the appeal to identify with the queen as a grandmother is particularly strong.

Her own tribute to Diana is brief but direct. She begins by stating, "First, I want to pay tribute to Diana myself. She was an exceptional and gifted human being. In good times and bad, she never lost her capacity to smile and laugh, nor to inspire others with her warmth and kindness."[61] In this initial part of her remarks about Diana, the queen lets her audience know that she is speaking for herself, and that her following comments can be seen as her own view of Diana. She makes an appeal to the emotions of the audience by recalling that through all the highs and lows of Diana's life, her vivacity and her care for others were among the hallmarks of her own personal appeal. By invoking these images of the caring and humane princess, the queen continues to identify with her subjects' grief.

As she concludes her remarks about the princess, the queen returns to invoking her own direct personal statements about Diana. The queen notes, "I admired and respected her—for her energy and commitment to others, and especially for her devotion to her two boys. This week at Balmoral, we have all been trying to help William and Harry come to terms with the devastating loss that they and the rest of us have suffered."[62] The underlying emotional appeal of this passage is the queen's statement that she held her former daughter-in-law in high esteem, which was due in part to Diana's strength as a mother to the queen's two grandsons. The queen then makes the connection that as part of continuing to take care of these two motherless boys, she and the other members of her family remained at Balmoral in order to support them, rather than staying there out of indifference to the death of Diana. There is also an appeal here to those members of the audience who have experienced a sudden loss in their family which requires the care of young children. The queen is providing grounds for those who have gone through that same experience, as well for those that can empathize with this situation, to identify with the royal family's sense of grief as they comfort William and Harry.

The Audience's Grief

After discussing her feelings about Diana's death and the grief of her family, the queen addresses what she believes will be Diana's final legacy. She says, "No-one who knew Diana will ever forget her. Millions of others who never met her, but felt like they knew her, will remember her. I for one believe that there are lessons to be drawn from her life and from the extraordinary and moving reaction to her death, I share in your determination to cherish her memory."[63] Part of the critical reaction to the queen's absence from the public view was the idea that the royal family had wanted to ignore Diana in death as well as in life, to treat her as though she was nothing more than a nuisance. In this passage, the queen seeks to overturn that view by noting that Diana is an unforgettable figure, and that she will not fade from public memory. The queen uses her *ethos* here to make an appeal to the *pathos* of the audience, by using her position to assure them that Diana will not be forgotten. This is also an appeal to identity, in that the queen is stating that "I share in your determination to cherish her memory," which indicates that she and her audience share a common goal that binds them together, although she is vague enough on what actions she will take to keep that memory alive.

Acknowledging Condolences

The queen then changes roles somewhat, speaking more as the head of her family, rather than as the monarch. Once she has memorialized Diana, she then thanks the public for their condolences. The queen invokes her family, particularly her grandsons, when she thanks her audience for their responses to Diana's death: "This is also an opportunity for me, on behalf of my family, and particularly for Prince Charles, and William and Henry, to thank all of you who have brought flowers, sent messages, and paid your respects in so many ways to a remarkable person. These acts of kindness have been a huge source of help and comfort."[64] The queen speaks to her audience in the way of a family matriarch, thanking people for their notes of condolence and acts of kindness at the death of a loved one. The queen makes a further appeal to emotion by letting her audience know that their acts of remembrance of Diana have not gone unnoticed by the royal family and how appreciative they are of them.

Acknowledging Other Victims of the Crash

The queen then transitions back into the role of monarch through her comments on the surviving families of those who died in the car crash along with Diana. The queen doesn't mention any of the survivors by name, but instead speaks of them as an unnamed group. It is the families of the survivors that she addresses directly. She reminds her audience that "Our thoughts are also with Diana's family and the families of those who died with her. I know that they too have drawn strength from what has happened since last weekend as they seek to heal their sorrow and then to face the future without a loved one."[65] The queen directly addresses her audience by assuring them that their expressions of sympathy for all of the victims of the car crash are felt by those families. This is also an expression of identifying the larger scope of the tragedy, which is that two other people were killed in the crash, without taking too much attention away from Diana's death.

Preparing for the Funeral

As she concludes the speech, she continues in her role as monarch by preparing her subjects for Diana's funeral the next day: "I hope that tomorrow, we can all, wherever we are, join in expressing our grief at Diana's loss, and gratitude at her too-short life. It is a chance to show the whole world the British nation united in grief and respect."[66] In this passage, the queen makes an appeal to *ethos*, speaking as the leader of the British nation, telling her audience that their expressions of sorrow and their honoring of Diana's death will be part of the history of Britain, and that the international audience that will be watching the funeral obsequies for Diana will see that the British people have come together to participate in the funeral marking Diana's death. This passage also demonstrates the queen's appeal to *pathos*, as she emphasizes the "grief and respect" that she knows will be demonstrated the following day at the funeral service. Finally, the queen is also making one last observance of identification, in which she places the nation's current mourning of the princess into historical context, saying that their emotions that will be on display at the funeral will only show the unification of the British people.

The final sentence of the speech is brief but telling. The queen issues something of a benediction to her audience, saying, "May those who died rest in peace, and may we, each and every one of us, thank God for someone who made many, many people happy."[67] For a speech that was meant to reassure her subjects, not specifically identifying Diana by name in this last passage stands out. Perhaps because Diana was the specific focus of the speech it was felt that addressing her by name wasn't necessary, or perhaps by not identifying her specifically along with the others who died in the car wreck, that the speech became a more universal statement of the grief of the nation. Yet by not doing so, it seems as if the queen is trying to lessen the impact of Diana's untimely death. The appeal to emotions here is an appeal to the solemnity of the moment by invoking those who had died, and by reminding everyone that Diana ultimately had "made many, many people happy," which will hopefully give them comfort as they watched the televised funeral the following day.

REACTION TO THE SPEECH

The reaction to the speech was beneficial for the monarchy in the short term and the long term. In the short term, the reaction to the speech was positive. A past critic and the prime minister at the time weighed in with their views: "John Grigg, the former Lord Altrincham pronounced it 'one of her very best speeches,' and said she had 'stabilized the situation,' while Tony Blair considered the broadcast 'near perfect. She managed to be a Queen and a grandmother at one and the same time.'"[68] The reaction of the general public seemed to echo their responses; although "support for a republic peaked in the days following her [Diana's] death, it dropped to 12 percent after the Queen's televised speech, and in the following month it return to around 19 percent, where it had been for three decades."[69] So the short-term goal of reassuring her subjects about her ability to react with sympathy to Diana's death had been reached, and the speech also went on to create long-term benefit as well.

CONCLUSION

As of 2014, Elizabeth II's reign is still in progress, and it's fair to say that she will be a subject of historical interest in a manner similar to Elizabeth I and Victoria. Not only will she be a focus of interest because of her longevity, but also because of the way in which she, as the leader of her country, navigated the changing times of her era in much the same way Elizabeth I and Victoria had to. All three of these women also faced the additional challenge of facing the perceived gender expectations of their times as they represented their country and empire in troubled and prosperous times. Elizabeth I came to the throne during the political and religious upheaval of the Tudor era, and by successfully eluding the wishes of her government and people to marry, she brought stability to the British people through her own political cunning and shrewdness. Although Victoria's place in line to the throne had been questioned as her predecessor's had been, she ascended the throne with less controversy than Elizabeth I did. Victoria was also wary of marrying, but she eventually fell deeply in love with and married her cousin Albert. After deciding that he would lead their household and she would lead their country, they became the living embodiment of the British monarchy upholding British middle class values. Elizabeth II came to the throne without any cloud over her ascension, and unlike her predecessors, she was already a wife and mother before becoming queen. But like them, Elizabeth II established her *ethos* as a monarch through her ability to make the rhetorical choices necessary to communicate to her subjects and the world her ability to lead the British people and the citizens of the British Commonwealth.

The ways in which Elizabeth II's entire life has been influenced by speech and communication, will continue to provide a rich area of study long after her death. Dating from her grandfather's decision to broadcast his speeches, to the issue of her father's stammer and how that might have an effect on his ability to be king, along with the changes in media that have ended most recently with the establishment of her own YouTube channel[70] and Facebook account,[71] the life of Elizabeth II has been molded by media as the dominant avenue for her to establish herself as the head of her country. Because of political turmoil that happens in any monarch's reign, the queen has relied on television most prominently, particularly in the case of the Princess Diana speech, to reach out to her people in times of upheaval and in times of peace. As she moved to using television as the primary means of speaking to her people, while never forgetting to utilize radio, Elizabeth II may not upload her own videos to her own YouTube channel, and she probably doesn't post messages on her own Facebook wall, but the fact that she has these forms of social media established in her name shows that she understands the necessity of establishing her presence in the mediums in which her subjects communicate with each other.

What this chapter has illustrated is how Elizabeth II's strengths and weaknesses as a monarch came into play with her single speech after the death of

Princess Diana, an event that has been acknowledged as perhaps the most serious threat to the monarchy during her lifetime. Princess Diana challenged many of the long-held beliefs of the monarchy that Elizabeth II had learned from her grandmother and her parents, in which stoicism and reserve were considered the appropriate ways with which to cope with crisis. In that speech, the queen demonstrated how she had not lost complete touch with her subjects and how she was able to use the abilities that she had displayed earlier in her reign to compromise on the issues that most disturbed the British public in her observance of Diana's death. Through her use of emotional appeals in her speech, she was able to acknowledge to her people that she felt their sense of grief and loss over the loss of Princess Diana, and that she would not be forgotten. Through her use of identification, she reminded her people that the loss of Diana was a personal, as well as a national, tragedy, and that together they would survive her loss and preserve her memory. Ultimately, Elizabeth II was able to quell the rising interest of establishing a different form of government in Britain; the British peerage expert Harold Brooks-Baker thought the monarchy might come to an end after Diana's death, but within a year, he believed that "there was a 70–to 80–per-cent chance the monarchy will be with us for many, many generations. And by that, I mean not only Charles and William, but their children and grandchildren."[72] Future research will determine just how successful she was in heading off what might have been a serious threat to the monarchy, as of 2014, she is poised to be considered the greatest British monarch ever, no matter the gender.

NOTES

1. Robert Lacey, *Majesty*, (New York: Harcourt, Brace, Jovanovich, 1977), 8.

2. Sally Bedell Smith, *Queen Elizabeth II: The Life of a Modern Monarch*, (New York: Random House, 2012), 499.

3. Ibid.

4. Among the successes would be the celebrations of her 25th and 50th anniversaries on the throne; her 50th wedding celebration, and her ability to keep many former colonies inside the Commonwealth. As for the disappointments, certainly her sister's decision to give up her divorced lover as a potential husband caused her grief early in her reign, as well as the subsequent divorces of three of her four children.

5. Lacey, 3.

6. Dorothy Laird, *How the Queen Reigns: An Authentic Study of the Queen's Personality and Life Work.* Cleveland and New York: The World Publishing Co., 1959), 227.

7. Ben Pimlott, *The Queen: A Biography of Elizabeth II*, (New York: John Wiley and Sons, Inc., 1996), 279–80.

8. Within his family and among his intimates, the Prince of Wales was known as David, one of his given names.
9. Lacey, 39–40.
10. Lacey, 68.
11. Ibid.
12. Prince Albert was known to his family and intimates as Bertie, a diminutive of his name. Like his brother, he would choose another name to rule: as David became Edward VIII, Bertie became George VI.
13. Lacey, 74.
14. "Historical Speeches and Writing," *The Official Website of the British Monarchy*, last modified 2009, accessed December 18, 2013, www.royal.gov.uk/pdf/edwardviii.pdf.
15. Ibid.
16. Ibid.
17. Lacey, 107.
18. Lacey, 110.
19. "The Rent She Paid for Her Room on Earth," *The Telegraph*, last modified April 1, 2002, accessed January 2, 2014, www.telegraph.co.uk/comment/telegraph-view/3574827/The-rent-she-paid-for-her-room-on-earth.html.
20. Ibid.
21. "Wartime Broadcast," *The Official Website of the British Monarchy*, last modified 2009, accessed January 4, 2014, www.royal.gov.uk/ImagesandBroadcasts/Historic%20speeches%20and%20broadcasts/Wartimebroadcast1940.aspx.
22. Ibid.
23. Ibid.
24. Ibid.
25. Ibid.
26. Lacey, 118.
27. Camilia Tominey, "The Real Value of the Royal Family: Queen's Accounts to Be Audited," *The Express*, February 17, 2013, accessed February 23, 2014, www.expresss.co,uk./news/uk/378183/The-rela-value-of-the-Royal-family-Queen-s-accounts-to-be-audited.
28. Laird, 26.
29. Laird, 27.
30. Robert Hardman, *Her Majesty: Queen Elizabeth II and Her Court*, (New York: Penguin Books, 2012), 235.
31. Lacey, 156–57.
32. Smith, 127.
33. Smith, 128.
34. Smith, 129.
35. "Christmas Broadcast 1953," *The Official Website of the British Monarchy*, last modified 2009, accessed on November 30, 2013, www.royal.gov.uk/ImagesandBroadcasts/TheQueensChristmasBroadcasts/ChristmasBroadcasts/Christmasbroadcast1953.aspx.

36. Ibid.
37. Smith, 128.
38. Smith, 129.
39. Roya Nikkah, "Princess Margaret: Recently Unearthed Letter Sheds New Light on Decision Not to Marry," *The Telegraph*, last modified November 7, 2009, accessed December 3, 2013, www.telegraph.co.uk/news/uknews/theroyal family/6520837/Princess-Margaret-recently-unearthed-letter-sheds-new-light-on-decision-not-to-marry.html.
40. Pimlott, 286.
41. Pimlott, 280.
42. Pimlott, 283.
43. Pimlott, 287.
44. Ibid.
45. Lacey, 165.
46. Smith, 179–80.
47. Smith, 179.
48. Smith, 198.
49. Ibid.
50. Ibid.
51. Ibid.
52. Ibid.
53. Pimlott, 413.
54. Lacey, 302.
55. Aristotle, *The "Art" of Rhetoric*, trans. John Henry Freese (Cambridge: Harvard University Press, 1926), 17.
56. Kenneth Burke, *A Rhetoric of Motives*, (Berkeley, University of California Press, 1950), 21.
57. "Speech Following the Death of Diana, Princess of Wales," *The Official Website of the British Monarchy*, last modified 2009, www.royal.gov.uk (accessed on December 13, 2013).
58. Ibid.
59. Ibid.
60. Karlyn Kohrs Campbell and Kathleen Hall Jamieson, *Presidents Creating the Presidency: Deeds Done in Words*, (Chicago and London: The University of Chicago Press, 2008), 77.
61. "Speech Following the Death of Diana, Princess of Wales," *The Official Website of the British Monarchy*, last modified 2009, accessed December 13, 2013, www.royal.gov.uk.
62. Ibid.
63. Ibid.
64. Ibid.
65. Ibid.
66. Ibid.
67. Ibid.

68. Smith, 405.
69. Smith, 417.
70. Smith, 487.
71. George Pascoe-Watson, "Queen of the Spinners," *New Statesman* 141, no. 5108 (June 4, 2012): 22–24, accessed on January 4, 2014, ehis.ebscohost.com.zeus.tarleton.edu:81/eds/pdfviewer.
72. Barry Came, "Diana's Legacy," *Maclean's* 111, no.35 (August 31, 1998): 44, accessed on December 21, 2013, ehis.ebscohost.com.zeus.tarleton.edu: 81/eds.

Part Two

MAATHAI, OGOT, AND NGILU: WOMEN AND LEADERSHIP IN KENYA

Chapter Three

Environmental Conservation, Peace, Democracy, and Development

A Case Study of Wangari Maathai's Speeches

Catherine Waithera Mwangi and Oscar Gakuo Mwangi

Wangari Muta Maathai was not only the first woman in East and Central Africa to earn a doctorate degree in Veterinary Anatomy but also the first to attain the position of Associate Professor of Veterinary Anatomy in the region. She was also the first African woman to be awarded the prestigious Nobel Peace Prize in 2004. Maathai was an acclaimed national and international environmental conservationist, human rights supporter, a defender of democracy, and a principled politician. She founded the Green Belt Movement (GBM) that became a formidable movement dealing with environmental and political issues. Given her national and international status she managed to create her own subjective representations of environmental problems effectively, indicating at the same time how the problems could be solved. This chapter utilizes elements of both classical and modern rhetorical theories to determine how Maathai, in the context of social constructivism, constructs environmental problems and attempts to secure adherence to her views on environmental conservation, peace, democracy, and development in her speeches.

The chapter is divided into three sections. The first section examines the relationship among social constructivism, environmental conservation, peace, democracy, and development with a view to demonstrating that environmental problems are socially constructed by agents in such a way that they are perceived as serious thus needing to be urgently solved. The second section is an analysis of the selected speeches. The conclusion points out that Maathai utilizes the three Aristotelian modes of persuasion to effectively construct the relationship among environmental conservation, peace, democracy, and development.

SOCIAL CONSTRUCTIVISM AND ENVIRONMENTAL CONSERVATION

Social constructivism pays attention to the role of ideas, norms, knowledge, culture, and argument in politics, emphasizing the role of collectively held ideas and understandings of social life. It stresses that human interaction is shaped mainly by ideational factors, not merely by material ones, and that most of these ideational factors are commonly shared beliefs that are not reducible to individuals. The major concern of constructivist analysis is to explain how social facts change and influence politics. Most social constructivists indicate that in politics, behavior is rule-guided and that actors try to do what is socially acceptable rather than maximizing or optimizing their given preferences. Socially shared ideas both regulate behavior and constitute the identity of actors. These norms also define the basic rules of politics in which actors find themselves when interacting. Constructivists argue that actors are shaped by the social milieu in which they live, hence agents and structures are mutually constituted in ways that explain the *reality* of the political world. It therefore becomes essential to understand the constitution of things so as to explain how actors behave and what causes political outcomes. The constitution of things is causal since it affects political behavior. In short, social constructivism views politics as socially constructed.[1]

Social constructivism can be characterized into three broad variants: conventional, interpretative, and critical/radical. In general, conventional constructivism examines the role of norms and identity in shaping political outcomes by advocating bridge-building among diverse theoretical perspectives. Interpretative constructivists focus on the *how possible* questions as opposed to the explanatory *why* kind. They adopt an in-depth inductive research strategy that pays attention to the reconstruction of identities and also makes use of methods that involve a variety of discourse-theoretical techniques. Critical variants add an explicitly normative dimension by examining a researcher's own implication in the reconstruction of the identities and world being studied. In this variant, discourse-theoretical methods are also emphasized but with greater emphasis on the power and domination inherent in language. The latter two variants derive their theoretical inspiration from linguistic approaches.[2] It is the third variant that focuses on discursive constructivism, which this chapter is primarily interested in.

Discursive constructivism emphasizes the role of language in the construction of social reality. There are various approaches to the discursive construction of the environment and environmental issues. They range from, among others, the Foucaultian ideas of power and knowledge relations, to phenomenological approaches to discourse analysis in linguistics and social psychology, to ethnographic traditions of intersubjective dialogue, to literary theories of textuality. Despite the theoretical diversity of discursive constructivism, the various approaches share something in common: a concern with power relationships. Advocates of discursive constructivism engage in political critique and emphasize that what is important is not just describing the ways environmental issues are constructed but also trying to understand the effects of those constructions, hence change them positively.[3] This perspective points out that environmental problems do not occur themselves but are socially constructed by individuals or organizations that define such problems as serious, hence seek to solve them. The social construction of environmental problems is influenced by one's social, economic, and political milieu especially the way in which the dynamics of power relationships in environmental governance are perceived. As such, environmental problems are not very different from other socio-political problems. The main objective is to understand why they are perceived as problems and how those who understand these problems command political attention in their bid to solve them. Environmental problems are not, however, merely socially constructed through language or symbolically but are also created through human activity as human behavior affects the environment. Environmental problems are both physical phenomena and social constructions. Social constructivism does not deny the importance of material factors of environmental problems. Rather, it emphasizes that actors operate on the basis of the meaning attached to these factors. The ways in which environmental problems are socially constructed has important theoretical and policy implications.[4]

The relationship among environmental conservation, peace, democracy, and development is best understood in the context of environmental change, environmental security, environmental degradation, and human security. Environmental change threatens both environmental security and human security when it leads to environmental degradation as the latter may lead to the depletion of natural resources in terms of quantity or quality. Environmental change is one of the main sources of scarcity of such resources, and environmental problems are therefore characterized as resource scarcities. The most salient impact of environmental change is the way that it threatens human security.[5] In this context, the discursive perspective of social constructivism attempts not only to describe the way environmental problems are socially constructed but also to understand the effects of such constructions with the aim of solving them positively. They are constructed in such a way that they become concerns of high politics; therefore, they become priority issues that require an urgent response at top political level. If they become part of low politics, environmental concerns lose their sense of political importance, urgency, and public interest.[6] Peace, democracy, and development can be achieved through environmental conservation if the latter is socially constructed as fundamental to the former.

It is in regard of the foregoing context of social constructivism that this chapter utilizes elements of both classical and modern rhetorical theories to determine how Maathai constructs environmental problems and attempts to secure adherence to her views on the relationship among environmental conservation and peace, democracy, and development in her speeches. It examines how she employs *logos*, that is, appeal to intellect, *pathos*, appeal to emotion, and *ethos*, appeal to character in her speeches.[7] Maathai was an uncompromising environmental conservationist, an ardent human rights supporter, an effective non-governmental organizations networker, a champion of democracy, and a principled politician. Her work on environmental conservation and human rights earned her several honorary degrees and international academic appointments. She founded the GBM, which became synonymous with her, in 1977 and transformed it into a formidable movement through the idea of planting trees using ordinary people. Using her unique skills, she managed to combine and balance science, social commitment, and politics to protect the environment. The GBM focused mainly on organizing, inspiring, and mobilizing grassroots women groups. These groups planted trees to conserve the environment and in the process empowering women by improving their human security. More than 30 million trees were planted in Kenya. Given its successes in Kenya, the GBM established a Pan-Africa Green Belt Network in 1986.[8] Due to her international recognition in environmental conservation and human rights, Maathai was also accorded the privilege of addressing the United Nations (UN) on several occasions. She also spoke on behalf of women at special sessions of the General Assembly during the five-year review of the Earth Summit and served on the Commission for Global Governance and the Commission on the Future. Maathai was also a member of parliament and an Assistant Minister for Environment and Natural Resources in Kenya.[9]

AN ANALYSIS OF WANGARI MAATHAI'S SPEECHES

This section provides an analysis of Maathai's speeches. The analysis examines Maathai's use of *logos*, *pathos*, and *ethos*.[10] For each speech analyzed, the claim, data and warrant(s) for the different arguments found are identified.[11] Throughout this chapter, the term *claim* is used in the Toulminian sense.[12] The emotions Maathai attempted to provoke are also identified, and an explanation of how and why she did this offered. The analysis also examines how she uses expertise and training and common ground to portray herself as a trustworthy person. Three key speeches are analyzed: the Nobel Peace Prize acceptance speech that she delivered on 10 December 2004; the "Inaugural World Food Law Distinguished Lecture" that she delivered on 10 May 2005; and the "Sustained Development, Democracy, and Peace in Africa" speech, which she delivered at the Summit of Nobel Peace Laureates held in Gwangju, South Korea on 16 June 2006.

Nobel Peace Prize Acceptance Speech

The Norwegian Nobel Committee awarded Maathai the Peace Prize for "her contribution to sustainable development, democracy and peace."[13] It also felt that she was "a strong voice speaking for the best forces in Africa to promote peace and good living conditions on that continent."[14] The construction of environmental and environmental-related social facts and knowledge can be analyzed through the usage of *logos* as it appeals to the intellect of the audience. *Logos* is effectively employed in Maathai's Nobel Peace Prize acceptance speech.

Maathai's claim that environmental conservation, democracy, human rights, and equality between men and women are all crucial for the attainment of peace is implicit, emerging from this statement: ". . . countless individuals and groups across the globe . . . work quietly and often without recognition to protect the environment, promote democracy, defend human rights and ensure equality between women and men. By so doing, they plant seeds of peace."[15] The statement "countless individuals and groups across the globe,"[16] creates the idea that teamwork is necessary for the realization of the itemized values. It is reinforced by the following statement: "The honour is also for my family, friends, partners and supporters throughout the world."[17] This claim is justified by the fact that she has been awarded the Nobel for her efforts in promoting peace by protecting the environment and fighting for democracy. The warrant is her experiences as an environmentalist.

The claim that democracy and environmental conservation are achievable in Kenya is also implicit, emerging from this statement: "I am also grateful to the people of Kenya—who remained stubbornly hopeful that democracy could be realized and their environment managed sustainably."[18] This claim is justified by the fact that she has been awarded the Nobel for her efforts toward attaining these. The warrant is her experiences as a Kenyan. Another implicit claim is that peace, democracy, and development are crucial for improved livelihoods in Africa. This is captured in the following statement: "My fellow Africans, as we embrace this recognition, let us use it to intensify our commitment to our people, to reduce conflicts and poverty and thereby improve their quality of life."[19] The word intensify is intended to impress upon Africans that these efforts have been existing but now need to be strengthened for the desired livelihoods to be achieved and also that she has been involved in these efforts. This claim is justified by the fact that she has been awarded the Nobel for her efforts in improving the livelihoods of Africans by fighting for peace, democracy, and development. The warrant is her experience as a politician.

Maathai expresses the view that there is a relationship among peace, democracy, and development when she explicitly claims: "Recognizing that sustainable development, democracy and peace are indivisible is an idea whose time has come."[20] This is justified through the fact that she has been awarded the Nobel: "In this year's prize, the Norwegian Nobel Committee has placed the critical issue of environment and its linkage to democracy and peace before the world."[21] Her warrant is also explicit: "Our work over the past 30 years has always appreciated and engaged these linkages."[22] Maathai also explicitly claims: "Indeed, the state of any country's environment is a reflection of the kind of governance in place, and without good governance there can be no peace."[23] This is supported with the following explanation: "Many countries, which have poor governance systems, are also likely to have conflicts and poor laws protecting the environment."[24] She emphasizes the logic that good governance is an essential precondition for environmental conservation, peace, democracy, and development.

Maathai maintains that the environment and livelihood are inextricably linked. She explicitly claims: ". . . when the environment is destroyed, plundered or mismanaged, we undermine our quality of life and that of future generations."[25] Testimony of rural women whom she worked with in 1977 is used to support this claim. Maathai notes that these women said they that they could not meet their basic needs of firewood, clean drinking water, balanced diets, shelter, and income due to environmental degradation and commercial farming. This testimony also serves to evoke sympathy by highlighting the agony that ordinary women have undergone due to environmental degradation.[26] Two explicit warrants are in this argument: (a) "Throughout Africa, women are the primary caretakers, holding significant responsibility for tilling the land and feeding their families";[27] and (b) ". . . international trade controlled the price of the exports from these small-scale farmers and a reasonable and just income could not be guaranteed."[28] The rationality behind these arguments is to demonstrate that the livelihoods of rural women, which are a function of small-scale farming, are inextricably linked to the status of the environment.

The claim that tree planting is a natural solution to the lack of basic needs is implied. It is supported by the following reasons: (a) ". . . tree planting is simple, attainable and guarantees quick, successful results within a reasonable amount of time";[29] and (b) "The activity also creates employment and improves soils and watersheds."[30] The argument contains seven warrants. The explicit warrants are: (a) "This sustains interest and commitment";[31] (b) ". . . we have planted over 30 million trees that provide fuel, food, shelter, and income to support their children's education and household needs";[32] and (c) ". . . a degraded environment leads to a scramble for scarce resources and may culminate in poverty and even conflict."[33] The implicit warrants are: (a) Poverty is the lack of capital but not the lack of knowledge and skills to address environmental problems; (b) Solutions to problems in Africa must come from Africa itself; (c) Satisfaction of basic needs rests on the environment being healthy and well managed; and (d) International economic arrangements are unjust.

Maathai tactfully impresses upon the audience that environmental problems are not very different from other socio-political problems by describing the civic education program of the GBM:

> . . . we developed a citizen education program, during which people identify their problems, the causes and possible solutions. They then make connections between their own personal actions and the problems they witness in the environment and in society. They learn that our world is confronted with a litany of woes . . . [34]

She proceeds immediately to explicitly claim: ". . . [there are] many human activities that are devastating to the environment and societies."[35] The following examples justify this claim: ". . . widespread destruction of ecosystems, especially through deforestation, climatic instability, and contamination in the soils and waters . . ."[36] It, therefore, becomes important to protect the environment from human activities that are destructive.

Maathai has two solutions to the problem of human activities that devastate the environment and societies. She presents them as arguments, the first being captured in this explicit claim: ". . . [citizens] must be part of the solutions."[37] The reason that supports this claim is that ". . . [citizens] are the primary custodians and beneficiaries of the environment that sustains them."[38] The warrant here is citizens have a hidden potential to conserve the environment. The second solution is also captured in an explicit claim: ". . . [we] need to revive our sense of belonging to a larger family of life, with which we have shared our evolutionary process."[39] This claim is supported by the following observation: "Activities that devastate the environment and societies continue unabated."[40] The warrants for these arguments are, first, the earth is a living thing and, second, "it is 30 years since we started this work."[41] For Maathai, environmental conservation must, therefore, be society centered, long term, and sustainable.

In an effort to develop the idea that the solutions to problems in Africa must come from Africa itself, she argues that local trees have been used for conflict resolution in African communities. She explicitly claims: "Using trees as a symbol of peace is in keeping with a widespread African tradition."[42] This is immediately followed by the data: "For example, the elders of the Kikuyu carried a staff from the thigi tree that, when placed between two disputing sides, caused them to stop fighting and seek reconciliation."[43] The *thigi* tree is used to reconcile warring Kikuyu communities. The warrant, which is explicit, follows immediately after the example: "Many communities in Africa have these traditions."[44] And in a move to intensify reverence[45] to positive African traditions, she claims: "Africans, especially, should re-discover positive aspects of their culture."[46] The explanation she gives to justify this follows immediately: "In accepting them, they would give themselves a sense of belonging, identity and self-confidence."[47] Two explicit warrants complete the argument: "Culture plays a central role in the political, economic and social life of communities"[48] and "culture is dynamic and evolves over time, consciously discarding retrogressive traditions, like female genital mutilation (FGM), and embracing aspects that are good and useful."[49] Maathai logically demonstrates that informal process-orientated systems are more effective than formal goal-oriented ones in providing solutions to problems in Africa.

In this speech, *logos* is, in sum, employed to convince the audience that there is a link among environmental conservation, peace, democracy, and development that is crucial for enhancing human rights, equality between men and women, and good governance in society. Environmental conservation, Maathai emphasizes, is crucial for development to be realized.

The construction of the identity of actors can be analyzed through the use of *ethos*, which appeals to the personality of the speaker. Maathai highlights several virtues that she would like Africans, African leaders and Kenyans to embrace. She therefore portrays herself as one who has the best interests of these groups by foregrounding the racial and national identities that she shares with them. In other words, builds her identity as an African as well as a Kenyan. At the onset of the speech, she says: "As the first African woman to receive this prize, I accept it on behalf of the people of Kenya and Africa, and indeed the world."[50] Later she says: "I am immensely privileged to join my fellow African Peace laureates . . ."[51] Maathai also says: "I know that African people everywhere are encouraged by this news. My fellow Africans, as we embrace this recognition . . ."[52] She intensifies her image as an African by displaying reverence to African traditions. This is seen where she cites the use of a staff from the *thigi* tree, noting that many African communities have similar traditions. Maathai therefore urges Africans to rediscover positive aspects of their culture so that they can revive their sense of belonging, identity, and self-confidence.

Having constructed her identity as a recipient of the Nobel, and as both an African and Kenyan woman, she proceeds to portray herself as a caring mother. She immediately says: "I am especially mindful of women and the girl child. I hope it will encourage them to raise their voices and take more space for leadership. . . . As a mother, I appreciate the inspiration this brings to the youth and urge them to use it to pursue their dreams."[53] These identities as an African woman and mother help intensify her image as one who knows about and has experienced the challenges faced by African women, subsequently, one who has the best interests of the women she supports through the GBM.

Her image as a person of good character is pronounced. She calls attention to several virtues, reiterating them all through the speech. In the following statement, she urges African leaders to embrace democracy and human rights, while promoting environmental security to a virtue by listing it alongside: "Let us embrace democratic governance, protect human rights and protect our environment."[54] She also identifies with Burmese Peace Prize Laureate Aung San Suu Kyi who received the Nobel in 1991 "for her non-violent struggle for democracy and human rights,"[55] calling for her release "so that she can continue her work for peace and democracy for the people of Burma and the world at large."[56] Maathai has drawn attention to democracy, peace, human rights and environmental security, perseverance, selflessness, and equality by associating with the "countless individuals and groups across the globe"[57] who strive for these virtues and with "the people of Kenya—who remained stubbornly hopeful that democracy could be realized and their environment managed sustainably."[58] The aim here is to portray herself as a staunch defender of environmental conservation, peace, democracy, and development.

Maathai makes a direct call to Kenyan leaders and citizens alike to embrace justice, integrity, and trust: ". . . it is equally important that in their own relationships with each other, [entire communities] exemplify the leadership values they wish to see in their own leaders, namely, justice, integrity and trust."[59] Later in the speech, African leaders are urged: ". . . expand democratic space and build fair and just societies that allow the creativity and energy of their citizens to flourish."[60] This also creates the image that she is a democracy-promoting crusader.

Gratitude is displayed by appreciating the role that others have played in her winning the Nobel: "This honour is also for my family, friends, partners and supporters throughout the world."[61] She also thanks the Norwegian Nobel Committee: "In this year's prize, the Norwegian Nobel Committee has placed the critical issue of environment and its linkage to democracy and peace before the world. For their visionary action, I am profoundly grateful."[62] Maathai's vision is, therefore, associated with that of the Norwegian Nobel Committee thereby enhancing her international status.

Practical wisdom is demonstrated by informing the audience about her expertise and training. She tells them that since its formation, the GBM has been involved in solidifying the link among environmental conservation, peace, democracy, and development: "Our work over the past 30 years has always appreciated and engaged these linkages."[63] Later in the speech she notes:

> Although initially the Green Belt Movement's tree planting activities did not address issues of democracy and peace, it soon became clear that responsible governance of the environment was impossible without democratic space. Therefore, the tree became a symbol for the democratic struggle in Kenya. . . trees of peace were planted to demand . . . a peaceful transition to democracy.
>
> . . . the tree also became a symbol for peace and conflict resolution . . . to reconcile disputing communities. During the . . . re-writing of the Kenyan constitution, similar trees of peace were planted . . . to promote a culture of peace . . .[64]

Maathai also reveals that her interest in the environment goes back to when she was a child, having had the advantage of growing up in a rural setting: "My inspiration partly comes from my childhood experiences and observations of Nature in rural Kenya. . . . As I was growing up, I witnessed forests being cleared and replaced by commercial plantations, which destroyed local biodiversity and the capacity of the forests to conserve water."[65] In the conclusion of the speech she adds:

> . . . I would visit a stream next to our home to fetch water for my mother. I would drink water straight from the stream. Playing among the arrowroot leaves I tried in vain to pick up the strands of frogs' eggs, believing they were beads. But every time I put my little fingers under them they would break. Later, I saw thousands of tadpoles: black, energetic and wriggling through the clear water against the background of the brown earth.[66]

She lets the audience know that this interest was intensified by her formal education, which she received in Kenya, the United States, and Germany.[67]

In sum, Maathai portrays herself as one who has the best interests of Africans, African leaders and Kenyans, all of whom are a target audience, by foregrounding the racial and national identities that she shares with them. She also foregrounds her identity as an African mother so as to emerge as one who has the best interests of the women she supports through the GBM. Her image as a person of good character is paramount, and it is constructed by accentuating gratitude, democracy, human rights, environmental security, justice, integrity, and trust. She demonstrates knowledge and expertise in environmental matters by tracing her interest in the environment to the rural setting she grew up in and her educational background as well as by outlining the GBM's role in environmental conservation, peace, democracy, and development.

The social construction of environmental issues meant to appeal to emotions can be analyzed through the usage of *pathos*. In this speech, Maathai attempts to evoke sympathy for the environment by portraying the earth as a "wounded woman": "We are called to assist the Earth to heal her wounds and in the process heal our own..."[68] Sympathy for the earth, Maathai hopes, would activate engagement in activities that protect it. There is also an attempt to trigger respect and sympathy for environmental conservationists by portraying them as a humble team playing against hostile opponents. This is evident when she says: "They work quietly and often without recognition... I know they, too, are proud today."[69] She also notes that the GBM has accomplished its work "under hostile conditions."[70] There is an attempt to provoke pride in African women from African men by portraying herself as a heroine: "I know the honour also gives a deep sense of pride to our men, both old and young."[71] By portraying herself as a heroine and instituting pride in Africans, Maathai is in a position to appeal to emotions that are required for mobilizing the people for environmental conservation.

There is also an attempt to stir bravery in the struggle for democracy in Kenya by describing the efforts of the GBM in emotive and connotative terms. Maathai says: "Through the Green Belt Movement, thousands of ordinary citizens were mobilized and empowered to take action and effect change. They learned to overcome fear and a sense of helplessness and moved to defend democratic rights."[72] She also notes: "In 2002, the courage, resilience, patience and commitment of members of the Green Belt Movement, other civil society organizations, and the Kenyan public culminated in the peaceful transition to a democratic government and laid the foundation for a more stable society."[73] Maathai expresses confidence that African leaders will succeed in achieving democracy, human rights, and environmental security so as to evoke the hope necessary for them to strive for these: "Let us embrace democratic governance, protect human rights and protect our environment. I am confident that we shall rise to the occasion."[74] In the speech, *pathos* is, in sum, created through imagery, emotive terms, and connotative terms.

Inaugural World Food Law Distinguished Lecture

The lecture delivered in Washington, D.C. in the United States of America in May 2005, was the inaugural address for the Howard University World Food

Law Institute's Distinguished Lectures. This institute seeks to "improve the understanding of issues faced by the millions of persons living and working in rural areas around the world and to provide support for those seeking food security."[75] The theme of the speech is "Forests and Food."[76] This speech is also analyzed using Aristotle's three strategies of persuasion.

With regard to *logos*, in this speech too, Maathai expresses the view that the environment, democracy, and peace are linked. She explicitly claims: "... you cannot achieve peace without looking at the environment."[77] She justifies this through the fact that she was awarded the Nobel for her contribution to this: "Those of us who have been working on peace, democratisation, environment [*sic*] movements, in women's movements, we always felt that indeed these issues are related, but nobody could have said it so dramatically and with so much persuasion as the Norwegian Nobel Committee."[78] Maathai also justifies that the environment, democracy, and peace are linked using this extended metaphor:

> A traditional African stool is actually made from one log and then three legs are chiseled out and a seat is also chiseled out in the middle so that when you sit, you sit on this basin, which rests on three legs.
>
> I compare the three legs to the three pillars that the Norwegian Nobel Committee identified. One leg is that of peace. The other is that of democratic space, where rights are respected ... The third leg is the environment, that needs to be managed sustainably ... the resources of which also need to be shared equitably.
>
> ... these three pillars ... are extremely important for any state that intends to be stable. For when a state rests on these three pillars then the basin of the seat becomes the space, the environment, the milieu in which we can do development ...
>
> ... we cannot keep that basin up, if those three legs are not stable ... we have to invest in those three legs. We have to invest in the environment ... in cultures of peace ... in cultures of democratisation. ... We can do all that if the three pillars are safe.[79]

In this metaphor, "three" is repeated for emphasis and to aid recall of the elements in the linkage. Equal importance is attached to these three elements through the parallel structure "the pillar of peace, the pillar of the environment, and the pillar of democratic space."[80] The tautological parallel structure "we feel secure, we feel safe"[81] emphasizes the confidence enjoyed by donors, states, and financiers when they invest in democratic and peaceful societies with environmental security.[82] The idea that no development can occur where these three aspects do not exist, hence the vital need to pay attention to them, is enforced through the anaphora[83] "we cannot" and "we have to invest in"[84] respectively. The concept democratic space is amplified through the anaphora "a space to."[85] This amplification is deemed important considering that democratic space creates an enabling environment that provides the opportunity for citizens to exercise, fully, the environmental-related fundamental rights and freedoms required to establish peace, democracy, and development in a society.[86] The warrant in this argument is her having been selected for the Nobel as well as the Norwegian Nobel Committee's belief that she was sincerely committed to promoting peace and good living conditions in Africa.

Social constructivism takes into account social facts or knowledge which have no material reality, a position Maathai adheres to in her speeches. Maathai implicitly claims the key to development for any country is peace, environmental security, and democratic space, not money. She justifies this with the observation that in the last forty years Africa has received money from development agencies yet no development has occurred. She also justifies the claim through the following details:

> Where you see a stable state and a state where people are appreciated, governments are investing in people rather than in weapons, they are investing in education, quality education, giving people the skills and the technology they need in order to exploit the resources that are within their borders, that's a state that feels stable, that doesn't feel threatened. Then it is able and willing to invest in its people.[87]

The warrant is that governments value development. This warrant stems from her experience as a politician.

Maathai maintains that environmental degradation and food insecurity are related. She explicitly claims: ". . . you cannot have security in food if you do not have that pillar of the environment."[88] She supports this with the example of Kenya where the clearing of natural forests in the mountains and their replacement with commercial plantations of trees from Australia and what she refers to as the northern hemisphere has led to loss of biodiversity and unexpected rainfall patterns that have caused low crop yields. She notes that the unexpected rainfall patterns have also been because of the illegal logging and charcoal burning, both of which have been going on for years. The warrant here is that sustaining natural forests is the only means of environmental conservation. This develops from her training and expertise in environmental issues.

Maathai refutes the view that climate change solely causes unexpected rainfall patterns by indicating that those that hold this view have not done enough research:

> . . . some people say it is climate change and they say, 'Well, you know, even on Mount Kenya the glaciers are receding.' . . . It's possible that it is part of climate

change. But climate change does not happen at a global level at once. Climate change starts at a local level . . . it is happening in Kenya, it is happening in Africa, it is happening in Europe, it's happening elsewhere. And sooner or later . . . climate . . . in certain areas will become extremely harsh, especially for people who don't have alternatives, such as the people in our region.[89]

She also refutes the view of Christian farmers that the unexpected rainfall patterns are caused by religious factors, particularly God, by indicating they believe this because they do not understand the importance of environmental conservation:

If you ask an ordinary Kenyan woman why the rains do not come, the farmer will probably say, 'God has not yet brought the rain, and we must pray so that God brings us the rain.' . . . But if the rains don't come, it has nothing to do with God. It has everything to do with the way they are managing their environment.[90]

Maathai maintains that the solution to the food crisis in Kenya is not buying food and receiving food aid but protecting the environment. She explicitly claims: ". . . if we destroy the mountain, the waters, when they take the soil, they take away the soil in which the farmer plants his seed."[91] She justifies this with a fact that she has relied on before in the speech:

. . . the Norwegian Nobel Committee said: The environment is an intricate way joined, is related, is intertwined, in our lives on an everyday basis. It is not something we think about or talk about or learn about sometimes. The air we breathe, the water we drink, the food we eat: everything we do has to do with the environment.[92]

The warrant is her belief that everything depends on the environment. In sum, *logos* is employed to show that environmental security, democracy, and peace are the pillars of development and that environmental degradation is the main cause of food insecurity in Kenya.

In the case of *ethos*, Maathai demonstrates that she knows about the unexpected rainfall patterns in Kenya by refuting that climate change and God are the causes. This not only shows that she is aware of the different positions in the debate but also that she respects those that advocate them otherwise she would not have responded to them. She also shows that she is experienced in environmental management by pointing out that the GBM has been planting trees on public land, which includes in the forests. She displays good character by calling attention to justice and gratitude. She highlights the injustice faced by Kenyan coffee and tea farmers who not only never get a fair price for their produce from the international market but also have to buy inputs for these products at a price set by somebody else, calling upon those with the capacity to intervene. Gratitude emerges when, at the onset of the speech, she thanks the other participants present for having invited her and received her so warmly.

This speech also makes use of *pathos* to achieve its intended objectives. Maathai draws attention to Africans living and working in rural areas by using the traditional African stool to clarify the linkage among democracy, peace and the environment. Her allusion to this African artifact attaches importance to African culture, which is important for she tries to convince Kenyans that the food insecurity they are facing is due to the destruction of natural forests and their replacement with trees from Australia and the northern hemisphere. If Kenyans are to accept to prioritize natural forests, they need to have reverence to African culture which they can do only if the positive elements of it are entrenched in their minds.

There is an attempt to evoke love for the environment by alluding to the Garden of Eden in the Bible: "... it is very important ... to see the connection between the book of Genesis and what is happening to the environment, and to begin to tell the faithful that they must take care of the Garden of Eden that God created in the book of Genesis...."[93] Emotions of love can easily be evoked through religious analogies. An attempt is also made to evoke sympathy for the Kenyan coffee and tea farmers who trade in the international market:

> Somehow there is a law that does not create justice for this farmer, and as a result, because he doesn't get enough for his labor, he continues to scrape, to scratch this land and get very little out of it. So we call him poor, and we begin to say that it is partly because of his poverty that the environment is being degraded. Well, it is not true. The farmer is doing his best.[94]

The aim here is evoke emotions of sympathy by establishing a link among small-scale farming, international trade, exploitation, and environmental degradation. Maathai, in sum, tries to create an emotional environment conducive for the revival of positive African traditions, participation in environmental protection, and intervention on behalf of Kenyan farmers dealing with the international market.

Sustained Development, Democracy, and Peace in Africa Speech

This speech is also analyzed using Aristotle's three strategies. It was delivered at the Summit of Nobel Peace Laureates in June 2006 at Gwangju, South Korea. As in other speeches, *logos* is used effectively to appeal to the intellect of the audience so that they can perceive the way in which she creates her own subjective representations of environmental issues. Maathai claims that there is a "close linkage between good governance, sustainable management of resources, and peace."[95] She justifies this with the fact she was awarded the Nobel for her contribution to these: ". . . when the Norwegian Nobel Committee honoured me with the Nobel Peace Prize in 2004 it intended to send a new and historic message to the world: to rethink peace and security."[96] There are two warrants: the Committee's value for peace and the fact that environmental resources are limited.

Good governance is crucial for sustainable management of environmental resources, a claim explicitly expressed: "Sustainable management of the resources is only possible if we practice good governance. . . ."[97] She justifies this through explaining the concept good governance by listing the following details:

> . . . good governance . . . calls for respect for the rule of law, respect for human rights, a willingness to give space and a voice to the weak and the more vulnerable in our societies; that we respect the voice of the minority, even while accepting the decision of the majority, and respect diversity. Good governance seeks justice and equity for all irrespective of race, religion, gender, and any other parameters, which man uses to discriminate and exclude. Good governance is indeed inclusive and seeks participatory democracy.[98]

Good governance, coupled with the sustainable management of resources, promotes peace. Maathai explicitly claims: "When we manage our resources sustainably and practice good governance we deliberately and consciously promote cultures of peace. . . ."[99] This claim is justified with details: ". . . cultures of peace . . . include the willingness to dialogue and make genuine efforts for healing and reconciliation, especially where there has been misunderstanding, loss of trust, and even conflict."[100] The warrant is that peace is desirable. Bad governance, poor management of resources, and the lack of peace are the three main causes of conflict, Maathai claims. She cites the conflicts in the Darfur region of Sudan, Somalia, Ivory Coast, Democratic Republic of Congo, and Chad as examples. Here too, the warrant is that peace is desirable.

Having shown the role of good governance in both the environment and peace, she claims that there is need for such governance in Africa in the following statement: "A good number of African leaders have recognised the need for good governance in Africa."[101] She justifies this with the following reasons: (a) ". . . despite all the resources in Africa, development continues to lag behind due to lack of peace and sustainable management of resources";[102] (b) "Corruption and mismanagement of resources frustrates development and exacerbates poverty";[103] and (c) It is a peaceful resolution of conflict and violence. She further gives this fact: ". . . no development will take place in a state of conflict and mismanagement of state affairs."[104] The warrants are that development and peace are desirable in society.

In sum, *logos* is employed to convince the audience that there is a close link among good governance, sustainable management of resources, peace, and development. Good governance enables sustainable management of resources and peace prevails where the two exist. Development flourishes in societies characterised by good governance and peace; in short, good governance is fundamental for sustainable management of resources, peace, and development.

The speech also portrays the speaker as an authority on environmental conservation issues. The audience is informed about her expertise and training in the issues she addresses. With respect to sustainability, Maathai first informs them of her involvement in sustaining the Congo Forest Ecosystem: ". . . I have been invited by the Heads of States in the Central African sub-region to be a Goodwill Ambassador for the Congo Forest Ecosystem . . . The forest is the second largest: only second to the Amazon forest."[105] She informs them of, second, her exposure to the campaign to reduce, reuse, and recycle resources:

> . . . while visiting Japan, I learned of the wonderful concept of mottainai, which . . . teaches us to be grateful, to not waste, and to be appreciative . . . I was very impressed to learn that by using technology many new items were being made from recycled materials like plastic waste, from which companies could make beautiful furoshiki.[106]

Japan is highly developed; by pointing out how technology is being utilized there, she is skillfully validating her view that African leaders should invest in technology. Maathai also informs the audience of, third, the GBM's contribution to reducing pollution: "The Green Belt Movement is partnering with some organisations by planting trees in our region to offset some carbon and contribute toward the reduction of the greenhouse gases."[107] With respect to democracy, she notes her role in mobilizing the African Civil Society:

> I have . . . been requested by the African Union to preside over the mobilisation of the African Civil Society in order to form a forum, which will advise the Union on how to manage African affairs more justly and responsibly . . . strengthening civil society would also strengthen the democratization process.[108]

Regarding conflict, she notes that Africa "has known many conflicts for a long time."[109] Her concern about the adverse effects of perverse conflicts upon the environment, peace, democracy, and development builds her image as one who cares about humanity.

Maathai's image as someone of good character is established by calling attention to several virtues. Among these is gratitude. She praises the Japanese concept of *mottainai*, which she notes teaches people to be grateful. Gratitude emerges at the onset of the speech when she thanks the Organizing Committee for the warm welcome as well as hospitality received in South Korea. A second virtue is democracy. She portrays herself as a champion of democracy by recognizing the occasion as an opportunity for the participants to ". . . honour and respect those who lost their lives in search of democracy."[110] She further commends the former President Kim Dae-June for initiating "democratic governance, peace, and reunification of the two Koreas,"[111] adding that the Laureates in attendance bring goodwill to the people of Gwangju and all Koreans as they continue in their "search for democracy and peace in the Peninsular."[112] These issues raised by Maathai in her speech delivered in South Korea, portrays her as one who advocates unity and stability in conflict-prone regions. The image of someone knowledgeable and experienced is, in sum, created by informing the audience about her expertise and training in the issues of sustainability, democracy, and conflict, all three of which she addresses. She calls attention to gratitude, democracy, and peace to build her image as someone of good character.

The use of *pathos* is also evident in the speech. There is an attempt to stir sympathy for all those that have perished, suffered, or are suffering in the fight for democracy. This is done through images of riots and bondage. This emotional state is crucial if her views on democracy are to be accepted. Maathai says:

> We value the opportunity to participate at the commemorations of the May 18 Democratic Movement and honour and respect those who lost their lives in search of democracy. May all the citizens of the Korean peninsular realise the dream for which so many lives were lost when the military opened fire on the defenseless citizens, killing about 150 and injuring more than a thousand.
>
> We regret that even as we continue to preach democracy and peace some of the Laureates like Madame Aung San Suu Kyi of Burma, remains a prisoner in her country and the 14th Dalai Lama, Tenzin Gyatso, was not facilitated with a Visa to attend this Laureate Summit.[113]

Maathai also evokes emotions of anxiety by trying to secure support for sustainable management of resources and good governance. She does so by associating mismanagement of resources and bad governance with conflict:

> When we manage our resources sustainably and practice good governance we deliberately and consciously promote cultures of peace, which include the willingness to dialogue and make genuine efforts for healing and reconciliation, es-

pecially where there has been misunderstanding, lost of trust, and even conflict. Whenever we fail to nurture these three themes, conflict becomes inevitable.[114]

In the speech, *pathos* is, in sum, established through imagery and association. Maathai attempts to evoke sympathy for democracy activists as well as fear of bad governance.

CONCLUSION

The discursive constructivist variants of social constructivism emphasize the role of language in the construction of social reality, particularly in the construction of environmental problems and how such problems can be positively solved. Maathai effectively manages to create her own subjective representations of environmental problems and further indicates how such problems can be adequately tackled. This is evident in her speeches as demonstrated through the application of Aristotelian and Toulminian rhetorical theories.

Maathai extensively employs *logos* to construct the adverse effects of environmental change and degradation especially on human and physical security, and goes ahead to emphasize that environmental conservation is the solution to these detrimental effects. Hence through the use of *logos*, she logically demonstrates the relationship between environmental conservation and good governance and subsequently peace, democracy, and development. Environmental conservation can be enhanced through the use of indigenous knowledge and greater public participation.

Maathai also employs *ethos* to demonstrate that given her socio-political background as a national and international acclaimed environmental conservationist and human rights crusader, as well as a Nobel Peace Prize winner, she is in an authoritative position to construct environmental problems. She effectively creates the image that she is in a position that makes her perceive the dynamics of power relationships in environmental governance much more clearly than ordinary persons. Maathai also builds her identity as an African and a Kenyan and portrays herself as a person of good character who is sincere in her undertakings. In a nutshell, she creates the image that she is trustworthy, which Aristotle maintains is necessary for a persuasive speech.

Through the use of *pathos*, she creates her own subjective representations of environmental problems by stirring emotions on the detrimental effects of environmental degradation by personifying the earth as a wounded woman, and that the solution to this problem is healing thorough environmental conservation hence the attainment peace, democracy, and development worldwide.

NOTES

1. Alexander Wendt, *Social Theory of International Politics* (Cambridge: Cambridge University Press, 1999), 1; Jennifer Sterling-Folker, "Competing Paradigms or Birds of a Feather? Constructivism and Neo-Liberalism Compared," *International Studies Quarterly* 44, no.1 (2000): 99; Thomas Risse, ""Let's Argue!": Communicative Action in World Politics," *International Organization* 4, no. 1 (2000): 4–6; Martha Finnemore and Kathryn Sikkink, "Taking Stock: The Constructivist Research Program in International Relations and Comparative Politics," *Annual Review of Political Science* 4 (2001): 393–394; Keith Grint, "Problems, Problems, Problems: The Social Construction of 'Leadership,'" *Human Relations* 58, no. 11 (2005): 1470–72; Richard Price, "Moral Limit and Possibility in World Politics," *International Organization* 62, no. 2 (2008): 193–94.

2. Jeffery Checkel, "Social Constructivisms in Global and European Politics a Review Essay," *Review of International Studies* 30 (2004): 230–31.

3. David Demeritt, "What Is the 'Social construction of Nature'? A Typology and Sympathetic Critique," *Progress in Human Geography* 26, no. 6 (2000): 772–75.

4. John Hannigan, *Environmental Sociology: A Social Constructionist Perspective* (London: Routledge, 1995), 2; Grahanm Woodgate, and Michael Redclift, "From a 'Sociology of Nature' to Environmental Sociology: Beyond Social Construction," *Environmental Values* 7 (1998): 6; Karen Liftin, "Constructing Environmental Security and Ecological Interdependence," *Global Governance* 5 (1999): 359–60; Jill Belsky, "Beyond the Natural Resource and Environmental Sociology Divide: Insights from a Transdisciplinary Perspective," *Society and Natural Resources* 15 (2002): 270.

5. Thomas Homer-Dixon, "Environmental Scarcities and Violent Conflict: Evidence from Cases," *International Security* 19, no. 1 (1994): 7–9; Cyril Obi, "Globalised Images of Environmental Security in Africa," *Review of African Political Economy* 27, no. 83 (2000): 50–51; Oscar Mwangi, "Environmental Change and Human Security in Lesotho: The Role of the Lesotho Highlands Water Project in Environmental Degradation," *African Security Review*, 17, no. 3 (2008): 59–61.

6. Mwangi, "Lesotho Highlands Water Project," 59–61.

7. For details on these three modes of persuasion, see Aristotle, *The 'Art' of Rhetoric*. John Freese, trans. (London: William Heinemann, 1926); Stephen Toulmin, Richard Rieke, and Allan Janik, *An Introduction to Reasoning*. 2nd ed. (New York: Macmillan Publishing Co, 1984); Stephen Lucas, *The Art of Public Speaking*. 7th ed. (Boston: McGraw-Hill, 2001).

8. Green Belt Movement,"Wangari Maathai Biography," 2013, accessed September 24, 2013, www.greenbeltmovement.org/wangari-maathai/biography; University of Nairobi, "A Brief on Founding Distinguished Chair of WMI Professor Wangari Muta Maathai," 2013, accessed September 24, 2013, www.uonbi.ac.ke/node/3946

9. Ibid.

10. See Aristotle, *'Art' of Rhetoric*; Toulmin, Rieke, and Janik, *An Introduction to Reasoning*; Stephen Lucas, *Art of Public Speaking*.

11. Stephen Toulmin, *The Uses of Argument* (Cambridge: Cambridge University Press, 1958): 94–107.

12. For more on this term, see Toulmin, Rieke and Janik, *Introduction to Reasoning*, 29.
13. "The Nobel Peace Prize for 2004 to Wangari Maathai—Press Release," *Nobelprize.org,* Nobel Media AB 2013, accessed February 28, 2014. www.nobelprize.org/nobel_prizes/peace/laureates/2004/press.html.
14. Ibid.
15. Wangari Maathai, "Nobel Lecture," Oslo, 10 December, 2004, accessed September 23, 2013. ogiek.com/indepth/NobelPeacePrizeAcceptanceSpeech.pdf
16. Ibid.
17. Ibid.
18. Ibid.
19. Ibid.
20. Ibid.
21. Ibid.
22. Ibid.
23. Ibid.
24. Ibid.
25. Ibid.
26. Peer testimony is particularly useful for the authenticity and emotional impact that it introduces. See Lucas, *Public Speaking*, 180.
27. Maathai, "Nobel Lecture."
28. Ibid.
29. Ibid.
30. Ibid.
31. Ibid.
32. Ibid.
33. Ibid.
34. Ibid.
35. Ibid.
36. Ibid.
37. Ibid.
38. Ibid.
39. Ibid.
40. Ibid.
41. Ibid.
42. Ibid.
43. Ibid.
44. Ibid.
45. Reverence is one of the emotions commonly evoked by speakers. See Lucas, *Public Speaking*.
46. Maathai, "Nobel Lecture."
47. Ibid.
48. Ibid.
49. Ibid.
50. Ibid.

51. Ibid.
52. Ibid.
53. Ibid.
54. Ibid.
55. "Aung San Suu Kyi—Facts," *Nobelprize.org*, Nobel Media AB 2013, accessed March 2, 2014, www.nobelprize.org/nobel_prizes/peace/laureates/1991/kyi-facts.html
56. Maathai, "Nobel Lecture."
57. Ibid.
58. Ibid.
59. Ibid.
60. Ibid.
61. Ibid.
62. Ibid.
63. Ibid.
64. Ibid.
65. Ibid.
66. Ibid.
67. Ibid.
68. Ibid.
69. Ibid.
70. Ibid.
71. Ibid.
72. Ibid.
73. Ibid.
74. Ibid.
75. Wangari Maathai, "Inaugural World Food Law Distinguished Lecture," Howard University, Washington, DC, May 10, 2005, accessed September 23, 2013, www.greenbeltmovement.org/wangari-maathai/key-speeches-and-articles/inaugural-world-food-law-distinguished-lecture.
76. Ibid.
77. Ibid.
78. Ibid.
79. Ibid.
80. Ibid.
81. Ibid.
82. Parallelism is recurrent structure or length in clauses but with continual variation. Its intended effects include emphasizing, balancing and making ideas memorable and increasing attentiveness. See Catherine Mwangi, "A Rhetorical Analysis of African Unification Oratory" (Ph.D. thesis, National University of Lesotho, 2009), 287.
83. Anaphora is repetition of a word or phrase at the beginning of consecutive phrases, clauses, sentences, or paragraphs. Its intended effects include emphasizing, enforcing and making ideas memorable, amplification, rhythm, emotionalism, and increasing attentiveness. See Mwangi, "African Union Oratory," 287.
84. Ibid.

85. Ibid.
86. In the speech, Maathai notes that she uses democratic space instead of democracy because some people might feel like the latter is "not exactly what they want to describe." See Maathai, "World Food Law."
87. Maathai, "World Food Law."
88. Ibid.
89. Ibid.
90. Ibid.
91. Ibid.
92. Ibid.
93. Ibid.
94. Ibid.
95. Wangari Maathai, "Sustained Development, Democracy, and Peace in Africa." Gwangju, South Korea, June 16, 2006, accessed September 23, 2013, www.greenbeltmovement.org/wangari-maathai/key-speeches-and-articles/sustained-development-democracy-and-peace.
96. Ibid.
97. Ibid.
98. Ibid.
99. Ibid.
100. Ibid.
101. Ibid.
102. Ibid.
103. Ibid.
104. Ibid.
105. Ibid.
106. Ibid.
107. Ibid.
108. Ibid.
109. Ibid.
110. Ibid.
111. Ibid.
112. Ibid.
113. Ibid.
114. Ibid.

Chapter Four

The "Extension of Self in Service"

An Analysis of Female Kenyan Political Leaders

Joy Williams-Black

In my previous research involving educational access, I explored the expansion of study abroad opportunities for Kenyans from late colonialism to early nationalism, emphasizing women's participation.[1] I examined educational opportunities and constraints using gender as an analytical framework and sought to uncover the voices of women that have been lost to imperial histories on Africa, which tended to exclude, ignore, or marginalize women. However, in surveying thousands of documents at the Kenya National Archives in 2004–2005, I found myself generalizing about the data I collected based purely on the binary categories of women and men. Since this was a problem of early gender research, which I did not want to duplicate, it created a dilemma. While sitting in the living room with the family who sponsored my visit, I vaguely remember watching a Kenyan news program. Although I didn't know the woman in the interview, she made a comment that caught my attention. The interviewer asked the woman how she reconciled her many roles—wife, mother, and politician. The woman stated that she did so as an extension of herself in service.[2] She stated that she extends herself in her nurturing role as wife and mother; she extended herself as a parliamentarian in service to the government; and she was extending herself in service to her constituency. She went on to explain that the extension of one's self in service pertained to what individuals put their efforts to the most. What an interesting concept, I thought. Afterwards, the family revealed the woman was Charity Ngilu who was a businesswoman and the Minister of Health. However, it was only after I saw an interview of another high profile Kenyan woman, Grace Ogot, a few days later, discussing how she extended herself in service that opened up a potential space to explore the multiple identities of the individuals under study. I decided to shift my research focus to one of multiple identities or the ways in which Kenyan men and women extended themselves in pursuit of higher education—as husbands, wives, uncles, aunts, brothers, and sisters. As a result, I was able to create a space for women's voices to be heard, in spite of the fact that a relatively small number were able to take part in early higher educational access.

This chapter explores the extension of self in service as a paradigm in the analysis of Kenyan women who held elected positions in government. However, instead of a top-down examination of issues facing women, I use books, YouTube, interviews, speeches, blogs, newspapers, and television programs to explore their lives using their own words. This chapter specifically examines the lives of Nobel Laureate and former Assistant Minister of the Environment Wangari Maathai, author and former Minister of Culture, Grace Ogot, and businesswoman and Cabinet Secretary in the Ministry of Land, Housing and Urban Planning Charity Ngilu—all three women also held elected positions as Ministers of Parliament. By examining their rhetoric of leadership, this chapter contextualizes the lives of these three high-powered women who not only served their country as leaders, but also as wives, activists, and politicians, and just as importantly, mothers. The next section lays an historical foundation for women's protest and collective activism in Kenya.

MASS PROTESTS, THE MAU MAU, AND KENYAN WOMEN'S PARTICIPATION

Dating to the early twentieth century, women in Kenya have participated mass mobilization and protests. Women demonstrated activism during the imprisonment of labor activist Harry Thuku in the 1920s, as well as during Kenya's Land and Freedom Army rebellion, deemed Mau Mau, during the 1950s.[3] Thus, the importance of their participation can't be underscored. On March 14, 1922, Thuku was imprisoned in Nairobi and crowds quickly gathered to rally for his freedom.[4] Kenyan *askari* (police) fired into the crowd of demonstrators. On March 16, 1922 the demonstration turned deadly as 7,000 to 8,000 men and women gathered at the jail outraged over Thuku's imprisonment and demanded for his release.[5] Male African leaders tried to disperse the crowd without success. Mary Muthoni Nyanjiru and many of the other women challenged the male leadership and began to yell insults trying to spur the men into action. Nyanjiru taunted, "You take my dress and give me your pants."[6] She and the other women began to practice *Guturamira Ng'ania* to defend their collective interest. *Guturamira Ng'ania* is a curse where women raise their skirts, bare their genitals and hurl insults at their opponents.[7] Nyanjiru and the other women called the men cowards and pushed toward the *askari* who were armed with rifles. In the ensuing agitation, the *askari* fired gunshots into the crowd. Muthoni was one three casualties in what became one of Nairobi's first mass labor demonstration.[8] Nyanjiru's role in the demonstration is an example of Kenyan women's agency. In his autobiography, Thuku recognized Nyanjiru's contribution to Kenya's fight for freedom, noting that women were in the forefront of Kenyan nationalism.[9] Women did not just organize around their own issues of common interest. They joined with the dominant political party to show solidarity with and loyalty to the nationalist movement as well.

Although the role and importance of Mau Mau is still hotly debated, the revolt ultimately came to involve more than just those who were banished from the Highlands. Mau Mau developed out of racial discrimination in politics, in social life, and in the economics of the country.[10] This culminated into insurrection in 1952, led by the majority ethnic group, the Kikuyu. The insurrection ended in 1956. Early scholarship characterized the movement as brutal and masculine.[11] However, newspaper articles of the period addressed the important role women could play in rebuilding the country as well as ending the Mau Mau revolt. A headline in the *East African Standard* on June 24, 1995 read "Women May Lead the Way Back."[12] It encouraged women to take a lead in coaxing their male relatives to leave the forests and surrender to the colonial government. Alternatively, a headline in the same paper on June 26 read "Women Main Support of Gangs in Reserves: Rehabilitation Difficulties."[13] The article noted that there were 1,800 people sentenced to complicity in the movement and 48,000 detained in 50 camps, and that in one camp there were 2,309 were women and 350 were children.[14] Thus, women's support of Mau Mau rebels was blamed as the reason why the government was unable to squash the movement. So, while women were seen as pawns who might help rebuild a stable foundation for their disrupted families and communities on the one hand, they were deemed to be troublemakers and non-cooperatives on the other hand.

As colonialism ended, women were ignored once again as the Kenya African National Union (KANU) restructured a new Africanized government. As KANU took power in 1963 and became a *de facto* one-part state, no women were elected to office. Kenya became a *de jure* one-party state in 1969, which was the first year a woman was elected to Parliament; two others were appointed to Parliamentary positions.[15] Since independence, Kenya has had four presidents—Jomo Kenyatta, Daniel Arap Moi, Mwai Kibaki, and Uhuru Kenyatta. Still, the political landscape of the country is complex, especially in light of regional and cultural differences, ethnic conflicts, corruption, continued land disputes, and violence. Although women represent half of the country's population, the participation of women in the electoral process has not reflected this demographic reality.[16] Yet, Wangari Maathai, Grace Ogot, and Charity Ngilu carved a small space in the political sphere. The next section specifically examines the language of these women in order to understand how they successfully navigated elected office and the ways in which they extended themselves in service to their country.

KENYAN WOMEN AND LEADERSHIP: SITUATING THE SELF IN SERVICE

Women's participation was de-emphasized or ignored in academic works that referenced Kenya's national struggle until the mid-1980s.[17] Women and gender scholars revealed the need for research that specifically examined women's contribution to their countries, particularly nationalist struggles in Africa. However, Western theories, methodologies, and research was problematic for African and Third World scholars who challenged gender as a theoretical framework appropriate for women in developing countries.[18] African historian Eric Aseka said, "all social life is theoretical and therefore all theory is real social practice."[19] Or as social historian Louise Tilly put it "gender analysis should be a social history that gives due respect to human initiative."[20] Perhaps we can escape the analytical quagmire of women/gender studies by examining women's leadership within in the context of indigenous analytical frameworks. This work seeks to integrate a Western mentality with an African sensibility that does justice to the lives of Kenyan women leaders. It does so through the exploration of the extension of one's self in service as demonstrated by the lives of Maathai, Ogot, and Ngilu. In her autobiography, *Unbowed*, Maathai described herself as a member of Parliament and government, founder and president of the Green Belt Movement, and mother and friend.[21] In a 1998 interview, Grace Ogot described herself as a politician, wife, and writer.[22] Charity Ngilu described her life as a concerned politician, Minister of Health and of Land and Water, and a mother.[23] Thus, I will examine these three Kenyan women leaders through their rhetoric and roles as leaders at the local, national, and global level in order to better understand the extension of self in service.

WANGARI MUTA MAATHAI: POLITICIAN, ACTIVIST, MOTHER, FRIEND

Wangari Muta (Mary Jo) was born in Nyeri District in 1940. She had five siblings and attended primary and secondary Catholic mission schools. After graduating from secondary school with high marks, she received the opportunity to attend Mount St. Scholastica in Kansas and studied biology as part of the Africa Airlifts, which brought hundreds of African students to U.S. colleges and universities beginning in 1959. After graduating in 1964, Maathai received an African Scholarship Program of American Universities (ASPAU) award to attend graduate school at the University of Pittsburgh in Pennsylvania where she earned her master's degree in biological sciences. Before returning to Kenya, she tried to secure a position; however, she stated she didn't get it due to sexism and tribalism.[24] She noted it was the first time she had encountered that form of discrimination where "both ethnic and gender barriers now were placed in the way of my self-advancement."[25] The problem was that she was a Kikuyu woman and had studied abroad. Additionally, she received a higher education at a time when few African men had the opportunity to attain a tertiary education in comparison to the population, and even fewer women. After returning to Kenya in 1966, Maathai secured a position at the University of Nairobi as a research assistant. She noted that her male colleagues constantly questioned her abilities as well as her truly having a master's degree in biological science and stated "I also knew I was better qualified than they were."[26] Maathai took their questioning of her abilities with a grain of salt. Instead of allowing them to intimidate her, she focused on ways to outsmart them—she continued her education.

Wangari Muta got married and had her first child in 1969; she had her second child in 1971, the same year she earned her doctorate from the University of Nairobi. Earning the Ph.D. was an accomplishment as she became the first African woman to do so in East or Central Africa.[27] She had her third child in 1974, but was very much involved with the first United Nations Decade for Women in 1975. She remarked that "I listened to the women from the country side."[28] She noted that their needs coincided with her own, but their condition was worse than her own as a child. As such, she became very much concerned with the lives of women. She believed "all issues go directly back to the government."[29] She noticed that the government was concerned with women organizing, but only because she and the women she interacted with, and trained, spoke out. Kenya women successfully negotiated space for themselves, their families, and their communities, many times under extremely restrictive conditions. One of the major women's organizations in Kenya, the *Maendeleo ya Wanawake* (Women for Progress) was established during the colonial period.[30] However, African women assumed leadership of the organization post-independence, and used women's collective activity to work with as well as boycott the government. As a result of women's historical collective activism, they created alternative forms of combat against colonial and post-colonial governance by using organizations to address basic needs as a means of survival. Maathai was elected chairman of the National Council of Women in Kenya (NCWK) in 1980.[31] However, her election caused a rift between the two organizations. She noted "for the next twenty years, the government ignored the NCWK and promoted *Maendeleo Ya Wanawake*."[32] Maathai had to continually overcome being a highly educated woman. She recalled how even some women in the NCWK suggested that she not run, and stated, "I knew was due in part to my ethnicity, in part to my education, and was again partly due to my marital status."[33] Maathai had worked her way to professor in 1976 and chair of the department of veterinary medicine at the University of Nairobi in 1977, becoming the first woman to attain these positions in the region.[34]

Maathai lived her beliefs through activism, worked with women to empower themselves economically, and in the process sacrificed herself for the environment, for peace, and for the well-being of women. She began an organization in 1977 that fought environmental degradation and conducted educational campaigns to raise awareness about women's rights, civic empowerment, and the environment throughout Kenya and Africa.[35] It paid rural women to plant trees in their villages. This empowered women to stand up for themselves since they were able to support themselves. In 1977, Maathai suffered personal turmoil when her husband of 10 years left a year after the birth of their third child. In *Unbowed* she stated "nobody told me that men would be threatened by the high academic achievements of women like me . . . it was an unspoken problem that I and not my husband had a Ph.D. and taught in the university."[36] He demanded that she stopped using his family name, Mathai. Although she accepted that the marriage was over, she refused to give up his name since it identified her personally and professionally. When the settlement was finalized, she received a court order stating that she had to stop using her husband's name, but instead, "adding another 'a' to Mathai.[37] As had been her nature throughout her life, Maathai found a way to get what she wanted, in spite of cultural and even legal constraints against women. She agreed to the children living with their father during that difficult time.[38] She achieved her highest professional achievement at the university level, and one of her lowest personal challenges, divorce. Maathai leaned on her activist organization during periods of much hardship, including her divorce. Not surprisingly, Maathai titled that period of her life "Difficult Years" in *Unbowed*.[39] She was pleasantly surprised when her focus on planting trees morphed from an organization to the Green Belt Movement. However, Maathai's activisms lead to violent clashes with Kenya's second president, Daniel Arap Moi. Maathai described the violent clashes she had with Moi over preservation of Kenya's forest in greater detail in *Unbowed*.[40] However, she noted that "awards brought international attention to our efforts, as well as making news at home. Both helped protect me from the increasing criticism and threats I experienced in subsequent years from the Kenyan government."[41] Aside from being physically harassed by the *askari*, she often found herself sitting in jail or under house arrest, particularly after The Greenbelt Movement was evicted from its office space and she moved the staff into her home in 1989.[42] Although Maathai experienced intimidation and physical violence, she didn't just go away because she was perceived as a problem. Instead, she used those challenges, and her challengers, as motivation to speak up, speak out, and take action against social injustice.

Kenya remained a *dejure* one-party state until 1992 when President Moi reinstated multi-party elections. In 1997, Maathai ran for a Minister of Parliament (MP) position and for president of Kenya. However, she lost both. In *Unbowed*, she revealed that "a rumor was circulated that I'd dropped out of both races . . . it was a dirty lie."[43] Maathai believed in democracy, and felt leadership, or the lack thereof, was a major problem for Africa. In stating why she entered politics, she recalled "I knew all too well the connection between bad governance and mismanagement of resources, environmental destruction, and poverty of millions of Kenya's people."[44] Thus, her activism at the grassroots level prompted her to seek political office, which would enable her to work for change at the bureaucratic level.

In 2002, Maathai ran for office again in the Tetu district but this time as a candidate on the successful National Rainbow Coalition (NARC) ticket. She touted "together we could lift ourselves up and address the conditions of our poverty and disempowerment and regain our sense of self-respect."[45] When she used the word we, it referred to Kenyans generally, but most of Maathai's work and activism included women specifically. Fortunately, this message connected with her constituency. Political parties united under the NARC ticket and were more prepared to challenge Moi's 22 years in office in the 2002 election. The following year, Kenya's third President, Mwai Kibaki, appointed Maathai to the position of Assistant Minister of the Environment and National Resources.[46] Still, it was an accomplishment, indicating that the brutal battles she fought with the government had at least come to an end. Although the appointment recognized and acknowledged her qualifications and experience, the man appointed as the Minister of the Environment had earned post-graduate diplomas in Law and Business Management.[47]

I was undertaking fieldwork in Kenya in 2004 when it was announced that Maathai would receive the Nobel Peace Prize. Kenyans were excited for her and proud of the honor. Finally, she received validation for her hard work and sacrifice through the colonial and independence periods. Interestingly, of those I encountered the same topic arose—Maathai gaining international accolades but not local recognition. Students, professors, and individuals I encountered in general conversations at lunch, workshops, and in meetings wondered how she could win the Nobel Peace Prize for her work on the environment and be the Assistant Minister of the Environment in Kenya.[48] Although individuals who posed the question regarding Maatha's ministerial position didn't come up with a definitive answer, conversations noted that earning a Ph.D., holding professional positions in the university, fighting with the government due to her activism, and protesting the destruction of deforestation were problematic within the framework of a traditional woman. In *Unbowed*, she related that President Moi had once offered the following suggestion, "if I was to be a proper woman in 'the African tradition'—I should respect men and be quiet."[49] However, as was Maathai's nature, she rarely took bad advice. She continued to fight for what she felt was right in the name of her community, country, and the world.

In her 2004 Nobel Prize speech presented in Oslo, Maathai began by acknowledging her country, women and girls, leadership and men, and her role as a mother. In her first full paragraph, she stated "I am especially mindful of women and the girl child. I hope it will encourage them to raise their voices and take more space for leadership."[50] Maathai had several encounters in her life where men tried to silence her: her husband, her male colleagues, the police, President Moi. She went on to mention women nine more times. She referenced motherhood twice, but each instance framed her speech overall. In the same paragraph that began her speech on women, she stated "As a mother, I appreciate the inspiration this brings to the youth and urge them to use it to purse their dreams."[51] Once again, receiving the award was not just a personal accomplishment, but a future inheritance the youth could use as inspiration in their personal pursuits. Maathai also referred to her childhood and reflected on her mother teaching her to love the environment as child—a gift she stated she "inherited from my parents."[52] One can easily see that she stood at the podium alone, but was surrounded by the women of her country in spirit. Maathai's speech codified her sense of duty to the women of Kenya and the world, particularly to help them "gain some degree of power over their lives."[53] And, although the majority of her speech addressed the linkage of the environment to peace, she began by identifying with women and ended by addressing women.

After becoming a Nobel Laureate in 2004, Maathai gave numerous interviews to media outlets from television, newspapers, radio, and the web interviewed Maathai after 2004.[54] The world became fascinated by this African woman who planted trees, organized the Green Belt Movement, was a scholar and educator, and a politician. The one thing that stood out in Maathai's interviews was her passion for the environment and how she extended herself in service, particularly to other women. However, in her memoir, Maathai described herself as a politician, activist, mother, and friend.[55] She referenced her dedication of herself in service to protecting the environment, preserving Kenyan culture and promoting good governance in Kenya and around the world. Earlier in the year she gave a speech in Oslo for winning the Sophie prize. Maathai discussed the importance of helping women empower themselves, taking care of the environment, and the connection of the environment to peace. She thanked women whom she had partnered with as central to her Green Belt Movement and to making her the woman she became, and for inspiring and encouraging her in her work and life, "especially rural women"[56] in the beginning of the speech; and "especially women who have contributed to this success"[57] at the end of it. In that speech, she grounded her life experiences through a discussion of women's well-being and motherhood. She contributed to her own success by ensuring that those at the grassroots level succeeded.

However, it was a face-to-face interview in 2008 with feminist and activist Marianne Schnall that provided insight into why Maathai so passionately extended herself in service. Schnall asked Maathai about her life's journey and the obstacles she has had to overcome. Maathai responded, "the more I observed resistance, the more I was encouraged."[58] Maathai also noted that she had witnessed fewer violations and saw problems of women's rights, human rights, and destruction of the environment nearly eliminated abroad and envisioned the same for Africa. Maathai credited her studies locally in Kenya and internationally in the U.S. and Europe for the worldview she developed. She stated that she imported her observations of more equal access to natural resources back to her country.[59] She knew she'd have to fight for this vision of equality. In a 2010 interview, she argued that the "biggest challenge is governance because the people at the top have power, because they have power they control the resources . . . and the public at the grassroots continue to suffer."[60] Maathai fought at the grassroots level by planting trees, training women to empower themselves economically and speaking up for their rights. She fought from the top as a politician against the detrimental effects of government policies against those at the grassroots by focusing on the well-being of women.

As a mother, Maathai raised three children, doing so alone after her divorce in 1979. As an activist, Maathai's Green Belt Movement planted trees and placed a focus on natural resources, environmental issues, and peace internationally. And as a friend, mentor and role model, she provided income and sustenance to millions of women in Kenya. Thus, she did not fit the traditional role of an African woman. She achieved a level of education even most men couldn't obtain. Nontraditional women like Maathai increasingly occupied the public sphere—a space that was masculine. She spoke out vehemently against the government and politicians, once again occupying a male dominant sphere. In the 2008 interview with Schnall, Maathai shared the one thing she learned from teachers, who were mostly missionaries, which guided her in her journey: "I really admired their sense of service. . . . And I think that one thing that they taught me, by the way they lived, and that I still value very, very much, is that sense of service."[61] And Maathai lived a selfless, caring, giving life focused on others. These and other lessons she learned epitomized Maathai's life and a strong sense of self in service to others.

GRACE AKINYI OGOT: POLITICIAN, WIFE, WRITER

Grace Akinyi was born in Butere in 1930. She attended Ng'iya Girls School, graduated from Butere High School, and trained as a nurse in Uganda and England, also serving as a midwife.[62] She also worked as an announcer and script writer with the BBC in London.[63] In her autobiography, *Days of My Life*, she detailed the opportunities for girls in the 1950s: "they could only be nurses or teachers."[64] Ogot followed her sister in nursing and became a midwife after receiving a scholarship to study in England for three years. She married Bethwell Ogot in 1959 and had four children. He was the one who encouraged her to pursue her talent for writing. Who Grace Ogot ultimately became was partly addressed in a 1998 interview that sought to explored gender issues in Kenya. The interviewer stated to Ogot "you are a politician, mother, a writer . . ."[65] She replied that she didn't deny those labels, but that she accomplished them as a result of her family, women groups, her community, and particularly her husband.[66]

Ogot's direction was also due in part to her Luo culture. In describing how the decision on whether she would study in England was a family and community decision, she noted, "Opposition was total. . . . My parents decided to seek advice from other relatives, uncles, aunts, grandmothers, grandfathers . . ."[67] Even her father, who believed girls should have the opportunity to attain a higher education, was in opposition. Ogot was young, would be away from home for three years, and would have to postpone finding a husband in order to take advantage of the scholarship opportunity. She stated many believed if she left, she would not return. Communal decision-making for such an important a monumental event was part of Luo culture. Her decision to marry was also a discussion made with her immediate family.[68] However, Ogot had to find ways to overcome the obstacle of culture, which could be oppressive. Still, even in oppressive cultures, Ogot noted there was room for choice. When she discussed ways husbands and wives should show respect to each other, she stated women, "You never quarrel with your husband when there are visitors"[69] and men, particularly Luo men will "take care of his family."[70] Was she advising women to be silent in order to have financial stability? For a woman who had to fight to have her voice in a male-dominated arena—politics—it was difficult to reconcile Ogot advising women to silence themselves for any reason. However, in fact, Ogot was making the opposition argument. Women should speak up for themselves; but, they should do so taking into account the position of their husbands. Not speaking out wasn't what she advocated. Actually, it was more akin to not berating or embarrassing your mate in public but display respect as a woman and wife.

Ogot stated that even though some customs were oppressive, she wrote about and lived life as "a rebel."[71] In describing how she gained strength from being a wife and mother she said, "I think that in motherhood you can change the course of life for a society and for a people."[72] Being a mother and wife gave Ogot the freedom she sought. It made her a wise woman, nurturing, and loving. Caring for her own family and others outside of her family gave her strength. Perhaps it was her time as a nurse and midwife that gave her a sense of empathy and selflessness, attributes she took with her as she served in politics. In asserting her authority, she stated, "I have been a member of parliament and a leader for the last 20 years."[73] As a result, Ogot had to learn how to balance her various careers with that of her renowned husband, Kenyan historian Bethwell.

Ogot entered politics in 1983 when President Moi nominated her for a seat in Parliament; but was elected as a Minister of Parliament (MP) for Gem in 1985, beating nine male opponents.[74] The same year, Kenya the Year of the Woman Conference, and President Moi appointed Ogot as the Assistant Minister of Culture and Social Services—she held both positions until 1993.[75] Historically politics had been a masculine arena. Yet, Ogot stated, "I stand in Gem because that is where I am a mother."[76] Thus, she ran for political office because of her position as a mother. In Gem, the community identified her by her husband and children as opposed to her male relatives. Marriage gave her status, stability, and a place of her own. As a KANU-backed candidate, Ogot received promotions from President Moi; however, she experienced violence for her political stance as well. She discussed the unsavory part of politics by saying, "The politics I was involved in were not only those of the constituency or Ministerial. There were also party politics which were amorphous, dirty, full of intrigues and sometimes vicious and bloody."[77] Ogot's husband often accompanied her on the campaign trail. He stated he accompanied her to political rallies because constituents got worked up, often calling her unprintable names.[78] In 1989 when KANU's one-party political rule was nearing an end, Ogot and her husband had to deal with an even more tenuous political environment. Both were involved in a car accident that she described as "an attempted assassination."[79] But Ogot wrote off the violence and politics of the period as a time that was "exciting, directionless, and occasionally tragic."[80] Perhaps it was exciting because she was breaking boundaries few women had the opportunity to do in the public sphere. Directionless seemed to be a response not solely to being unorganized but directed to her male colleagues who didn't work with her because she was a woman. Occasionally tragic was a good description of her disappointment at being a target of violence, but also may reflect the violence and death of those in political position.

As a MP, Ogot focused on providing education, especially to girls. Unequal access to education was a major obstacle to girls' and women's advancement in addition to institutionalized patterns of discrimination that limited their access to employment, healthcare, and land. Early missionary, colonial and cultural restrictions limited girls' educational opportunities, particularly beyond primary school. Ogot's interest in educational attainment for girls and activism was stimulated by a 1953 decision to close the second oldest girls' secondary school in Nyanza. She was passionate about the cause because as she explained, "I was one of the women leaders who decided to oppose with all the women power we could generate in Kenya, this thoroughly discriminatory policy."[81] Thus, she mobilized the women and used their power to affect a different outcome. Ogot argued "to abolish the oldest girls' secondary school in Nyanza could only mean one thing—lack of interest in girls' education."[82] Ogot fought the government because in her eyes, it was a bad policy decision. However, she took the closure personally as an alumna and organized other women to affect change. One reason she took action was because even when girls and women, particularly those from more rural areas, had the desire to pursue education, religion, tradition, cultural biases, and access prohibited them from attainment of an education. As Minister of Parliament in Gem, she helped set up over 18 secondary schools in her district.[83] Having the opportunity to receive an education inspired Ogot. She appreciated the opportunities she had, realized those opportunities were still limited for girls, and took action by using her position as MP to practically affect her community.

Ogot has written several short stories and is a renowned writer and novelist.[84] She published her first books in English in 1966 and revealed in a 1985 interview why she began to write in her native language. She showed the publication of her books in English to her mother who responded "If only you could write in Luo you would serve your people well."[85] Ogot took that criticism to heart, and wrote her next novel in the Luo language. She wrote books in Luo as well as English and also had a radio program in Luo. Having worked as at the BBC, you can see the influence of language in her written responses in the 1985 interview as a bit of the Queen's English crept into her vocabulary. She replied to one question the interviewer asked by explaining she had been delayed because "the chap who is doing my first editing wanted me to be around in case of any language difficulty since he does not speak my language, Luo."[86] Here was a European man, interviewing an African woman, who had a European editor who didn't speak her Luo language with her responding with a uniquely British word—chap. It's also interesting to contemplate whether the word choice was a result of her studying abroad and picking up foreign words and phrases or if it was the result of a colonial upbringing since Kenya was under British rule for nearly half of her life.

A 2003 interview shed light on Ogot's feelings about marriage for Luo women. She noted "When you are born your destiny is marriage."[87] This statement seemed to provide the answer to why Ogot survived being married for 51 years, especially when linked with her views on inheritance. She went on to say "there are things that must be done in a proper way and in continuity."[88] It could be argued that being married for nearly half a century was in part due to the need for a proper way/continuity, in addition to demands of Luo culture. However, as Ogot explained for Luo women, "In her political life she is carrying a husband with her . . . I must take care that my activism will not demean or hinder his progress."[89] In a 2008 interview, Ogot talked about the need to find balance being married for 51 years to a renowned scholar and public figure. She stated as a wife, she knew she needed to give her husband space because of his work. "I understood that Prof is a bookworm and was never interrupted whenever he pored over or wrote books."[90] Ogot was well aware of the need to make the house a home for her husband, but realized she needed her own space as well, especially as she began to focus more on writing. In turn, she noted he made space for her to have a political office in their home.[91] She seemed to gain strength from her experiences, her constituency, her husband, and, her family. At the end of her autobiography, she "thanked God for protecting [her] through this valley of death."[92] She leaned on religion as she had when she was younger. A religion handed down by her father who was one of the early converts to Christianity. Ogot found a way to effectively balance her roles as a politician, wife and mother, and writer. She overcame cultural constraints, operating as a lady when the situation called for it. However, the role she most had to exercise was one of rebel as she navigated the male-dominant sphere of politics in order to serve others.

CHARITY KALUKI NGILU: WIFE, MOTHER, MINISTER OF PARLIAMENT, MINISTER OF HEALTH

Charity Kaluki was born in 1952 and came from a poor family of 13. She attended Mbooni Intermediate School primary school and graduated from

Alliance Girls High School in 1972. After obtaining her high school diploma, she worked as a certified pubic secretary at a technical college in Kenya. From 1978 to 1981, Ngilu held various public and private sector jobs before starting her own business.[93] Charity Kaluki married Michael Mwengwa Ngilu in the early 1980s, and they had three children. Ngilu first entered politics in 1982, criticizing politicians who didn't stick to issues, but instead made promises to secure votes.[94] She successfully defeated the incumbent male opponent to become the MP in Kitui, maintaining her position in four successive elections.

In 1989, she served as the head of Kenya's national women's organization, *Maendeleo ya Wanawake*. In 1992, Ngilu was the first woman to announce her nomination to run for the presidency. Wangari Maathai announced her nomination after Ngilu and was accused of trying to sabotage Ngilu's run.[95] However, Maathai denied the accusations stating "it was nearly impossible to find a forum in which you can address them if you are not a candidate yourself . . . if you are not a candidate, it is much harder to reach the general public with your message.[96] An outspoken politician, Ngilu was the chairperson of NARC, which took power in 2002 under Mwai Kibaki. She was appointed to the position of Minister of Health in 2003. Unfortunately, her high hopes of Kibaki eliminating graft and addressing Kenya's most pressing problems—literacy, healthcare, and poverty—were not realized.

In a 2006 television interview, Ngilu stated she was leery of the unmet promises of Kenya's third president, Mwai Kibaki.[97] Thus, she supported the presidential candidacy of Orange Democratic Movement (ODM) leader, Raila Odinga, the son of Kenya's first independent vice president, Oginga Odinga.[98] She did not resign from government despite her support for President Kibaki's main rival, but a day after she backed Mr. Odinga, she was dismissed from her post.[99] Violence erupted across Kenya when Kibaki was declared the winner amidst allegations of voting fraud. In a power-sharing agreement, Kibaki assumed the presidency and Odinga served as the Prime Minister. Ngilu was appointed as the Minister of Water and Irrigation in 2008.

In a blogged interview in 2012, Ngilu addressed women's strength and power. She stated "I am not apologetic at all about emphasizing on women empowerment because I believe a woman is the pillar of the family. Look at the many women-led households in the country!"[100] Ngilu's statement about not being apologetic may stem from the fact that she was a woman running for the top position in her country, which required an individual who was stern, confident, and a skilled politician. In a televised interview, Ngilu discussed the reasons for a second run, and once again emphasized women's empowerment. She stated that she ran also because the promises of Kenya's first president—literacy, healthcare, and poverty—had yet to be realized. In yet another interview while discussing her second bid for president she asserted, "I have continued to serve, and serve very, very well. . . . It is about that mama who is walking barefoot, that mama who is dying in the hospital, that young man. . . . Leadership is about cushioning and taking care of everybody."[101] Once again, her presidential run was unsuccessful. However, she stunned her party when she placed her support behind the Jubilee Alliance presidential candidate, Uhuru Kenyatta, the son of independent Kenya's first president, Jomo Kenyatta. In explaining why she supported an opposition candidate instead of her own party's candidate, Ngilu stated "I don't support personalities . . . I support issues."[102] Perhaps she saw the winds of change blowing away from Mwai Kibaki after two terms in office. Perhaps she was an astute businesswoman and politician who situated herself for future promotion.

In 2013, Kenya's fourth president, Uhuru Kenyatta, appointed Ngilu to the position of Cabinet Secretary for Land, Housing, and Urban Development. She was successfully vetted on May 9 confirmed shortly after. Ngilu quickly took to social media to give accolades to her mother, children, and women in general for her success. Having a career in politics and raising children is a challenging task in its own right. Traditionally, in Kenya women are called mama and the name of their eldest child; however, since helping to birth the National Rainbow Coalition that defeated President Moi in 2002, the media deemed Ngilu Mama Rainbow.[103] Thus, Ngilu as nurturer and politician became one and the same. It is not surprising when she received the Cabinet Secretary position, she didn't think of it as an individual accomplishment; she had spent her life in service to others. Maathai, Ogot, and Ngilu overcame tragedies and life's difficulties while participating in the public sphere and raising a family. They all situated motherhood at the core of their sense of self.

CONCLUSION

Marriage, motherhood, and politics ground the sense of self identity for Maathai, Ogot, and Ngilu. Marriage, although different for all women, was a factor in developing their sense of self. Maathai overcame the challenges of a public divorce. Ogot had a 51-year marriage that required her to balance her own aspirations with those of a well-renowned educator and public figure. Ngilu had to deal with being widowed at a relatively young age. All three women felt the need to take action. They had been impacted by experiences during the colonial, post-colonial, and independence periods. As a result they had personal knowledge of failures in leaderships, poor decision-making and ineffective government policies, which negatively impacted them directly in addition to women generally. This served as an impetus for organizing women, participating in women organizations, and running for political offices. However, it was motherhood that ground the lives of the women, which was priority as well. They praised both their children and mothers for being understanding and supporting them in spite of the taxing demands of their careers. Maathai and Ogot talked extensively about their families in their autobiographies. In *Unbowed*, Wangari talked about the difficulties of raising her children amidst divorce, imprisonment, and her activism and political life. She spoke proudly of her children and the works she's engaged in to help make a better life for them, including allowing her husband to raise them immediately after their divorce. *In Days of My Life*, Ogot spoke proudly of her children as well, noting that as adults they held positions in education and politics. Over the previous five years, Ngilu mourned the sudden loss of her husband, continued to fight political battles, supported her children in their endeavors, and earned a college degree. Ngilu talked proudly about her deceased husband, her political career, the lives of her children, and aspirations. So, while these women were nurturers because of their maternal status, they also gave of themselves in a political climate that was not always welcoming to women's leadership. Other categories that helped ground their sense of self was religion and education. Maathai studied in Germany and the U.S. and Kenya; Ogot studied in England and Uganda; and Ngilu studied in Kenya.

By using an indigenous category of analysis, this study has shown that it is very appropriate for understanding and questioning power relations by highlighting women's roles, their leadership styles, and their language in order to understand how they see themselves and the power they exert. This chapter examined women's organizing, their public and private selves, and their agency, which helps to better understand why they extended themselves in service and what their impact has been locally, nationally, and internationally. Third World and non-Western feminist movements refashioned how we think about gender in terms men/women, victim/agency, others/self and public/private, The extension of self in service reexamines how we think about women within the context of family, work and society, and politics, specifically addressing these issues through the lens of the women themselves. Global women leaders like Wangari Maathai worked closely at mobilizing women at the grassroots as well as the national and international level to in order to change women's lives. Women leaders like Ogot have impacted women's lives locally as a nurse, midwife, and politician and internationally as an author. Charity Ngilu has empowered women locally through policies as a politician. During the colonial period, both men and women had to fight against a system of subordination. Yet, women have had a prolonged struggle since independence in the fight for equality. This study has outlined the active role African women leaders have played. It gives voice to Kenyan women who were, and are, at the forefront of the struggle to gain independence, through nation-building, and as part of Kenya's indigenous-ruled governance.

This chapter explored Kenyan women leaders as agents of change in order to better understand ways in which African women impacted the world globally through the activism of Maathai, internationally through the writings of Ogot, and locally through politics as in the case of Ngilu. African women have not been silent on the struggle for equal distribution of resources and the incorporation of women into the political sphere. They actively worked for greater representation in politics. And, perhaps with greater representation of women will come the power to impact society and make positive, long-lasting changes for all. There is still a need for continued research on Kenyan women and how they have overcome constraints placed on them, particularly during periods of conflict and transition. I believe that research should, when possible, allow those women to be the authority, set the tone and agenda of the research, speak to their lived experiences, and do so in their own voices. Examining African women's lives locally, nationally, and globally through the extension of self in service is an indigenous category of analysis that meets this directive.

NOTES

1. The extension of self in service first appeared in my dissertation, *"The Expansion of Higher Education for Kenyans, with Special Emphasis on Women, 1959–1969"* (Ph.D. diss., University of Illinois Urbana-Champaign, 2008), However, I was unable to explore the paradigm in greater detail since my research focused on study abroad.

2. I originally became aware of this term while completing dissertation fieldwork in Nairobi, Kenya 2004; Charity Ngilu discussed why she extended herself in service while running for president a second time, Cheche News Program, "Interview with Charity Ngilu," September 5, 2012, accessed April 23, 2014, www.citizennews.co.ke/.

3. Wangari Maathai, *Unbowed: A Memoir* (New York: Alfred A. Knopf, 2006), 63.

4. Audrey Wipper, "Kikuyu Women and the Harry Thuku Disturbances: Some Uniformities of Female Militancy," *Africa: Journal of the International African Institute,* 59, no. 3 (1989).

5. Ibid.

6. Ibid.

7. Ibid.

8. Ibid., official government reports placed the total number killed at 21 while unofficial sources placed it at 56; see also Monica Udvardy, "Theorizing Past and Present Women's Organizations in Kenya," *World Development* 26 (1998), 1758.

9. Harry Thuku with assistance from Kenneth King, *Harry Thuku: An Autobiography* (Nairobi: Oxford University Press, 1970), 33.

10. Sorobea N. Bogonko, *Kenya 1945–1963: A Study in African National Movements* (Nairobi: Kenya Literature Bureau, 1980), 89.

11. See Cora Ann Presley, *Kikuyu Women, the Mau Mau Rebellion, and Social Change* (Boulder: Westview Press, 1992), 170, fn2 for a historiography of Mau Mau literature.

12. *East African Standard*, "Women May Lead the Way Back," June 24, 1955.

13. *East African Standard*, "Women 'Main Supports of Gangs in Reserves': Rehabilitation Difficulties," June 26, 1955.

14. Ibid., statistics taken from the article, which addressed a conference held in London that discussed the need for ore education among African women.

15. Katy Migiro, "Factbox: Women in Kenyan Politics by the Numbers," Thomas Reuters Foundation, December 6, 2013, accessed December 28, 2013, www.trust.org.

16. See National Democratic Institutions, Final Report, Kenya: Supporting Women's Political Participation, October 1997 for a report from independence to 1997; and for a detailed report on elections and the impact on women see "Key Gains and Challenges: A Gender Audit of Kenya's 2013 Election Process," published January 2013.

17. Muthoni Likimani, *Passbook Number F.47927: Women and Mau Mau in Kenya* (London: Macmillan Publishers, Ltd., 1985); E.I. Njiro, *The Women's Movement in Kenya* (Nairobi: Association of African Women for Research and Development, 1993); Marina Santoru, "The Colonial Idea of Women and Direct Intervention: The Mau Mau Case," *African Affairs* 95 (1996); Wambui Otieno, *Mau Mau's Daughter The Life History of Wambui Otieno*, edited and with an introduction by Cora Ann Presley (Boulder: Lynne Rienner, Publishers, 1998).

18. Joy Williams-Black, "Gender, (Under) Development and Globalization: A History of Development Theory and Practice in Sub-Saharan Africa" (paper presented at the Second Annual Graduate Symposium on Women's and Gender History, Champaign, Illinois, March 22–24 2001); Filomina Chioma Steady, "African Feminism: A Worldwide Perspective," in *Women in Africa and the African Diaspora*, Rosalyn Terborg-Penn, Sharon Harley, and Andrea Benton Rushing eds. (Washington: Howard University Press, 1987); Philomina E. Okeke, "Postmodern Feminism and Knowledge Production: The African Context," *Africa Today*, 43 (1996); Obioma Nnaemeka, ed., *Sisterhood, Feminisms and Power: From Africa to the Diaspora* (Asmara: Africa World Press, Inc., 1998); Chandra Talpade Mohanty, Ann Russo and Lourdes Torres, eds, *Third World Women and the Politics of Feminism* (Bloomington: Indiana University Press, 1997); Amrita Basu, ed., *The Challenge of Local Feminisms: Women's Movements in Global Perspectives,* with C. Elizabeth McGrory (Boulder: Westview Press, 1995).

19. Eric Masinde Aseka et al., *The Political Economy of Transition in Kenya; A Study of Issues and Social Movements in Kenya since 1945* (Nairobi: Eight Publishers, 1999), 2.

20. Louise Tilly and Vivian Patraka, eds. *Feminist Revisions: What Has Been and What Might Be* (Ann Arbor: University of Michigan, 1983).

21. Maathai, *Unbowed*, 302.

22. Mike Kuria, ed., "Grace Ogot: Introduction," *Talking Gender: Conversations with Kenyan Women Writers* (Nairobi: PJ-Kenya, 2003), 71, interview at KANU headquarter in Kenya, October 17, 1998.

23. Interview with Jeff Koinange, "Capital Talk," *K24TV*, YouTube, accessed December 28, 2013.
24. Ibid., 101.
25. Ibid.
26. Ibid., 104.
27. Maria Nzomo, *Empowering Kenya Women* (Nairobi: National Committee on the Status of Women, 1993).
28. Video Player, "Nobelprize.org." Nobel Media AB 2013, Web 28 Dec 2012, nobelprize.org/mediaplayer/index.php?id=120.
29. Ibid.
30. Audrey Wipper, "The Maendeleo ya Wanawake Movement in the Colonial Period," *Rural Africana*, 27–30 (1975–76): 195, This acknowledgement of Africana women laying the groundwork is usually not addressed in the literature but focuses, instead on the organization being established by the wives of colonial officers; see also Wipper, "The Maendeleo ya Wanawake Organization: The Co-optation of Leadership," *African Studies Review*, 18 (1975).
31. Maathai, *Unbowed*, 159.
32. Ibid.
33. Ibid., 157.
34. Wangari Maathai, "Biography," accessed February 24, 2014, greenbeltmovement.org.
35. www.greenbeltmovement.org.
36. Maathai, *Unbowed*, 139.
37. Ibid., 147.
38. Ibid., 154.
39. Ibid., 139.
40. Ibid., 184.
41. Ibid., 178.
42. Ibid., 198.
43. Ibid., 259.
44. Ibid., 255.
45. Ibid., 287.
46. www.Greenbeltmovement.org.
47. Curriculum Vita of Stephen Kolonzo Musyoka, accessed online March 2, 2014, utamu.ac.ug/research/publications/doc_download/40-hon-stephen-kalonzo-musyoka-cv.html. who served in the position from 2004–2005.
48. Author's informal conversations while undertaking fieldwork in Nairobi at Kenyatta University, 2004–2005.
49. Maathai, *Unbowed*, 196.
50. Video Player, "Nobelprize.org," Nobel Media AB 2013.
51. Ibid.
52. Ibid.
53. Ibid.
54. Wangari Maathai, "Key Speeches and Articles," accessed February 24, 2014greenbeltmovement.org.
55. Maathai, *Unbowed,* 302.

56. Sophie Prize, "Speech by Sophie Prize winner Wangari Maathai," Oslo Sophie Prize Ceremony June 15, 2004, 1, accessed February 24, 2014.

57. Ibid., 2.

58. Marianne Schnall, "Conversations with Wangari Maathai," *Feminist.com*, December 9, 2008, accessed December 27, 2013, Schnall is the executive director of feminism.com, a leading women's website and nonprofit organization, and cofounder of ecomall.com, a website promoting environmentally-friendly living.

59. Ibid.

60. Wangari Maathai, "Wangari Maathai and the Greenbelt Movement," Strides in Development, Youtube, uploaded July 9, 2010, accessed March 2, 2014.

61. Schnall, "Conversations."

62. Peter Ngangi Nguli, "Grace Ogot Took the African Story to the World," *Kenya National Standard*, September 11, 2013, accessed December 3, 2013, www.standard media.co.ke/?articleID=2000093261&story_title=grace-ogot-took-the-african-story -to-the-world.

63. Mike Kuria, editor, "Grace Ogot: Introduction," *Talking Gender: Conversations with Kenyan Women Writers* (Nairobi: PJ-Kenya, 2003), 71, interview at KANU headquarter in Kenya, October 17, 1998.

64. Grace Ogot, *Days of My Life: An Autobiography* (Kenya: Anyange Press, 2012), 42.

65. Kuria, *Talking Gender*, 94.

66. Ibid., 95.

67. Ogot, *Days of My Life*, 60.

68. Ibid., 82.

69. Kuria, *Talking Gender*, 84.

70. Kuria, *Talking Gender*, 85.

71. Ibid., 79.

72. Ibid., 89.

73. Kuria, *Talking Gender*, 75.

74. Ogot, *Days of My Life*, 254.

75. Ogot, *Days of My Life*, 291.

76. Kuria, *Talking Gender*, 94.

77. Ogot, *Days of My Life*, 298.

78. "The Academic and the Writer on Enduring Love," updated November 9, 2008, 2, accessed December 3, 2013, www.standardmedia.co.ke/?articleID=1143998852& story_title=the-academic-and-the-writer-on-enduring-love&pageNo=6.

79. Ogot, *Days of My Life*, 317.

80. Ibid., 324.

81. Ibid., 45.

82. Ibid.

83. "The Academic and the Writer," 5.

84. Nguli, "Grace Ogot," 3, she can be credited with being the first African woman writer in English to be published with two short stories in 1962 and 1964.

85. Don Burness, editor, "Grade Ogot," *Wanasema: Conversations with African Writers* (Ohio: Ohio University Center for International Studies, 1985), 60.

86. Ibid.
87. Kuria, *Talking Gender*, 75.
88. Ibid., 79.
89. Ibid., 93.
90. "The Academic and the Writer," 5.
91. Ibid.
92. Ogot, *Days of My Life*, 324.
93. Mzalendo, "Biography: Charity Ngilu," Mzalendo ('Patriot' in Swahili) is a non-partisan project started in 2005 whose mission is to "keep an eye on the Kenyan parliament," info.mzalendo.com/person/charity-ngilu/experience, accessed December 3, 2014.
94. Jeff Koinange, "Capital Talk," *K24TV*, YouTube, accessed December 28, 2013.
95. Maathai, *Unbowed*, 257.
96. Ibid., 256.
97. Koinange, "Capital Talk."
98. Ibid.
99. Wangui Kanina and Andrew Cawthorne, "Charity Ngilu Gets Sacked from the Cabinet," (Nairobi) Reuters, October 6, 2007 accessed March 1, 2014, wanjuna.blogspot.com/2007/10/charity-ngilu-gets-sacked-from-cabinent.html.
100. Njoki Chege, "Charity Ngilu: Back with a Bang," In *Politics Blog*, October 9, 2012, Chege works as a features writer with the Nation Media Group—Kenya, accessed January 3, 2014, njokichege.wordpress.com/tag/charity-ngilu/.
101. Cheche, "Interview with Charity Ngilu."
102. Koinange, "Capital Talk."
103. Ibid.

Part Three

WHEN NATIONS UNITE: A GLOBAL COMMUNITY OF FEMALE LEADERS IN THE UNITED NATIONS

Chapter Five

Women's Rhetorical Leadership within the United Nations

Valerie M. Hennings and Laura Steckman

Between 2004 and 2014, politicians and celebrities worldwide have predicted that the twenty-first century will become known as the "Century of Women."[1] Male and female global figures, including Hillary Clinton, Tom Brokaw, Malou Jacobs, Michele Bachelet, Phumzile Mlambo-Ngcuka, Ban Ki-Moon, and Dr. Kasuka Mutukwa, Ph.D. concur that not only is the "Century of Women" already in process, but that empowering women is vital for sustainable development.[2] One critical aspect of the "Century of Women" revolves around women leaders and how they choose to employ words and actions to advocate and implement policies locally, nationally, and globally.

This chapter analyzes the ways in which women provide leadership within an international institution—the United Nations (UN)—through their political speech. The primary policymaking body within the UN, the General Assembly (GA), serves as a unique forum in which women practice leadership globally—not only by holding positions as representatives from its member states or partners, but also through the issues and interests they advocate when speaking before an international audience. In particular, we analyze how women speaking within the GA lead through their speeches on the organization's signature, anti-poverty program: the Millennium Development Goals (MDG), a fifteen-year, multi-billion dollar campaign designed to alleviate poverty worldwide. We begin with a review of the literature on women's and rhetorical leadership discussion. We follow this with a discussion of the UN's structure and a brief history of the MDG. Then, we present our research questions, methods, and results, followed by our conclusions and suggestions for future research.

WOMEN AS LEADERS: RHETORICAL LEADERSHIP AND THE IMPORTANCE OF CONTEXT

The scholarship on women's leadership has striven to address key gaps in our understanding of the gendered factors influencing leaders and leadership. This includes studies that examine why women tend to be underrepresented in our examples and theories of leaders.[3] Scholars have considered how specific elements such as positive and negative gender stereotypes can present obstacles to women's leadership and emergence as leaders.[4] Studies have also explored whether differences exist between men's and women's leadership styles and strategies.[5] Another key development is the effort to move beyond focusing solely on leaders' traits and behaviors by contextualizing leadership. Klenke, a scholar on gender and leadership, argues that "at all levels—individual, group, organizational, and societal—leadership is tied to context. It is context that shapes the process of leadership."[6] Because of the social, cultural, historical and institutional forces associated with different contexts, women's leadership is not the same across situations and actors. This study builds upon this reasoning by expanding where we look to understand how women serve as global leaders. The UN provides a setting within which we can see how women exert their power as global leaders by participating in a particular practice—speaking on the floor of the UN GA—that is unique to the specific context of such a powerful, international institution.

In addition to the literature on women's leadership, this study is informed by work in the area of rhetorical leadership. Rhetorical leadership is a relatively new subfield in political and rhetoric scholarship; in 1981, a team of political scientists coined the term "rhetorical presidency" to describe what they perceived as a fundamental shift in U.S. politics from the nineteenth to twentieth centuries.[7] Associated initially with the U.S. presidency, they argued that presidents are conditioned to speak frequently starting with their campaign, a practice which continued due to demands of the media and the public until "presidents not only face the demand to explain what they have done and intend to do, but they also have come under increasing pressure to speak out on perceived crises and to minister to the moods and emotions of the populace."[8] Tulis, a professor of political theory and American politics, expounded on this idea by asserting that the president used rhetorical leadership to engage the masses, particularly in subverting legislative efforts to enact less popular laws.[9] Subsequent research has continued to draw on Tulis's initial conceptualization of rhetorical leadership, with little emphasis on defining or refining the concept.[10] Dorsey offered one of the first attempts to nuance the meaning of rhetorical leadership:

Suffice it is to say that political leadership and rhetoric constitute a complex dynamic. What, then, is "rhetorical leadership?" Is it simply merging the definition of rhetoric and leadership as an explanation for what presidents do? If so, rhetorical leadership could be defined as the process of discovering, articulating, and sharing the available means of influence in order to motivate human agents in a particular situation.[11]

Though he cautions this definition may be too simplistic and not cover all facets of rhetorical leadership, it provides a foundation from which to build. Zarefsky further contributed to the definition by clarifying that this type of leadership is neither innate nor ". . . predetermined. It comes about through the exercise of prudence, the practical art of balancing and accommodating competing interests to maximize opportunities and minimize constraints."[12] These contributions to defining rhetorical leadership disconnect the concept from the presidency, allowing it to be applied to other leadership positions and purposes, including to women and their political oratory, in and outside of American politics.

From these initial definitions, we define rhetorical leadership as a verbal and non-verbal communicative process wherein a speaker crafts and wields language in order to exert persuasive and symbolic influence over a target audience. More importantly, using the methods described below, we seek to understand how gender influences this process in relation to a particular agenda—the MDG—within the specific context of the UN.

THE UNITED NATIONS GENERAL ASSEMBLY AND ITS MILLENNIUM DEVELOPMENT GOALS

As one of the largest international forums for discussion and debate, UN's GA provides a platform for global leaders to advocate for their country's position on a wide variety of issues. To promote their country-specific viewpoints, these representatives have six committees in which to examine pre-determined problem sets. In order, these committees address disarmament and international security; economic and financial issues; social, humanitarian, and cultural concerns; special political situations and matters of decolonialization; administrative and budgetary concerns; and legal concerns. There are other, smaller committees that work on specific issues when called upon to do so.[13] It is within this structure that delegates meet to contribute to the discussion and work to resolve complex matters such as the global MDG initiative.

The MDG focus on improving the living standards of people across the world, with a special emphasis on populations in least developed countries

(LDCs). MDG development and implementation began with the 2000 Millennium Summit, wherein country delegations discussed the world's most critical issue sets and commenced a decade-long process that established the MDG and worked toward achieving the targets set as markers to gauge the success of these initiatives.

UN Secretary-General Kofi Annan produced a report in 2000 describing what he saw as the primary challenges for the international community. In his manuscript, he recommended multiple issues for the summit to consider adopting as priority targets.[14] UN Member Nations took his recommendations to heart, adopting resolution 55/2 in September 2000.[15] The Millennium Declaration iterated the organization's values and principles and selected seven broad sectors to address.[16] These broad-reaching themes became the foundation for the MDG, intended to bring higher levels of peace to the world.

In 2002, Annan commissioned the Millennium Project, an independent advisory body, to turn the goals into a practical, implementable plan.[17] He issued a report that included targets and indicators for the eight primary goals. His efforts became UN Resolution A/59/2005, the basis for discussion at the 2005 World Summit.[18] In 2005, 189 country representatives agreed to work collectively toward the major goals and their proposed targets. The finalized goals were to 1) eradicate extreme poverty and hunger; 2) achieve universal primary education; 3) promote gender equality and empower women; 4) reduce child mortality; 5) improve maternal health; 6) combat HIV/AIDs and other diseases; 7) ensure environmental sustainability; and 8) develop a global partnership for development.[19] This agreement envisioned reaching all targets by 2015.

Country delegations met again at the 2010 Summit on the Millennium Development Goals to reaffirm their commitment to meeting targets, to announce their progress, and to push forward a new funding initiative. The initiative received pledges for over forty billion dollars in funding over a five-year period. Government, private sector representatives, international and civil organizations, and research institutes promised contributions to focus on women's and children's issues.[20] The summit's outcome document, Resolution A/RES/65/1,[21] outlined the UN's progress toward and challenges remaining with the MDG project. By 2015, the UN and its partners anticipate reaching many targets in some countries, though not all MDG targets will be met universally.[22]

Based on the literature on women's and rhetorical leadership as well as the global significance of the UN and its MDG, we investigate three research questions in this study. First, are there differences in the issues, constituencies, and rhetorical style used in the UN GA speeches of women speakers as compared to men speakers? Second, are there differences in the issues, constituencies, and rhetorical style used in the UN GA speeches of women speakers from a particular world region as compared to men speakers from the same world region? Third, are there differences in the issues, constituencies, and rhetorical style used in the UN GA speeches of women speakers from a particular world region as compared to women speakers from a different world region?

METHOD

To answer these questions, we conducted a content analysis of speeches given during the 67th session—from September 18, 2012 to September 16, 2013—of the UN's GA, which included 193 member states. This session was chosen because it was the last with the sole focus on achieving the MDG.[23] The GA adopted the suggestion, making it one of the focal points of the 68th session agenda.

We assembled our collection of speeches by using UNBISnet, the UN's premier online documents collection.[24] This comprehensive database contains transcribed speeches and condensed reports of speeches made before the UN. Speeches and reports are made available in English and usually one or more of the UN's five other official languages in full-text versions.[25] Within the database's advanced search features, we chose to narrow the search to the GA, the body most likely to discuss the MDG formally and provide the largest amount of speeches from women and men representing all world regions and countries. We further limited the search to identify speeches most likely to engage the MDG.[26] In separating the session transcripts into individual speakers, we discovered that only records for the Plenary and First Committee, *with its focus on disarmament and other international security threats,* provided full-text speeches in their entirety.[27]

Ultimately, our collection of speeches included 1126 speeches from men and 179 speeches from women. These speeches spanned eight world regions: Africa, Asia, Australia and Oceania, Europe, Latin American and the Caribbean, Middle East, and North America (including Mexico) (see Table 5.1). Our collection also included 121 organizational speeches—112 by men and 9 by women. Organizational speeches are defined as speeches not made on

Table 5.1. Men's and Women's Speeches by World Region

	Men's Speeches	Women's Speeches
Africa	180	16
Asia	329	18
Australia & Oceania	23	10
Europe	227	37
Latin America & Caribbean	123	59
Middle East	116	8
North America	16	22

behalf of a country, but as a representative of a civic, corporate, or nongovernmental agency. Representatives speaking on behalf of other UN agencies or its administration are included in the organizational speaker count.

To code the content of these speeches, we conducted a computer-assisted analysis.[28] We conducted our analysis using Yoshikoder, which is open-source software that allows users to create custom dictionaries, creates concordances for examining the usage of text in-context, and provides word frequencies.[29]

As a part of our coding scheme, we first constructed a dictionary of terms in the areas of interest—MDG Issues, which included classifying items as female issues and male issues; MDG Constituencies (those groups and interests associated with the MDG); and Feminine Rhetorical Style, a rhetorical approach that uses a personal or self-disclosing tone, anecdotal evidence, and inductive reasoning.[30] To confirm that the words used in our dictionary accurately measured the concepts of interest, we manually coded a randomly selected 10 percent subset of our UN speeches (131 records of 1305). This manual check verified that terms included in the final dictionary were correctly associated with the relevant concepts 90 percent to 100 percent of the time.

The final dictionary included 153 terms that related to the multiple issues and constituencies associated with the UN's eight Millennium Development Goals. The words and phrases selected are listed in Table 5.2.[31]

We also categorized the selected MDG Issues items in terms of female and male policy issues.[32] Although there is some variation across studies as to which particular policy issues are deemed female versus male issues, we ground our categorization in the work of Kim Fridkin Kahn and other previous research on gender and politics.[33] Additionally, we coded our collection of UN speeches for indicators of what Campbell defines as "Feminine Rhetorical Style."[34] As a rhetorical approach, it includes addressing the audience as peers, inviting audience participation, encouraging the audience to enact change, and identifying with the experiences of others.[35] To capture elements of feminine style, we included the terms "I," "change," "transform," "us," and "we" in our dictionary. These specific words, which could be coded through our computer-assisted method, were chosen as indicators of Feminine Rhetorical Style because they reflect a personal tone ("I"), address the audience as peers ("we" and "us") and encourage the audience to be agents of change ("change" and "transform").

RESULTS

We began our analysis of women's leadership within the UN by comparing how women and men discussed the MDG in terms of Issues, Constituencies, and the use of a Feminine Rhetorical Style. Table 5.3 presents the results of

Table 5.2. Final Content Analysis Dictionary by Category

Millennium Development Goals Issues		Millennium Development Goals Constituencies	Feminine Rhetorical Style
Female Issues	Male Issues		
AIDS	agricultural support	Child	I
biodiversity	communication technology	DAC	change
birth rate	debt	developed country	transform
carbon dioxide emission	debt relief	developing country	us
child mortality	economic development	development assistance committee	we
climate change	export	ECA	
contraceptive	fair trade	ECE	
contraception	financial system	ECLAC	
drinking water	GDP	Economic Commission for Africa	
education	GNI	Economic Commission for Europe	
empowerment	gross domestic product	Economic Commission for Latin America and the Caribbean	
environment	gross national income	Economic and Social Commission for Asia and the Pacific	
environmental resource	information technology	Economic and Social Commission for Western Asia	
environmental sustainability	internet	ESCAP	
	MDRI	ESCWA	
gender equality	multilateral debt relief initiative	FAO	
gender equity	ODA	Food and Agriculture Organization	
global warming	official development assistance	heavily indebted poor country	
health care	personal computer	HIPC	
HIV	tariffs	IFAD	
		ILO	
		UN Children's Fund	
		UN Conference on Trade and Development	
		UN Department of Economic and Social Affairs	
		UN Development Group	
		UN Educational Scientific and Cultural Organization	
		UN Entity for Gender Equity and the Empowerment of Women	
		UN Environment Program	
		UN Habitat	
		UN Human Settlements Program	
		UN Industrial Development Organization	
		UN Office on Sport for Development and Peace	
		UN Population Fund	
		UN Refugee Agency	
		UN Relief and Works Agency for Palestine Refugees in the Near East	
		UN Women	
		UNAIDS	
		UNCTAD	
		underweight child	

(continued)

Table 5.2. Continued

Millennium Development Goals Issues		Millennium Development Goals Constituencies		Feminine Rhetorical Style
Female Issues	Male Issues			
hunger	technology	IMF	UNDESA	
malaria	technology transfer	International Fund for Agricultural Development	UNDG	
maternal health	telephone line	International Labour Organization	UNDP	
maternal mortality	trade	International Monetary Fund	UNEP	
measles	trading	International Telecommunications Union	UNESCO	
medication	unemployment	International Trade Center	UNFPA	
nutrition		ITC	UNHCR	
ozone depletion		ITU	UNICEF	
pharmaceuticals		Joint UN Program on HIV/AIDS	UNIDO	
pollution		landlocked state	United Nations Development Program	
poverty		LDC	UNOSDP	
poverty reduction		least developed country	UNRWA	
reproductive health		Millennium Campaign	UNWTO	
sanitation		Office of the High Commissioner for Human Rights	WFP	
tuberculosis		OHCHR	WHO	
universal primary education		OPEC	WMO	
women's empowerment		Organization of the Petroleum Exporting Countries	WTO	
women's rights		poor	women	
		private sector	World Bank	
		slum dweller	World Food Program	
		small island state	World Health Organization	
			World Meteorological Organization	
			World Tourism Organization	
			World Trade Organization	
			youth	

Note: As a part of our analysis, we coded for the use of acronyms in addition to the phrases for which they represent. To account for the fact that both the acronyms and full phrases were distinct dictionary items, they are listed separately in this alphabetized list.

Table 5.3. Differences in Issues, Constituencies, and Frames in UN General Assembly Speeches

Category	Women (All)	or	Men (All)	Women (Lat.Am./ Carib.)	or	Men (Lat.Am./ Carib.)	Women (Africa)	or	Women (Asia)/ Africa
N	179		1126	59		123	16		18
All MDG Issues	**Women** % Change: 40.56 Risk Ratio: 1.41 [1.27, 1.55]*			**Women** % Change: 49.96 Risk Ratio: 1.50 [1.21, 1.86]*			**Africa** % Change: 75.68 Risk Ratio: 1.76 [1.19, 2.59]*		
Female MDG Issues	**Women** % Change: 18.19 Risk Ratio: 1.18 [1.03, 1.36]*			**Not Significantly Different** % Change: -13.50 Risk Ratio: .88 [.62, 1.25]			**Africa** % Change: 145.33 Risk Ratio: 2.45 [1.41, 4.27]*		
Male MDG Issues	**Women** % Change: 62.89 Risk Ratio: 1.63 [1.44, 1.85]*			**Women** % Change: 129.12 Risk Ratio: 2.29 [1.77, 2.96]*			**Not Significantly Different** % Change: 16.33 Risk Ratio: 1.16 [.73, 1.84]		
MDG Constituencies	**Not Significantly Different** % Change: -.85 Risk Ratio: .99 [.85, 1.15]			**Not Significantly Different** % Change: 25.38 Risk Ratio: 1.25 [.93, 1.70]			**Africa** % Change: 1,487.95 Risk Ratio: 15.88 [3.89, 64.88]*		
Feminine Rhetorical Style	**Not Significantly Different** % Change: -3.82 Risk Ratio: .96 [.92, 1.01]			**Not Significantly Different** % Change: 3.10 Risk Ratio: 1.03 [.94, 1.14]			**Africa** % Change: 26.43 Risk Ratio: 1.26 [1.03, 1.55]*		

* $p \leq .05$.

Note: Each cell identifies which groups of speakers—according to gender and world region—were more likely to emphasize different issues and constituencies in their speeches and employ a feminine style. Percent change, risk ratio estimates, and 95 percent confidence intervals are also reported for each comparison.

this analysis by providing two types of information to illustrate our findings. First, we report risk ratios. Risk ratios reflect the relative probability of seeing each category of dictionary terms—MDG Issues, MDG Constituencies, and Feminine Rhetorical Style—in the speeches of different groups of speakers. This measure is calculated from proportions—the number of words coded for each category divided by the total number of words—which allows us to account for differences in the length of speeches being compared.[36]

As an example, to discern differences in the mentions of the MDG Issues between women and men speakers, we divided the proportion of words in women's speeches that were coded as MDG Issues by the same proportion of MDG Issues mentioned in men's speeches; this produced a risk ratio of 1.41 (see Table 5.3). Ratios that are greater than 1 mean that the proportion from the first group (all women, women from Latin America and the Caribbean, and women from Africa as listed in Tables 5.3 and 5.4) is greater than the second group. The farther away from 1 this ratio is, the greater the difference between the two groups compared.

We also report a 95 percent confidence interval for each risk ratio.[37] If that interval does not include 1, the difference between the two groups—in this example, between all women and all men speaking in the GA—is statistically significant.[38] When it comes to mentions of MDG Issues, we can interpret this result as saying women speakers emphasized issues related to the MDG in their GA speeches more often than men and that this difference is statistically significant.

Second, we report percent change as a way to show how much of a difference is detected between the groups compared. Positive percent change, in those cases where a statistically significant ratio is reported, shows a greater likelihood of that category of terms appearing in the speeches of the first group of speakers in each comparison we make. In the example noted above, the percent change in mentions of MDG Issues between all women and all men speakers is approximately 41 percent (see Table 5.3). This means that speeches given by women in the GA were 41 percent more likely than those by men to include mentions of the MDG Issues as coded with our dictionary.

In response to our first research question, we found statistically significant differences in how women and men discussed issues related to the MDG in their speeches before the GA. This held true when we classified the MDG Issues items in terms of female and male issues. Women were 18 percent more likely to discuss female issues and 63 percent more likely to mention male issues in our collection of speeches as compared to their male counterparts (see Table 5.3). The emphasis on female issues such as education and gender equality is illustrated by the following excerpt from a September 26, 2012, address by Julia Gillard, prime minister of the Commonwealth of Australia:

We will help improve education. We will be among the world's largest education donors in 2015.... We will help increase gender equality.... Australia will provide $320 million over 10 years to support women's political participation, to expand women's leadership and to spread economic and social opportunities in the Pacific. That is a principle underpinning every Australian aid intervention and initiative: empowering women and girls.[39]

This quote from Prime Minister Gillard demonstrates that one way women lead within the UN is by publically voicing support and commitment, often on behalf of their country, to the MDG. The following quote by U.S. philanthropist Cheryl Saban, given October 17, 2012, makes a similar public showing of rhetorical leadership by discussing commitment to economic growth (coded as a male MDG issue): "We agree with the Secretary-General's conclusion that creating the conditions for sustained and inclusive economic growth will permit African populations to benefit more broadly from better incomes and living standards."[40] Unlike our findings regarding MDG Issues, we did not detect any significant differences between women's and men's mentions of MDG Constituencies or use of Feminine Rhetorical Style.

To address our second research question, which seeks to understand how speakers from various world regions differ in their discussion of the MDG and use of Feminine Rhetorical Style, we then compared women and men from Latin America and the Caribbean. We chose this area as our focus because it was the world region with the highest number of women speakers during the GA's 67th session. As with our comparison between all women and men, we did not find any statistically significant differences in mentions of MDG Constituencies and use of feminine style between women and men of this region (see Table 5.3). We did find that women in Latin America and the Caribbean were 50 percent more likely to discuss MDG Issues than men. This difference, which was statistically significant, was driven by women's discussion of male MDG Issues. References to male MDG Issues were 129 percent, or 1.29 times, more common in speeches by women in this world region than by men. The excerpt below, by Paulette Bethel, the UN ambassador of the Bahamas, on October 17, 2012, provides an example of how such issues, like the economy, were discussed. It also illustrates how women, by calling for direct action and providing guidance in how to act, lead globally in this particular context:

The persistent global financial and economic crisis has impacted on [sic] the level of international cooperation and the provision of aid to developing States such as those in Africa. We nonetheless call on the international community and financial institutions to stay the course and help strengthen the platform of engagement between Africa and her development partners.... It is in this context that South-South cooperation and partnerships are also an essential part of the international response, offering viable opportunities to countries in their individual and collective pursuit of sustained economic growth and sustainable development.[41]

As noted above, our comparisons of women speakers to men speakers provide strong evidence that women were more likely than men to discuss issues related to the MDG. However, do any differences emerge between different subsets of women speaking before the UN? To answer this third research question, we compared women speakers in two world regions: Africa and Asia. We justified this comparison based on the United Nations Conference on Trade and Development's (UNCTAD's) 2013 report naming the world's LDCs. Of the 49 countries listed, the majority are from Africa (34) and Asia (8).[42] All eight MDG goals, focused on alleviating poverty and improving living standards, are applicable to LDCs, whereas in more developed regions, some of the goals have been achieved previously.

We found multiple statistically significant differences between the speeches by women from Africa and those from Asia. Women from Africa were 76 percent more likely than women from Asia to emphasize issues related to the MDG. More specifically, women from Africa were 145 percent, or 1.45 times, more likely to mention female MDG Issues than women from Asia (see Table 5.3). Additionally, we detected a very large difference between these two groups of women and their mentions of constituencies related to the MDG. Women from Africa were approximately 15 times more likely than those from Asia to mention different groups associated with the MDG. They also employed a Feminine Rhetorical Style 26 percent more often than women from Asia. The following September 26, 2012, quote from Joyce Hilda Mtila, president of the Republic of Malawi, illustrates how women as a constituency were referenced in relation to the MDG:

> At this moment, I say to the Assembly that Malawi is on a journey—a journey to change its trajectory; a journey to make real change happen . . . I would like to share that we are certain that we will be able to achieve five of the eight MDGs by 2015. And we will continue to strive to achieve our goals of the three remaining MDGs: universal primary education, promoting gender equality and empowering women, and improving maternal health. Coincidentally, these three MDGs are related to issues that I have worked on throughout my life, and I will personally ensure that Malawi redoubles its efforts to make improvements in those areas.[43]

This excerpt also highlights elements of feminine style through its personal tone and use of the words "change," "I," and "we." Additionally, it showcases how women within this context serve as global leaders by expressing an individual commitment and responsibility, not just that of the country or organization they represent within the UN, to those issues and constituencies for which they advocate.

To gain a clearer understanding of how women discussed the MDG, we broadened our examination by conducting a word frequency analysis to determine which female and male MDG Issues terms from our dictionary were the most commonly mentioned in our collection of speeches. Our sample of 1305 records included a total 708,467 words. Overall, 15,958 different words were used. Among our dictionary terms for female MDG Issues and male MDG Issues, the most commonly mentioned items were "malaria" (21 percent of all female issues mentions), "poverty" (19 percent of all female issues mentions), "education" (18 percent of all female issues mentions) and "environment" (17 percent of all female issues mentions). The male MDG Issues mentioned the most were "trade" (61 percent of all male issues mentions), "technology/ies" (21 percent of all male issues mentions), "export/s" (7 percent of all male issues mentions) and "debt/s" (5 percent of all male issues mentions). We then compared the use of these eight dictionary terms across our three sets of speakers. The results of this analysis are presented in Table 5.4.

In our initial analysis comparing all women and men speakers, we learned that women were more likely to mention both female and male issues as compared to men. Our extended analysis shows a statistically significant difference in how often women referenced the particular issues of malaria, trade, exports, and debt (see Table 5.4). This additional analysis shows that women were not significantly more likely than men to discuss education, the environment, poverty, and technology. The greatest difference detected was in discussions of debt—women were 1.82 times more likely than men to mention this male MDG issue.

Our primary analysis of women and men from Latin America and the Caribbean showed that women were significantly more likely than men from this region to mention male MDG Issues. We see in Table 5.4 that this applies to three of the four most common issue items in this category: trade, technology, and debt. As with the comparison between all women and all men speakers, the largest difference detected between women and men of this region was in how often debt was mentioned. Women from Latin America and the Caribbean were 9.6 times more likely to discuss the topic of debt in relation to the MDG than men of this region (see Table 5.4). This emphasis is illustrated in the excerpt below by Christina Fernández, president of the Argentine Republic, on September 25, 2012:

> Today, as emerging countries, we are being condemned as protectionist by the very countries that survived by protecting themselves through agricultural subsidies and all sorts of special breaks at the expense of our economies and, above

Table 5.4. Differences in the Most Common Female and Male MDG Issues Mentioned in UN General Assembly Speeches

	Women (All)	or	Men (All)	Women (Lat.Am./Carib.)	or	Men (Lat.Am./Carib.)	Women (Africa)	or	Women (Asia)
N	179		1126	59		123	16		18
Female MDG Issues									
Malaria	**Women** % Change: 35.09 Risk Ratio: 1.35 [1.01, 1.81]*			**Not Significantly Different** % Change: N/A Risk Ratio: N/A			**Africa** % Change: 252.88 Risk Ratio: 3.53 [1.05, 11.83]*		
Poverty	**Not Significantly Different** % Change: 36.06 Risk Ratio: 1.36 [1.00, 1.85]			**Not Significantly Different** % Change: 9.17 Risk Ratio: 1.09 [.62, 1.92]			**Africa** % Change: 429.32 Risk Ratio: 5.29 [1.24, 22.57]*		
Education	**Not Significantly Different** % Change: 24.64 Risk Ratio: 1.25 [.90, 1.73]			**Not Significantly Different** % Change: -75.72 Risk Ratio: .57 [.27, 1.20]			**Not Significantly Different** % Change: 504.93 Risk Ratio: 6.05 [.79, 46.52]		
Environment	**Not Significantly Different** % Change: 14.49 Risk Ratio: 1.15 [.82, 1.61]			**Not Significantly Different** % Change: 6.99 Risk Ratio: 1.07 [.48, 2.37]			**Not Significantly Different** % Change: 227.67 Risk Ratio: 3.28 [.74, 14.52]		

Male MDG Issues

Trade	**Women** % Change: 69.44 Risk Ratio: 1.69 [1.44, 1.99]*	**Women** % Change: 75.13 Risk Ratio: 1.75 [1.26, 2.43]*	**Not Significantly Different** % Change: 37.49 Risk Ratio: 1.37 [.69, 2.74]
Technology	**Not Significantly Different** % Change: 32.20 Risk Ratio: 1.32 [.99, 1.77]	**Women** % Change: 162.69 Risk Ratio: 2.63 [1.19, 5.79]*	**Not Significantly Different** % Change: 126.85 Risk Ratio: 2.27 [.77, 6.70]
Export	**Women** % Change: 71.69 Risk Ratio: 1.72 [1.08, 2.74]*	**Not Significantly Different** % Change: 91.05 Risk Ratio: 1.91 [.56, 6.53]	**Asia** % Change: -1,685.32 Risk Ratio: .056 [.01, .44]*
Debt	**Women** % Change: 182.08 Risk Ratio: 2.82 [1.73, 4.61]*	**Women** % Change: 958.73 Risk Ratio: 10.59 [4.23, 26.51]*	**Not Significantly Different** % Change: N/A Risk Ratio: N/A

* $p \leq .05$.

Note: Each cell identifies which groups of speakers—according to gender and world region—were more likely to emphasize the most commonly mentioned female and male MDG issues. Percent change, risk ratio estimates, and 95 percent confidence intervals are also reported for each comparison. N/A indicates that one of the two groups compared did not have any mentions of the MDG issue.

all, of millions of our people who only now are being incorporated into the labour force. It is crucial for developed countries to understand the contribution that emerging countries can make to the international economic recovery with the millions of dollars we still owe, on top of our costs for social benefits and production. Besides, we have paid down our debt to levels never seen before. Argentina, whose foreign debt represented 160 per cent of its gross national product, today owes only 14 per cent of its gross national product.[44]

The excerpt by Fernández not only shows how women discuss issues such as debt within the UN, but also illustrates how women's rhetorical leadership in this arena includes acknowledging and addressing a power imbalance that exists, in this example, among countries.

Our initial comparison between women from Africa and Asia showed that women from Africa were significantly more likely to discuss MDG Issues, particularly female MDG Issues, as well as MDG Constituencies. They were also more likely to utilize a Feminine Rhetorical Style when compared to women from Asia. Our extended analysis reveals that women from Africa were more likely than those from Asia to mention the particular female MDG Issues of malaria and poverty, but not education and the environment (see Table 5.4). Interestingly, we also see that women from Asia were 16.85 times more likely to discuss exports as compared to women from Africa. In expressing support and commitment to the MDG, Preneet Kaur, India's Minister of State for External Affairs, focuses on the topic of trade in her October 17, 2012, address:

Given the sheer potential of untapped trade, we have raised our bilateral trade target to $90 billion by 2015 from the $70 billion target set earlier. We are already making available duty-free and quota-free market access for goods from 34 of the least developed countries in Africa, which covers 94 percent of India's total tariff lines and provides preferential market access on tariff lines that add up to 92.5 per cent of the global exports of all LDCs.[45]

This excerpt, in contrast to that of President Mtila above, showcases how women also expressed a collective responsibility to the MDG through their speeches by speaking on behalf of an organization, or in this case, a nation.

CONCLUSION

From the above analysis of women's speeches within the UN's GA, we gain two key insights to women's roles as global leaders. First, our content analysis reveals that women are in many ways taking the lead on a significant, multi-year, international program—the UN's Millennium Development Goals. Our collection of speeches reveals that women are consistently more likely than men to discuss issues related to the MDG. This holds true when comparing speakers within and across world regions. This finding indicates that international women leaders are being included in the conversations about MDG. Through their participation in these conversations, women thus have an opportunity to shape the discussion, which can lead to how the MDG are ultimately implemented, assessed, and perceived by the global community.

Second, our results show that women's leadership within the context of the UN and the MDG is dynamic. We found that women's discussion of the MDG Issues are not constrained to a subset of topics defined as female issues. Instead, women were more likely than men to discuss both female and male issues pertaining to the MDG. We also see that women's rhetoric on the MDG included elements as diverse as individual and collective expressions of support, direct calls for action, concrete suggestions for achieving policy goals, and critiques of power imbalances. Additionally, although women were not more likely than men to utilize a Feminine Rhetorical Style, we did see a difference in the use of this style between women from different world regions.

These insights provide an important starting point for future research. A fundamental understanding advanced by this study is that context shapes who leads and how leadership is practiced. A simple, but critical step for future work is to continue to expand the contexts in which we examine women's emergence as leaders and how they choose to lead. Also, this study strives to build upon the rhetorical leadership literature by considering how gender influences this form of leadership. Additional research in this area should continue to develop a more nuanced understanding of the gendered dimensions of rhetorical leadership across local, national, and international contexts.

NOTES

1. Florence Howe and Tobe Levin, eds. "Beijing and Beyond: Toward the Twenty-first Century of Women: Includes the Complete Text of the Platform for Action," *Women's Studies Quarterly* 25, nos. 1 & 2 (1996).

2. Hillary Clinton, "First Lady Hillary Rodham Clinton Remarks for the United Nations Fourth World Conference on Women," Fourth World Conference on Women by the United Nations Development Programme (UNDP), September 5, 1995, accessed January 4, 2014, www.un.org/esa/gopher-data/conf/fwcw/conf/gov/950905175653.txt.; *NBC Today*, "Tom Brokaw: Welcome to the Century of Women," aired May 2, 2013, accessed February 22, 2013. www.today.com/video/today/51745555#51745555; Amadís M Guerrero, "War and Peace–and Literature," *Philippines Daily Inquirer*, December 19, 2013, accessed February 22, 2014, lifestyle.inquirer.net/141545/war-and-peace-literature.; UN Women, "The Twenty-First Century Will Be the Century of Girls and Women," September 23, 2011, accessed February 22, 2014, www.unwomen.org/en/news/stories/2011/9/the-21st-century-will-be-the-century-of-girls-and-women; UN Women, "'Taking Action Together, We Can Make the Twenty-First Century the Century of Women'-UN Women

Executive Director," Accessed February 21, 2014, www.unwomen.org/ca/news/stories/2013/10/ed-addres-to-third-committee-of-the-general-assembly; UN News Center, "UN Chief Urges World Leaders to Answer Demands of their People for Dignity, Development," Accessed February 22, 2013, www.un.org/apps/news/story.asp?NewsID=45950&Cr=general+debate&Cr1#.Uwimq_1dWTk; Speedwell Mupuchi, "Zambia: 'Twenty-First Century Must Be a Century of Women,'" *AllAfrica.com*, Originally from The Post (Zambia), October 19, 2001, accessed February 22, 2014, allafrica.com/stories/200110190422.html.

3. Valerie Stead and Carole Elliott, "Common Understandings: Leadership and Leadership Development," in *Women's Leadership* (New York, NY: Palgrave Macmillan, 2009), 15–39.

4. Todd L. Pittinsky, Laura M. Bacon, and Brian Welle, "The Great Women Theory of Leadership? Perils of Positive Stereotypes and Precarious Pedestals" in *Women and Leadership: The State of Play and Strategies for Change*, ed. Barbara Kellerman and Deborah Rhode (San Francisco, CA: Jossey-Bass, 2007), 93–116; Valerie Stead and Carole Elliott, "Visualising Women's Leadership: Stereotypes and Metaphors," in *Women's Leadership* (New York, NY: Palgrave Macmillan, 2009), 40–59.

5. Alice H. Eagly and Linda L. Carli, "Are Men Natural Leaders?" in *Through the Labyrinth: The Truth About How Women Become Leaders* (Boston, MA: Harvard Business School Publishing, 2007), 29–48.

6. Karin Klenke, *Women in Leadership: Contextual Dynamics and Boundaries* (Bingley, UK: Emerald Publishing, 2011), 7.

7. James W. Ceaser, Glen E. Thurow, Jeffrey Tulis, and Joseph M. Bessette, "The Rise of the Rhetorical Presidency," *Presidential Studies Quarterly* 11, no. 2 Presidential Power and Democratic Constraints: A Prospective and Retrospective Analysis (1981); Jeffrey Tulis, "On the Forms of Rhetorical Leadership," in *Beyond the Rhetorical Presidency*, ed. Martin J. Medhurst (College Station: Texas A&M University Press, 2008).

8. James W. Ceaser, Glen E. Thurow, Jeffrey Tulis, and Joseph M. Bessette, "The Rise of the Rhetorical Presidency," 161.

9. Jeffrey Tulis, *The Rhetorical Presidency* (Princeton: Princeton University Press, 1987).

10. For examples see Matthew Eshbaugh-Soha and Jeffrey S. Peake, *Breaking Through the Noise: Presidential Leadership, Public Opinion, and the News Media*. (Stanford: Stanford University Press, 2011); B. Dan Wood, "Presidential Rhetoric and Economic Leadership," *Presidential Studies Quarterly* 34 The Public Presidency (2004): 573–606.

11. Leroy G. Dorsey, *The Presidency and Rhetorical Leadership* (College Station: Texas A&M University Press, 2008), 9.

12. David Zarefsky, "The Presidency Has Always Been a Place for Rhetorical Leadership," in *The Presidency and Rhetorical Leadership,* ed. Leroy G. Dorsey (College Station: Texas A&M University Press, 2008), 39.

13. General Assembly of the United Nations. Last updated December 2013. www.un.org/en/ga/.

14. Kofi Annan, *We the Peoples: The Role of the United Nations in the Twenty-First Century* (New York: United Nations Department of Public Information, 2000).

15. UN General Assembly, 55th Session. "United Nations Millennium Declaration" (A/RES/55/2). Published Sep 18, 2000. www.unmillenniumproject.org.

16. UN General Assembly, 55th Session, "United Nations Millennium Declaration" (A/RES/55/2). Published Sep 18, 2000. www.unmillenniumproject.org.

17. Pan American Health Organization, "History of the MDGs." Last updated 2010. www.paho.org.

18. UN General Assembly, 59th Session, "In Larger Freedom: Towards Development, Security and Human Rights for All" (A/59/2005). Published March 21, 2005. www.unmillenniumproject.org.

19. UN Statistics Division, "Official List of MDG Indicators." Published January 15, 2008. mdgs.un.org.

20. Every Woman Every Child, "About Every Woman Every Child: An Unprecedented Effort to Save Lives." Last updated 2013. www.everywomaneverychild.org.

21. UN General Assembly, 65th Session, "Keeping the Promise: United to Achieve the Millennium Development Goals" (A/RES/65/1). Published October 19, 2010. www.un.org.

22. UN Department of Economic and Social Affairs, *The United Nations Development Strategy Beyond 2015* (New York: United Nations, 2012).

23. While the 68th session continues discussing progress and challenges to meeting MDG targets, on September 25, 2013, Secretary-General Ban Ki-Moon urged the UN to shift its agenda to consider a post-2015 action plan. See UN General Assembly, 68th Session, "Outcome Document of the Special Event to Follow up Efforts Made towards Achieving the Millennium Development Goals" (Draft resolution A/68/L.4). Published on October 1, 2013. www.un.org; United Nations, "Report of the UN Secretary-General: A Life of Dignity for All." Published online in 2013. www.un.org.

24. The collection contains a speech database, the Index to Speeches, which includes data from 1983 to the present.

25. UN Dag Hammarskjöld Library, "United Nations Bibliographic Information System." Last updated in November 2013. unbisnet.un.org/.

26. We accomplished this by selecting the search string "Millennium OR Development" to capture all possible related records. We reduced these results further by using the years 2012 and 2013, and then chose all records falling within the official 67th session dates.

27. The process resulted in a total of 1305 records, which included all substantive and procedural speeches resulting from the search.

28. Computer-assisted content analysis provides a number of advantages. When compared to human coding, computer-assisted procedures allow researchers to analyze a large amount of data in an efficient, reliable, and replicable manner. This approach is particularly useful when the coding unit is a word or phrase, as described in the coding scheme below. See Kimberly A. Neuendorf, *The Content Analysis Handbook* (Thousand Oaks, CA: SAGE, 2002); and Daniel Riffe, Stephen Lacy, and Frederick Fico, *Analyzing Media Messages: Using Quantitative Content Analysis in Research*, 2nd ed. (Mahwah, NJ: Lawrence Erlbaum Associates Inc., 2005) for additional discussion of the advantages and disadvantages of computer-assisted content analysis.

29. Will Lowe, "Yoshikoder: An Open Source Multilingual Content Analysis Tool for Social Scientists" (Paper presented at the Annual Meeting of the American Political Science Association, Philadelphia, PA, August 31–September 3, 2006).

30. Karlyn Kohrs Campbell, "The Discursive Performance of Femininity: Hating Hillary," *Rhetoric & Public Affairs* 1, no. 1 (1998): 1–19.

31. The words included in our final dictionary were coded using a wildcard search so as to include singular and plural versions of the word.

32. In this study, we use the terms "female issues" and "male issues" as a way to classify subsets of the dictionary terms used to code issues related to the Millennium Development Goals. These categories are also known as "feminine issues" and "masculine issues" as well as "women's issues" and "men's issues."

33. See Kim Fridkin Kahn, *The Political Consequences of Being a Woman: How Stereotypes Influence the Conduct and Consequences of Political Campaigns* (New York, NY: Columbia University Press, 1996); Kim L. Fridkin, Jill Carle, and Gina S. Woodall, "The Vice Presidency as the New Glass Ceiling: Media Coverage of Sarah Palin," in *Women and Executive Office: Pathways and Performance*, ed. Melody Rose (Boulder, CO: Lynne Rienner Publishers, 2012), 33–52.; Miki Caul Kittilson and Kim Fridkin, "Gender, Candidate Portrayals, and Election Campaigns: A Comparative Perspective," *Politics & Gender* 4 (2008): 371–92; Jennifer Lawless, "Women, War, and Winning Elections: Gender Stereotyping in the Post September 11th Era," *Political Research Quarterly* 53 (2004): 479–90.

34. Karlyn Kohrs Campbell, *Man Cannot Speak for Her: A Critical Study of Early Feminist Rhetoric* (New York, NY: Greenwood, 1989).

35. Karlyn Kohrs Campbell, "The Discursive Performance of Femininity: Hating Hillary," *Rhetoric & Public Affairs* 1, no. 1 (1998): 1–19.

36. Stated as a formula, the risk ratio (RR) is: RR = where and .

37. To generate a 95 percent confidence interval, we first calculate $Ln(RR) \pm 1.96$ and then take the antilog (exp) of the lower and upper limits. When the 95 percent confidence interval does not include the null value (RR = 1), the result is statistically significant.

38. Lowe, "Yoshikoder."

39. Julia Gillard, Address to the United Nations General Assembly, September 26, 2012.

40. Cheryl Saban, Speech to the United Nations General Assembly, October 17, 2012.

41. Paulette Bethel, Speech to the United Nations General Assembly, October 17, 2012.

42. UNCTAD, *The Least Developed Countries Report: Growth with Employment for Inclusive and Sustainable Development* (New York, United Nations, 2013).

43. Joyce Hilda Mtila Banda, Address to the United Nations General Assembly, September 26, 2012.

44. Cristina Fernández, Address to the United Nations General Assembly, September 25, 2012.

45. Preneet Kaur, Speech to the United Nations General Assembly, October 17, 2012.

Chapter Six

Samantha Power

Before and After "Hell"

William Carney

In late 2013, violence flared in the Central African Republic. The country, bordered by Sudan and Chad, was a former French colony that had received its independence in 1960. Its evolution toward democracy has been tenuous with a series of military coups ousting elected governments.[1] In 2013, the United Nations (UN) warned that the latest crisis in the tiny country (around 240,000 square miles with a population of 4 million)[2] a complex affair in which religiously affiliated militias had negotiated and then suspended a power-sharing agreement with the government, was dangerously close to spiraling out of control. Competing Christian and Muslim militias fighting over land claims had spurred the African Union to send peacekeeping forces. By Christmas Day 2013, roughly 600 people had been killed in the fighting.[3] This crisis placed a spotlight on the Central African Republic and the world took notice of the long-time human rights abuses that had occurred in that country, a nation long ignored as it was deemed to have no strategic importance to the United States or to most nations in the West.[4] A 2010 U.S. State Department document listed a pattern of extrajudicial punishment, torture, rape, human trafficking, corruption, and ethnic discrimination that existed no matter which government was in power.[5] Movement throughout the northern part of the country was limited due to bandits and the Christian and Muslim militias. Also, roughly 68 percent of all marriages performed in the country from 2000 through 2008 were considered to be "child marriages."[6]

In December 2013, United States Ambassador to the United Nations Samantha Power visited the Central African Republic to draw attention to the crisis and to pressure the transitional government there to pursue a course of reconciliation between Christians and Muslims and to hold free elections no later than 2015.[7] Power also held a series of meetings with the victims of the violence and sought, through her questioning, to drive home the point that the nation was on the verge of genocide. In one exchange with a victim of the religious conflict:

> In a small room on Thursday, the young man who alluded to joining a militia told her that he had counted 22 corpses on a small stretch of road after the rebels who overthrew the government and seized power this year—a group known as Seleka that is mostly Muslim—went on a rampage. He said his cousins were among the dead in the countryside, adding that if nothing changed in the next couple of months, he could himself join the Christian militias that have sprung up in defense. Ms. Power, who had been taking notes, looked up and asked: Does that mean killing people because they are Muslim?[8]

Such a question ("Does that mean killing people because they are Muslim?") seems simple enough and not out of place coming from an Ambassador to the United Nations. But, in the context of Samantha Power's career, one can suggest that such a question underscores her life-long interest in and advocacy for victims of genocide. It also serves as a window into the complex role this former investigative journalist must now negotiate on the world stage. A Pulitzer Prize winner for her work on genocide and an internationally recognized advocate for humanitarian intervention across the globe, Power seemed, at first glance, to be uniquely well-suited to serve as Ambassador to the United Nations.[9] But, it is one thing to document atrocities all over the world and to advocate for strong international responses to quell violence. It is quite another thing to work within a series of complex institutions often at odds with each other to bring about the sorts of outcomes she advocated for as a journalist. Power's career serves as a lesson about the power of public rhetoric and how it is shaped by one's own role and by the context in which one operates. For Samantha Power, her advocacy for the victims of genocide led to greater recognition of atrocities that occur and the need for international response. It has also, however, led to a rather controversial public life in which she has received both praise and trenchant criticism for her broadsides against injustice, culminating in government service in an administration under fire itself for what some would call missteps in foreign policy.[10] For Ambassador Power, her detailed and impassioned descriptions of human rights abuses have made her someone who commands the attention of the world when she speaks or writes. But this *ethos* also makes for challenges in her new role in the United States government in which the limits of her rhetoric are well-circumscribed and the often controversial things she has said in the past seem to surface at some inopportune times, as was the case during the 2008 Presidential campaign with her remarks about Hillary Clinton.[11] This chapter discusses Samantha Power's career, her award-winning journalism, and her new role with the United Nations. It explores the impact of her work as an advocate for victims of genocide and how this simultaneously informs and presents challenges in her present work with the United Nations. As her position with the United Nations almost certainly limits what she can say, her reputation as a plain-spoken reporter of genocide provides her an *ethos* many diplomats do not possess.

SAMANTHA POWER: BACKGROUND AND *RAISING HUMAN RIGHTS*

Samantha Power was born in Dublin and raised in Castlenock, Ireland until she was nine years old, at which time she and her mother emigrated to Pittsburgh after the break-up of her parents' marriage.[12] She graduated from Yale University in 1994 with a degree in history.[13] Upon graduation, she covered the conflicts in the Balkans from 1993–1996 as a correspondent for several magazines including *The Economist* and *US News and World Report.*[14] She refers to herself as a "child of Sarajevo" and writes about the lasting impressions of the genocide in the region.[15] Power was dismayed by what she saw as the unwillingness of the United States to intervene in a crisis that was becoming more and more out-of-control. The final straw for her came in Srebrenica, an area designated a "safe haven" by the United Nations and its international peacekeeping forces, where in July 1995 an estimated 7,000 Muslim men and boys were massacred by Bosnian Serbs.[16]

Power then realized that journalism, per se, does not change policy.[17] She left the region in anger and frustration. "It wasn't about me, Samantha," she said. "It was about impotence."[18] Ms. Power's response involved enrolling at Harvard University where she earned a J.D. and the writing and editing of a 600 page book, which would grow out of a paper she wrote in law school, *Realizing Human Rights*, a volume she would go on to co-edit with Graham Allison. She graduated in 1999 and from 1999 to 2002 she served as the Founding Executive Director of the Carr Center for Human Rights Policy at Harvard University's Kennedy School of Government and later as Anna Lindh Professor of Practice of Global Leadership and Public Policy.[19]

Her book, the previously mentioned *Realizing Human Rights: Moving from Inspiration to Impact*, featuring essays on human rights struggles throughout the world, was published. Contributors included President Jimmy Carter, Chinese dissident Wei Jingsheng, and Kofi Annan.[20] Her introduction to the book provided a clear exposition of her approach to intervention in human rights cases. The notion of military intervention by international organizations such as the United Nations or North Atlantic

Treaty Organization (NATO) and by countries such as the United States has long been a controversial idea. Certainly, it is at odds with the idea of national sovereignty, that nations should be free from interference in their own affairs. Power, however, skewers this idea. She writes that, "The sovereignty of states has never been absolute, and concern for rights never entirely absent."[21] She goes on to detail interventions such as Great Britain, France, and Russia teaming up to defeat the Ottoman Fleet in the 1827 Battle of Navarino, in support of the Greek struggle for independence. These interventions, while part of a larger military project, served to protect ethnic minorities and place the value of individual and minority rights as a cornerstone of civilization.[22]

For Power, the 1948 United Nations Universal Declaration for Human Rights, the touchstone of *Realizing Human Rights*, is hardly a radical idea. She explains that it has its genesis in the policies of Edmund Burke, Disraeli, and Gladstone; in the Hague Conventions of 1899 and 1907; and in Woodrow Wilson's League of Nations.[23] But, it was the horror of the Holocaust that prodded Winston Churchill and Franklin Delano Roosevelt to call for something that might guarantee the protection of human rights.[24] Violations of these rights imperil the value of the individual citizen and the responsibility of holding states accountable for the protection of these basic rights. That these rights are held to be universal, she argues, can be seen in the cultural products of every nation (literature and visual art) which show a deep and abiding affinity for freedom, autonomy, and peaceful coexistence between peoples.[25]

Samantha Power was earning a reputation as one who spoke explicitly about human rights violations around the world. An example of her no-holds-barred style comes from this section of an *Atlantic Monthly* article about Rwanda and President Clinton's assertion that the United States could have done more to alleviate the situation:

> In reality the United States did much more than fail to send troops. It led a successful effort to remove most of the UN peacekeepers who were already in Rwanda. It aggressively worked to block the subsequent authorization of UN reinforcements. It refused to use its technology to jam radio broadcasts that were a crucial instrument in the coordination and perpetuation of the genocide. And even as, on average, 8,000 Rwandans were being butchered each day, U.S. officials shunned the term "genocide," for fear of being obliged to act. The United States in fact did virtually nothing "to try to limit what occurred." Indeed, staying out of Rwanda was an explicit U.S. policy objective.[26]

Analyses such as these gave Power a reputation as a consistent and plain-spoken advocate for victims of international conflicts.

CONSTRUCTING A RHETORIC OF GENOCIDE

In 2002, Power published *A Problem from Hell: America and the Age of Genocide*, a book that generated great interest and both positive and negative responses, and that served as a call for a robust military response to human rights violations around the world.[27] Power discusses the work of Raphael Lemkin, a Polish attorney who had emigrated to the United States in 1941 and who had coined the word "genocide."[28] For Power, Lemkin is a pivotal figure in the struggle for human rights during the twentieth century. In an article in *Dissent*, Power discusses Lemkin's linkage of the Armenian atrocities with the Holocaust and how this should color our understanding of both events. Lemkin's 1944 book *Axis Rule in Occupied Europe* provided details about the many laws and decrees enacted throughout Nazi-controlled Europe during World War II. His purpose, as he saw it, was to draw the world's attention to the barbarity of the Nazi enterprise, a barbarity that went beyond that of simply fighting a war for territory.[29] Lemkin called these acts "genocide," and he defined them as acts that are "systematic, purposeful, and brutal."[30] The word, somewhat surprisingly, became widespread rather quickly throughout Western nations even though defining an event as "genocide" would be something international actors were often hesitant to do.[31]

Power goes on to discuss the implications of this newly coined word. Although Lemkin was sorely disappointed that the Nuremberg Trials failed to consider his idea, his efforts led to the 1946 adoption of a United Nations Convention on Genocide and, in 1948, after several drafts of the Convention, the United Nations defined genocide as:

(a) Killing members of the group;
(b) Causing serious bodily or mental harm to members of the group;
(c) Deliberately inflicting on the group conditions of life calculated to bring about its physical destruction in whole or in part;
(d) Imposing measures intended to prevent births within the group;
(e) Forcibly transferring children of the group to another group.[32]

The United States was slow to ratify the Convention, only doing so (with reservations) in 1986.[33]

A Problem from Hell highlights the history of genocide in the latter half of the twentieth century. She discusses the Khmer Rouge in Cambodia, which she uses to explain the relationship between war and genocide. The Vietnam conflict, Power explains, almost necessarily gave rise to the "killing fields" of Cambodia, when the United States expanded the conflict into neighboring Cambodia.[34] And Powers goes on to suggest that for Pol Pot, just as for Lenin and Hitler, the eradication of specific groups of people was not just incidental to policy, but was itself a policy objective.[35] In the United States and in much of the West, however, reports of atrocities were met with either disbelief or with a sense of resignation that intervention would be futile.[36]

A Problem from Hell then shifts its focus to Iraq's use of chemical weapons against its own Kurdish minority in the late 1980s.[37] Certainly, as Power argues, Saddam Hussein did not set out to commit genocide. Indeed, the aggression against the Kurds was initially a response, however brutal, to an insurgency in rural areas. Initially, no actions were taken against Kurdish Iraqis in urban areas.[38] As the killing progressed, however, Saddam took a more and more systematic approach to the eradication of Kurds, simply because of their ethnic identity.[39] Peter Galbraith of the Senate Foreign Relations Committee was one of the first to chart the development of genocidal actions but was stonewalled by an administration, that of George H.W. Bush, hesitant to criticize the Iraqis because it was perceived that a common enemy, Iran, posed a much bigger threat.[40] Sanctions and other actions against Hussein faced a rather steep climb in Congress and with the administration. The administration's greater anxiety over Iran and the House's concerns about a growing Iraqi business lobby led to fairly watered-down sanctions, which still had a degree of success. Recognition by the United States that Hussein had engaged in genocide did not lead to the prosecution of any Iraqi perpetrators.[41]

Next, Power moves on to the Bosnian conflict, a situation Power directly experienced in her time as a journalist. When Yugoslavia split around ethnic lines, Slovenia and Croatia were the first republics to secede. Slobodan Milosevic used this opportunity to create Serb dominance in what was left of the former Yugoslavia.[42] The Republic of Bosnia was in a bind. If it remained in what was left of Yugoslavia, its sizeable Muslim population, 44 percent of its population, would be essentially marginalized in terms of economic opportunity.[43] If it left, the Muslims and the Croatian minority would be worse off with no protectors in the region.[44] The United States advised the leaders of a new Bosnian transitional government to ensure human rights but Serb hard-liners balked at such a move.[45] Soon, ethnic tensions between Serbs, Croats, and Muslims in Bosnia reached a crisis point. What followed was a period of targeted "ethnic cleansing" by well-armed Serb militias.[46] Diplomatic measures by the European Union and, finally, by the United States did little to aid the Muslims and Croats. National Security Adviser Brent Scowcroft and the Bush administration did not believe that "ethnic cleansing," as horrific as it became, was the equivalent of genocide and, thus, did next to nothing, according to Power.[47] Under the succeeding administration of President Clinton, a continuing hesitancy to call the conflict "genocide" also kept the United States from acting forcefully. Despite pleas from Elie Wiesel and senior members of Congress, defining the Bosnian situation as genocide was not something Washington wanted to do. It was not until 1995, that Clinton and NATO took any decisive action to quell the violence.[48]

Power's final conflicts covered in *A Problem from Hell* involve the Rwandan genocide of 1994, Srebrenica in 1992, and Kosovo throughout the 1990s, a situation Power herself covered as a journalist). She describes how these stories also fit the definition of genocide, also involved great hesitancy on the part of the United States, the UN, NATO, the African Union, and other multinational groups, and, most importantly, also could have seen an end to the systematic violence with quicker action and intervention.[49] For Power, the victims of genocide are victims precisely because of their collective identities, not because of anything they might have done as individuals. It is enough, she says, to be, for example "a Tutsi in Rwanda."[50] Power then makes the connection to the events of September 11, 2001 in which she suggests that the victims in the World Trade Center and the Pentagon were targeted solely because of national identity.[51] She suggests that, to ignore the perpetrators of genocide is to embolden them and to embolden others to take similar actions.[52] A robust and consistent willingness to counter genocide is, for Power, in the national interest. Although *A Problem from Hell* discusses events that were, essentially, foreign policy failures, Power notes that, "If anything testifies to the U.S. capacity for influence, it is the extent to which the perpetrators kept an eye trained on Washington and other Western capitals, as they decided how to proceed."[53] Further, she states that, "for all the talk of the likely futility of U.S. involvement, in the rare instances that the United States did act, it made a difference." Power argues that the sanctions against Iraq, albeit relatively mild, did lead to an end to Hussein's use of chemical weapons. NATO bombing in Bosnia, when it finally did occur, brought that war to a close.[54]

Thus, *A Problem from Hell* became a manifesto of sorts for Samantha Power and members of the Washington establishment who took a "hawkish" approach to matters of ethnic, national, and religious violence around the world.[55] Certainly, this was by no means a new approach. Former Secretaries of State Madeline Albright and Zbigniew Brzezinksi among others shared such a worldview. What made Power notable were her youth and her rather passionate commitment to the issue. She was an academic whose writing was easily understood by a general readership and compelling and persuasive. The book won the 2003 National Book Critics Circle Award and the Pulitzer Prize.[56] Certainly, there was criticism of the book from those on the political left. Joseph Nevins suggested in *The Nation* that Power's analyses tended to ignore instances in which American foreign policy itself led to ethnic cleansing and genocide.[57] Howard Zinn took her to task for a lack of nuance in her thinking.[58] In a rather stinging critique, Edward Herman, writing in the *Monthly Review,* took Power to task for her depiction of the conflict in Kosovo. For Herman, Power's simplistic views essentially whitewashed shared responsibilities for the conflict.[59] On the right, President George W. Bush expressed disagreement with her calls for robust responses to genocide, calling instead for a more cautious approach.[60] Yet, the book was, by anyone's reckoning, a success and led to Power being named one of *Time* magazine's "100 Most Influential People of 2004" and she was asked to write occasional columns for the magazine. In 2007, she began writing a regular column for *Time*.[61]

In 2005, Power became a Senior Policy Fellow and advisor in the office of Senator Barack Obama. Here, she was credited with sparking Obama's interest in the Darfur conflict.[62] In 2007, she joined Obama's presidential campaign and, during a particularly heated disagreement on foreign policy with the Clinton campaign, wrote a memo that was "leaked" describing Obama as going against the "conventional wisdom" on foreign policy.[63] Senator Obama's calls for robust diplomacy and military action, when warranted, barring the use of nuclear weapons, represented the sort of policies the world needed in the new millennium.[64] Still, Power often seemed anything but "cold" and purely analytical in her writing. Her style, indeed, still contained quite an "edge" as demonstrated by this section from an article in the *New York Review of Books*:

> In the 2000 election George W. Bush, who had shirked military service, succeeded in presenting himself as more reliable on national security than Al Gore. This was despite Gore's service in Vietnam, his seven years on the Senate Armed Services Committee, his four years on the House Intelligence Committee, his help in brokering a deal to dismantle the nuclear arsenal of former Soviet republics, and his creation of binational commissions with Russia, South Africa, Egypt, Kazakhstan, and Ukraine to deal with issues ranging from AIDS to disarmament. In 2004, too, even before the Swift Boat campaign, John Kerry, a decorated Vietnam veteran, had an uphill climb convincing voters that Democrats made reliable commanders in chief during wartime—even though a majority of Americans had already come to regret that the sitting commander in chief had chosen to wage war in the first place.[65]

Fiercely partisan but plain-spoken as always, Power lent a great degree of ethos to the Obama campaign.

In early 2008, she combined a book tour to promote her new book *Chasing the Flame: Sergio Vieira de Mello and the Fight to Save the World,* with a series of interviews in support of the Obama campaign. She appeared on the Charlie Rose program and various news programs in the United States, Great Britain, and her native Ireland and took every opportunity to give as many interviews as she could.[66] In a March 6 interview with *The Scotsman*, however, after the Ohio Primary, she said: "'We fucked up in Ohio. In Ohio, they are obsessed and Hillary is going to town on it, because she knows Ohio's the only place they can win.'"[67] Further, she added, 'She is a monster, too—that is off the record—she is stooping to anything . . . if you are poor and she is telling you some story about how Obama is going to take your job away, maybe it will be more effective. The amount of deceit she has put forward is really unattractive.'"[68] In the wake of a predictably negative reaction from the Clinton campaign and from the Republicans, Power resigned from the Obama campaign.[69] Here, the plain-spoken and often polemic language she employed as a journalist and author backfired when she was foreign policy advisor to a major presidential candidate.

Significantly, following a much-publicized but private apology, to Senator Clinton, Power served as a member of the State Department transition team and worked closely with Clinton when the latter became Secretary of State.[70] In January 2009 President Obama appointed Power to the National Security Council Staff, where she served as a Special Assistant to the President and Senior Director running the Office of Multilateral Affairs and Human Rights.[71] Thus, the Obama White House featured two women in foreign policy advisory roles (Power and Susan Rice, then Ambassador to the United Nations) who had themselves witnessed genocide first-hand and who were widely considered to be "hawkish" on questions of humanitarian intervention.[72] Both Power and Rice were seen as instrumental in persuading the administration to intervene in Libya.[73] Although critics on the left and right suggested that such a move was tantamount to another Iraq invasion, Power took great pains to suggest that the decision involved far more input that her own and was quite deliberate and cautious.[74] And, while the administration pursued the course advocated by Power as well as by Clinton and Rice, the tensions of her new role as an "insider" were again the focus of a number of Washington pundits as had happened similarly during her time on the campaign trail. "I think what she is doing is good," said Bill Nash, a retired Army general who commanded forces in Bosnia.[75] "But," he continued, "I suspect it is more black and white to her than the real world portrays."[76] Still, it was clear that she had a degree of influence in the administration. She was successful, for example, in urging the Obama administration to embrace congressional legislation calling for the arrest of the leader of the Lord's Resistance Army (LRA), which enslaves children as guerrilla fighters. The White House did, indeed, employ a full-time staff member devoted to monitoring LRA atrocities.[77]

THE UNITED NATIONS: CONSTRUCTING A RHETORIC FOR INTERVENTION

During 2013, President Obama nominated Power to serve as United States ambassador to the United Nations. She received great bipartisan support in the Senate with Senator John McCain praising her qualifications and Senator Joseph Lieberman calling Power a "friend of Israel."[78] But, her nomination was also opposed by a number of people including former U.S. Ambassador to the UN John R. Bolton.[79] The former U.S. Assistant Secretary of Defense for International Security Policy Frank Gaffney criticized her for a 2003 article in *The New Republic* that she wrote in which she compared the United States to Nazi Germany.[80] There also surfaced a video of her suggesting a "thought experiment" in forcing peace on Israel, remarks she said were both hypothetical and taken out of context.[81] Criticism notwithstanding, her nomination process was relatively easy, passing the Senate quickly by a vote of 87–10.[82]

Immediately after taking the post of ambassador, Power again seemed to court controversy. As the civil war in Syria went on into a third year, she expressed outrage and dismay about the inability of the United Nations Security Council to bring about a resolution. She briefed the United Nations Press Corps that the United States had been telling other member states of its intelligence assessment about an attack in the Damascus suburbs on Aug. 21.[83] The assessment concluded that banned chemical munitions had been used and that the forces of President Bashar al-Assad were responsible.[84] She said that more than 1,400 civilians were killed in the strike, including more than 400 children.[85] Yet, because Russia and China would almost certainly veto any action against Syria, the United Nations was essentially powerless to do anything. She went on to assert that, "Russia continues to hold the Council hostage," and that, "what we have learned—what the Syrian people have learned—is that the Security Council the world needs to deal with this crisis is not the Security Council we have."[86] Here, Power spoke more in the fashion of a journalist and commentator than in the manner one might expect from a diplomat.

The limits of her new position seemed to be especially confining. It would seem that Power's tendencies toward intervention ran up against some hurdles. A plan for intervention supported by Leon Panetta, Generals Petraeus and Dempsey, and Secretary Clinton in 2012, had already been dismissed by the administration.[87] Also, the "proceduralism" and support for multilateralism inherent in an ambassador's post argues against any public advocacy for unilateral action.[88] Indeed, the president agreed to pursue a diplomatic course with the Russians. In the aftermath of that decision, Samantha Power has essentially hewed the policy line of the administration with regard to Syria.[89]

Power's role as United Nations ambassador, however, is not as simple as her serving as a spokesperson for the White House. Her reputation as a champion for genocide victims allows the administration to use her talents in ways that they could not with other officials. Given Power's international stature as one of her generation's most eloquent voices for human rights, it seems no accident that the Obama White House chose Power to be the point person for Lesbian, Gay, Bisexual, and Transgendered (LGBT) concerns in the year leading up to the Sochi Olympic Games in Russia.[90] She authored the White House blog detailing the administration's position on LGBT rights, suggesting that LGBT citizens who were victims of discrimination and violence might qualify for refugee status.[91] She writes that, "Seventy-eight countries have laws that criminalize consensual same-sex acts between adults, resulting in unchecked human rights abuses and exploitation by police, security officials and private citizens."[92] She goes on to suggest that, in at least five countries, "the death penalty can be applied for being gay. Even where being LGBT is not a crime, violence by state and non-state actors alike often goes unpunished and LGBT communities live in fear and isolation."[93] Power says that the United States will support the rights of LGBT people across the world, stating in the blog that, "As we move forward with this work, we stand in solidarity with the many brave LGBT activists around the world—from Albania to Zimbabwe—who put their lives on the line every day."[94] In light of Russia's rather draconian laws about "homosexual propaganda" being illegal, Power seems to want the reader to contrast the freedom guaranteed by the United States with the discrimination LGBT people might face in Russia.[95]

CONCLUSION

With Samantha Power taking the lead in the Central African Republic, it seems certain that her celebrity will draw more attention to events in that country. It will be interesting to see what actions the United States and the United Nations take. It seems reasonably safe to say that someone with the *ethos* that Power possesses can create interest in issues for which it might have been difficult in the past to get any sort of action. It also seems a safe bet to say that Power will continue to be challenged as she negotiates the path between advocate and government official. As the parameters of her role as UN ambassador limit what she can say, her credibility as a reporter of genocide and her reputation as a plain-spoken advocate for what she believes will almost certainly draw attention to her actions, her statements, and to the position of UN ambassador. Whether her tenure as a government official will ultimately diminish the reputation she built early in her career as a journalist and advocate is anyone's guess. While her service to the Obama administration has provided a larger stage for her work, one wonders how perceptions of political partisanship will affect her work in the future.

NOTES

1. Somini Smgupta, "U.N. Ambassador in Central Africa, Vows Aid and Hears of a Unity Shattered," *New York Times*, December 19, 2013, accessed December 20, 2013, www.nytimes.com/2013/12/20/world/africa/us-ambassador-visits-central-african-republic-amid-bloodshed.html.
2. Ibid.
3. Ibid.
4. Ibid.
5. Ibid.
6. Ibid.
7. Ibid.
8. Ibid.
9. Ibid.
10. Ibid.
11. Ibid.
12. Samantha Power, "Once Upon a Nomar," *Boston Globe*, June 5, 2013, accessed December 20, 2013, www.bostonglobe.com/opinion/columns/2013/06/05/once-upon-nomar/uXl3d0AiplZj1IwaD9PRfK/story.html.
13. Ibid.
14. Ibid.
15. Celestine Bohlen, "On a Mission to Shine a Spotlight on Genocide: Samantha Power's Mind Leaps from Bosnia to Iraq," *New York Times*, February 5, 2003, accessed October 3, 2013, www.nytimes.com/2003/02/05/books/mission-shine-spotlight-genocide-samantha-power-s-mind-leaps-bosnia-iraq.html?pagewanted.
16. Ibid.
17. Power, "Once Upon a Nomar."
18. Samantha Power, *A Problem from Hell: America and the Age of Genocide* (New York: Harper-Collins, 2002), xx.
19. Ibid., xxi.
20. Samantha Power and Graham Allison, *Realizing Human Rights: Moving from Inspiration to Impact* (New York: Palgrave, 2000), xv.
21. Ibid., xv.
22. Ibid., xvi.
23. Ibid., xvii.

24. Ibid., xv.
25. Ibid., xvi.
26. Samantha Power, "Bystanders to Genocide," *The Atlantic Monthly*, September 2001, accessed December 1, 2013, www.theatlantic.com/magazine/archive/2001/09/bystanders-to-genocide/304571/2.
27. Ibid.
28. Power, *A Problem from Hell*, 40.
29. Ibid., 42.
30. Ibid., 44.
31. Power, "Bystanders to Genocide."
32. Power, *A Problem from Hell*, 57.
33. Ibid., 65.
34. Ibid., 90.
35. Ibid., 110.
36. Ibid., 114.
37. Ibid., 172.
38. Sheryl Gay Stolberg, "Still Crusading, but Now on the Inside," *New York Times*, March 29, 2011, accessed November 30, 2013, www.nytimes.com/2011/03/30/world/30power.html?_r=0.
39. Power, *A Problem from Hell*, 200.
40. Ibid., 210.
41. Ibid., 243.
42. Ibid., 264.
43. Ibid., 265.
44. Ibid., 266.
45. Ibid., 271.
46. Power. "Bystanders to Genocide."
47. Samantha Power, "Raising the Cost of Genocide," *Dissent* Spring (2002): 88.
48. Power, *A Problem from Hell*, 249.
49. Ibid., 385.
50. Ibid., 506.
51. Ibid., 507.
52. Ibid., 508.
53. Ibid., 512.
54. Ibid., 513.
55. Ibid., 517.
56. Ibid., 505.
57. Joseph Nevins, "On Justifying Intervention," *The Nation*, May 20, 2002, accessed November 30, 2013, www.thenation.com/article/justifying-intervention#.
58. Howard Zinn, "On Terror," *Z-Net*, August 21, 2007, accessed September 24, 2008, www.zmag.org/Zinn.
59. Edward Herman, "The Dismantling of Yugoslavia, Part IV," *Monthly Review*, October 1, 2007, accessed November 30, 2013, monthlyreview.org/2007/10/01/the-dismantling-of-yugoslavia-part-iv.

60. Sheryl Gay Stolberg, "Still Crusading, but Now on the Inside," *New York Times*, March 29, 2011, accessed December 20, 2013, www.nytimes.com/2011/03/30/world/30power.html?_r=0.

61. Ibid.

62. Bohlen, "On a Mission to Shine a Spotlight on Genocide."

63. Stolberg, "Still Crusading."

64. Ibid.

65. Samantha Power, "The Democrats and National Security," *The New York Review of Books* 55 (2008), accessed December 20, 2013, www.nybooks.com/issues/2008/aug/14.

66. Gerri Peev, "'Hillary Clinton's a Monster': Obama Aide Blurts Out Attack in Scotsman Interview," *The Scotsman*, June 3, 2008, accessed November 30, 2013, www.scotsman.com/news/hillary-clinton-s-a-monster-obama-aide-blurts-out-attack-in-scotsman-interview-1-1158300.

67. Ibid.

68. Ibid.

69. Stolberg, "Still Crusading."

70. Max Fisher, "What Do Susan Rice and Samantha Power Promotions Mean for Syria Policy? Probably Not Much," *The Washington Post*, June 5, 2013, accessed November 30, 2013, www.washingtonpost.com/blogs/worldviews/wp/2013/06/05/what-do-susan-rice-and-samantha-power-promotions-mean-for-syria-policy-probably-not-much.

71. Ibid.

72. Ibid.

73. Ibid.

74. Ibid.

75. Ibid.

76. Stolberg, "Still Crusading."

77. Ibid.

78. Ibid.

79. "Samantha Power Will Concede US Self-Determination to the UN." Center for Security Policy, accessed June 14, 2013, www.centerforsecuritypolicy.org/2013/06/14/samantha-power-will-concede-us-self-determination-to-the-un.

80. Ibid.

81. Christine Hauser and Robert Mackey, "Video of Samantha Power's 2002 Remarks on Imposing Peace on Israel Could Haunt Her, Israeli Paper Says," *New York Times*, June 5, 2013, accessed November 29, 2013, thelede.blogs.nytimes.com/2013/06/05/israeli-newspaper-focuses-on-samantha-powers-remarks-in-2002/?ref=samanthapower.

82. Ramsey Cox, "Samantha Power Confirmed as Obama's UN Ambassador," *The Hill*, August 1, 2013, accessed November 29, 2013, thehill.com/blogs/floor-action/senate/315137-senate-votes-to-confirm-power-as-un-ambassador.

83. Rick Gladstone, "New U.S. Envoy to U.N. Strongly Condemns Russia," *New York Times*, September 5, 2013, accessed December 20, 2013, www.nytimes.com/2013/09/06/world/middleeast/new-us-envoy-to-un-strongly-condemns-russia.html?_r=0.

84. Ibid.
85. Ibid.
86. Ibid.
87. Ibid.
88. Ibid.
89. Ibid.
90. Ibid.
91. "US Leadership to Advance Equality for LGBT People Abroad," *The White House Blog*, accessed December 13, 2012, www.whitehouse.gov/blog/2012/12/13/us-leadership-advance-equality-lgbt-people-abroad.
92. Ibid.
93. Ibid.
94. Ibid.
95. Ibid.

Part Four

GLOBAL FIGURES: SOCIAL ISSUES AND SOCIAL MEDIA

Chapter Seven

Assessing the Rhetoric of Sheikha Moza

Mistress of Ethos

Mohanalakshmi Rajakumar

The Middle East region has faced many challenges with regard to women's roles in public life, particularly in the countries of the Arabian Gulf, or Gulf Cooperation Council (GCC), which include Oman, Qatar, Saudi Arabia, Bah'rain, Kuwait, and the United Arab Emirates, where conservative interpretations of Islam mean gender segregation in public spaces and patriarchal attitudes toward women's roles inside the home. The GCC countries are perhaps best known for their oil rich economies or petro dollars, which ushered in foreign investment and labor in vast sums from the 1970s. As Allen Fromherz explains in his introduction to *Qatar: A Modern History,* economic development in the Arabian Gulf has not coincided with social reform.[1] Rather the opposite has become the case; whereas Bedouin women worked with their hands and were given responsibilities in overseeing the household or childcare, female nationals of these emirates now have the assistance of maids, cooks, and drivers to attend to their daily tasks. They are encased in gilded cages, their mobility hampered even as their well-adorned bodies must be protected as symbols of familial honor and purity. Very traditional men will not say the names of their female relatives to other men, even if they are not strangers.

In such a divided society, where primary schools and even government workplaces have separate areas—sometimes even buildings—designed to keep the two genders apart, the place and position of women in society is often seen as within the home, as sisters, cousins, and nieces are being groomed to become wives and mothers. Sheikha Moza Bint Nasser, the second wife of the former Emir, Sheikh Hamad Bin Khalifa Al Thani, is a rare exception. She exerts a visible public role, crossing boundaries for Qatari women and exerting significant influence at a key moment of modernization in Qatari history. Her Highness, as she is commonly referred to by nationals, is an embodiment of the delicate balance between modernization and tradition that the small emirate strikes in foreign policy as well economic development. Through her role as chairperson for the Qatar Foundation for Science, Technology, and Community Development, she espouses a plural, liberal interpretation of Islam, which focuses on the religion's emphasis on education, the role of the individual in society, and the betterment of the world. The sheikha's position as a modern traditionalist allows her to assert a religious nationalism within the safe, feminine space of educational policy.[2] Her speeches abroad increasingly demonstrate a blend of Arab identity, modern pragmatism, and keen drive to improve Qatar by importing the best educational models the world has to offer, making Qatar a hub for educational innovation in the Arab world:

> In the past, countries in our region sent students abroad to be educated. Upon their return, such citizens were often isolated from their societies, for they had acquired the education needed to analyze and participate in their societies, but their societies had not developed any mechanisms to accommodate the practice of citizenry. Such people either secluded themselves from others or returned abroad, initiating a process of brain drain in our region. In Qatar, we are bringing institutions to our region, rather than sending our people outside.[3]

Constant comparisons between the two Emirates have made Qataris adamant that they do not want to be as Western as Dubai, which has seen most of its Emirati population leave the city to other outlying states. The focus of the Qatari modernization project, as stated in the *Qatar National Vision 2030*, has four pillars of development: economic, social, human, and environmental—all of which have Qatari citizens at the center of its goals.[4] The Human Development pillar is focused on capacity building, which has the promotion of education reform and innovation at its core.

An ambitious policy development program for the nation, structured to move it away from dependency as an oil and natural gas exporter, *Qatar National Vision 2030* declared to the world the leadership's intentions to catapult the country into the international arena, serving as "the Guiding Principles of the Permanent Constitution and the directions of Their Highnesses the Emir, the Heir Apparent and Sheikha Mozah."[5] One-half of the ruling couple and mother to the heir apparent who ushered in unprecedented economic and social change, Sheikha Moza is a study in nuanced gendered rhetoric. In the same way the State of Qatar balances hosting the Al Jazeera television network and the largest American military base in the Middle East in a landmass roughly the size of the state of Connecticut, the sheikha vacillates from speaking to the General Assembly of the United Nations to demurring any personal credit for her country's advancements and lauding her husband's vision.

FASHIONABLE EDUCATION

While the areas of Sheikha Moza's influence lie in traditional feminine spheres, mainly education and community building, her prominent role in international organizations such as United Nations Educational Scientific and Cultural Organization (UNESCO) means that she is a considerable female presence in the socio-cultural landscape of the GCC and the greater Middle East. Feminist Islamic scholar, miriam cooke, explains how both Muslim fundamentalists and Western society attribute a singular identity to veiled women.[6] Yet, Sheikha Moza, as a well dressed, glamorous, English-speaking Arab woman, has the necessary credentials to resist the "singular religious and gendered identification that overlays national, ethnic, cultural, historical and even philosophical diversity" in the post 9/11 geo-political landscape.[7] Her use of self representation, is what cooke identifies as the only means around a monolithic notion of Muslim womanhood: "the more women represent themselves and project alternative notions of gender in the Muslim imaginary, the more control they will have over the Muslim woman."[8] Western media and institutions, such as *Forbes* magazine, and various educational arms of the United Nations, including UNESCO and the Alliance of Civilizations, have made Sheikha Moza their emblem of Arab promise. Her unique interpretation of her role as the public wife or consort of the emir of the state of Qatar demonstrates the type of savvy ability to carve out a role for Qatari women in public life that cooke defines as "cosmopolitan identity with local roots."[9] She is both mobile and modern, while still mindful of traditional practices. The sheikha was among the first of the royal wives of the GCC to have her photo published in local and then international newspapers.[10] Unlike the other women in public roles in Qatar, including her aunt, the well-respected president of Qatar University, Sheikha Al Misned, Ph.D., the sheikha has a glamorous visage who is as likely to appear on the front page of the newspaper next to the queen of England in satin and pearls as in the traditional abaya, or long black robe worn by Qatari women when inside Qatar. Her ability to challenge the stereotypical notion of Muslim women as cowering and covered head to toe in a burqa with her physical appearance is what cooke deems "Women's visible assumption of an Islamic identity . . . projecting a transnational imaginary."[11] Sheikha Moza's bejeweled luxury brand outfits are carefully considered material presentations through which she expresses her identity as modern, yet modest, Muslim woman, all the while confirming the vast resources of the country she represents.[12] As she is engaged in the process of reforming Qatari society through education, her movements and articulations embody her commitment to Arab culture and values.

The ultra-feminine, designer-wearing aspect of her persona softens the extent of her public influence because of the popularity among Qatari women of fashion and luxury brands. In the early stages of the twenty-first century, as global markets were in flux, the cash-rich economies of the GCC emerged on the global stage as more than mere exporters. Despite being unfavorably compared to Dubai, which is known for having the world's tallest building, the Burj Khalifa, or the largest fireworks display on New Year's Eve 2013. Qatar established itself as a serious geo-political player by being named host of the 2022 World Cup, and being the first Middle Eastern country to ever have the distinction of hosting the 18th Conference of the Parties on Climate Exchange.[13]

Sheikha Moza is an example of a female Arab leader who both tests the limits of social conventions for Qatari women and also plays within these boundaries. She cannot alienate her people and risk losing their support, but she can challenge their notions of what is acceptable for modern women. Her leadership *ethos* demonstrates Mansoor Moaddel's assertion that modernism in the Arab world does not always mean a discarding of traditional values;[14] in her role as wife and educational champion she balances the feminine *ethos* acceptable in Islamic society while at the same time empowering and enabling young Arab women to academic achievements previously not possible. She is listed as the co-founder and chairperson of the Qatar Foundation for Science, Education and Community Development (QF), alongside her husband, Sheikh Hamad. While she is active in the day-to-day operations of the foundation, her husband's power gives her the authority she needs to operate in a patrilineal society. Within the role ascribed to her, she has brought her own passionate belief in education as a force for change, a mission that has garnered the respect of the international community, as demonstrated in honorary degrees and countless awards. Her *ethos* is tied to his an innovator of the Qatari economy and industries; together they are an innovative force that has catalyzed what most of the world previously considered a sleepy, backwater country into one of the most rapidly growing economies.[15]

Sheikha Moza has directly and indirectly helped engender some of the most dramatic educational reform the country has ever known. The project oversees the largest university campus in the world, the Education City (EC) project, with branch campuses of six American universities, various graduate degree granting programs and a host of affiliate centers engaged in human capacity building in Qatar and the Middle East. Having Sheikha Moza as the leader and spokesperson for EC serves the double reinforcement of modernization of education as well as open access for female Qatari students.[16] She has spoken out against assumptions that religion alone is behind educational choices for young Muslim women. In 2007, in remarks at the Los Angeles

World Affairs Council, she said, "Muslim countries prohibiting the education of women is not because they are Muslim. There are other cultural aspects that guide those decisions."[17] In the case of Qatari women, traveling abroad without a male chaperon would deter families from allowing their female members access to education outside of the country; the development of the EC project means these ambitious young women now have six universities and an ever-increasing number of graduate programs to choose from.

Educational reform was also underway for students in their first years of schooling through the Education for a New Era project (2001),[18] a reconfiguring of Qatari public primary and secondary schools into an independent or character school-like system. The entire premise for the Education for a New Era project was a concern over the lack of the existing system to prepare the citizens Qatar would need for its modern economy. As Sheikha Moza explained in a keynote address at a conference on Arab Women at Georgetown University in Qatar:

> Scholars have affirmed that the "traditional" system of education in the Arab world, built upon the absolute power of those in authority, encourages learning by rote, and blind acceptance of power. In such schools, girls and boys are taught not to question their teachers, just as individuals in society are taught not to question their rulers. In short, the type of education prominent in the Middle East sustains autocratic regimes and inequalities—racial, class, and gender.[19]

The sheikha acknowledges the limitations of education that does teach students to question; she is critical of educational practices in the Middle East and conversely the inequalities they reinforce, including gender as a constraining category. The public acknowledgement of the need to reform power structures by someone playing a key role in a governing Middle East monarchy is unique. She highlights the negatives of "individuals in society [who] are taught not to question their rules"; the space she carves out for herself as a prominent woman who still respects tradition demonstrates her own negotiation as a Qatari woman. In so doing, the sheikha adapts on another acceptable role for women in the public sphere, that of teacher or scholar.[20] While her comments in the speech could be construed as subversive in a country ruled by a constitutional monarchy, her relationship to the ruler, membership in the ruling family, and status as mother of the heir apparent, means that her comments apply only to the arena for which they were intended: the academic community, as most of the members in the audience were faculty, staff, or students from Georgetown University. The public rhetoric used in speeches at the start of the EC project was inclusive of other academic institutions in the country, chiefly Qatar University. In her 2009 remarks to the graduating class of EC, the sheikha refers to the EC commencement while also acknowledging there are students on other campuses: "This is the true significance of commencement, whether here at Education City or at other universities in the country."[21] EC, a collection of American branch campuses, with an elite study body, was grouped with the national university, with a campus of thousands of students from a broad cross-section of the population. Such public pairing of disparate institutions, acknowledges that both groups of students (and their parents) are part of her constituency; underlying the importance of loyalty in wide a close-knit community. The 2009 reference to EC students within the context of the other students studying in Qatar, who are outside her official guidance in her capacity as chairperson, but within her constituency as the first lady of the nation, is not repeated in ensuing years as the EC project continues to add universities and programs.

The ambitious project began with one university, fifteen years ago, starting with an all-female design program at Virginia Commonwealth University in Qatar. The single-sex environment and largely traditional design of only one university building were created to inspire confidence in the families who would send their Qatari daughters to this new concept, an American university in their nation's capital:

> Virginia Commonwealth University in Qatar accommodated the cultural privacy women requested. Even the university's building was custom-made to maintain privacy as much as possible. Similar to older traditional architecture, [. . .] the patterns on the walls were geometric, and the designs and patterns were Islamic-inspired. The use of color all over the university is traditional and warm, and consists of earth tones. For Qatari families, walking into VCUQ was comfortable, familiar, and they could see that their culture and religion were respected and protected through the interior design of the institution.[22]

Since 2008, however, female students have entered engineering, medicine, and computer science at QF, and Qatar University continues to have large female enrollments in the sciences, indicating that change is happening among this generation of university students.[23]

In her 2013 convocation speech to the graduating classes of the American branch campuses at QF, Sheikha Moza equivocates on her expectations for the graduates' role in society: "I, personally, look forward to this day, a day when I see dreams take shape. When I look at you, I feel confident that you graduates are capable of transforming our world and ushering in long-lasting change."[24] Lasting change in a patriarchal society could mean elevating the status of women, not only in public life, but also in civil society. Under Islamic family law, daughters inherit half that of sons; Qatari women cannot pass nationality to their children, nor are they paid the same as men because male Qataris are eligible for allowances to maintain households while women are not. Considering that the enrollment of most universities in Qatar is heavily female, disproportionate to those of male university students, women have taken advantage of the benefits of the education reform more than their male counterpart. In developing their academic credentials, female students are ensuring future professional qualifications that may allow for greater financial autonomy from fathers or husbands. Before the advent of so many educational options, Qatari females were married at younger ages. Now with a variety of specializations, including those that place them in learning or professional environments with males, Qatari women are delaying marriage in order to pursue their academic or professional ambitions.[25] This burgeoning trend will take several generations to usher in the "long-lasting" change the sheikha mentions.

With restrictions on their mobility abroad, females must always have a male family member accompany them while traveling. The establishment of international degree programs within the country means that deterrent to pursuing education is lifted, at least for those who do not mind studying in mixed gender environments as all the QF programs are. Sheikha Moza's charge to the graduates outlines their role in a changing society, a role that the largely hierarchical workforce they will enter is unprepared for: "Remember, knowledge has value only when it is turned into achievement. So keep the spirit of achievement in your work and life [. . .] This environment is a result of our decision to establish progressive academic institutions in Qatar that would help the social, economic, scientific and cultural development of the country in a sustainable way."[26] The direct acknowledgement of the role young people will play in the further development of the social fabric of Qatar is at odds with the status quo in Qatar which remains largely tribal, with citizenship determined by the father's nationality, as it is in much of the Arab world.

THE ROYAL "WE," THE STATE OF QATAR, AND A SHEIKHA

When the sheikha says, "we," in her public addresses, she is using the royal sense of the pronoun, but also acknowledging her powerbase stems from her husband and his government; this is a necessary reminder to her audience who may see an Arab woman and wife, speaking often in front of Westerners and Western audiences, that she is aware of her place both in domestic politics and the domestic space. Lest she be accused of stepping outside of her bounds as a wife to the emir, the traditionally accepted source of power, she mentions her alliance early in most addresses. Once raised, the reference necessitates a shift from the "I" used earlier in speeches, such as the 2013 convocation address. Her remarks are then defined by partnership: "In our minds, we.... It is our aim.... It is our pleasure...."[27] Along with the royal "we" and references to the government come the alignment of her project with the goals of the State of Qatar, which one would not normally see for a private educational enterprise: "This environment is a result of our decision to establish progressive academic institutions in Qatar that would help the social, economic, scientific and cultural development of the country in a sustainable way."[28] The conflation of QF's goals, along with the priorities of the nation, protects the country against the accusations of being a campus run by foreigners, one of the worst charges in a country where expatriates outnumber nationals by the hundreds of thousands.

While publications like the *Christian Science Monitor* might describe her as "rival[ing] her husband in terms of influence in this land,"[29] the sheikha debunks any such idea, firmly establishing the power hierarchy: It's the emir, she says, who inspires *her*. "I live beside him, and know his worries, his hopes, and his dreams for his nation."[30] Her assertions include an earlier use of the "we" that presents itself in the 2013 convocation speech: "We believe it is our duty to make things happen."[31] Evidently, she convinced the reporter because the title of the pieces are "Backstory: Qatar Reformed by a Modern Marriage"[32] and "The Royal Couple that Put Qatar on the Map;"[33] there can be no clearer evidence that the partnership between the emir and his wife exerts a powerful influence that she would not have on her own.

The regional media cast her importance as linked to that of the good wife, contributing to her husband's mission, even when the sheikha is internationally recognized for her work in education, as was the case in 2007, when she won the UK Chatham House Award. The prize is given to a "statesperson who is considered to have made the most significant contribution to international relations in the previous year."[34] *The Business Intelligence Middle East* said of her, "Fully committed to her husband's vision to make Qatar a prosperous, developed and sustainable society, Sheikha Mozah works to promote the progress of Qatar and the wellbeing of its people."[35] The sheikha herself is wary of overstepping the bounds of her role as figurehead and ambassador, as she stated bluntly in the introduction of her acceptance speech for the prize: "When I was asked to speak about the 'Islam' versus 'West' conflict, I hesitated. I hesitated for a number of reasons, for I felt that speaking on this subject has become a political exercise. And certainly I do not consider myself a politician."[36] In public speeches, as well as in quotes for articles, she clarifies again and again her role as a community developer, someone who is avowedly not a politician, but who uses her platform to discuss issues about women, education, and Islamic society.

While accepting the platform to give an authoritative opinion about the discourse between the West and Islam, she simultaneously draws her own parameters by which she wants her comments understood. Her moves to reframe discussions demonstrate an active restructuring of the rhetoric of Islam and the West: the sheikha rejects the dominant categories in interesting ways. During remarks at the Baker Institute on the status of Arab women, for example, she rejects the notion that limited political participation is a surprise:

> I cannot understand how women's political participation can be discussed as if it is divorced from the political realities of the region. A region where the few control the many. Where basic political rights, such as freedom of speech, the right to assemble, to form associations, are still either non-existent or newly born. How can we, in all sincerity, talk about women's political participation? ... The truth is there is nothing in our religion to prevent women's political participation. Women are excluded for the same reasons men are excluded.[37]

Having said she is not officially someone with a political position, she expresses opinions about the state of the Middle East region for everyday citizens. Her criticisms are listed as observations; she equates disempowered women with repressed citizens. For someone who does not purport to be a politician, the sheikha in this instance appears to take a political stance against dictators, even while being part of a monarchical regime that does not permit the right to assembly within its own borders. Yet her political stance is really a defense of Islam from accusations that the religion limits women's participation in modern society—including political process—another example of her efforts to present a sophisticated, attractive type of Islam when she says "there is nothing in our religion to prevent women's political participation."[38] Her remarks that women have full access to society are attractive to both younger Muslims, as well as the Western audience she is addressing.

Her public commentary often redefines the roles possible for Muslim women. As she explains in her speech, "The 'Woman's Issue' in Context: Deframing the Discourse on Middle Eastern Women," tradition is often confused with religion both by the West and Islamic societies.[39] Her move to "deframe" women (her own term) and call for further research into women's presence in the political process is an attempt to assert control over a conversation that has been about Arab women without involving them. She sums up her argument by saying, "We have to position Muslim women not as objects of discourse, but as subjects of our past and our present. Let us dare break the frames of the Orientalist paintings in which we have been framed."[40] Each of the shekiha's actions fall in this category; her fashion sense has put her on the best dressed lists by *Huffington Post* and *Vanity Fair* since 2011, negating the idea of a Muslim woman wearing a burqa, covered from head to toe. Her cinched waists and satin turbans, posing next to women such as Carla Bruni, wearing strapless gowns at state dinners, are physical embodiment of the demureness expected of women who wear the Islamic head covering, the hijab, or the veil. She is a modern individual, balancing both parts of her identity with a strong sense of self. Her blend of fashion and Islamic values, including adapting designer Western wear with matching colored turbans and covered arms and legs, demonstrates her awareness of the conservative Muslim majority in Qatar.[41]

The well-phrased diplomacy abroad, situating her work within the overall mission of Qatar's modernization, is tempered by her rhetoric domestically, and most particularly at Qatar Foundation and the Education City project. Similar to her public presence and persona, the sheikha cannot help bring a personal touch to projects at home. She closes the 2013 convocation address with a very strong sense of self: "Each time I celebrate the graduation of a new class...."[42] The sheikha is much more likely to use the first person while at home; particularly in her role as the matriarch of the students at EC, she asserts a fuller sense of self than while abroad. As the recipient of honorary doctorates from Virginia Commonwealth, Texas A&M, Carnegie Mellon, and Georgetown universities, Sheikha Moza is not unlike the female students she champions;[43] her credentials also benefit from the educational allegiances QF has made possible for this generation of students.

A FINE BALANCE

This balancing act between the public or national and the private or personal is important in a tribal kinship structure such as Qatar where the collective is still more important than the individual. Sheikha Moza's rhetoric contrasts her own balance between the two factions since she challenges graduates: "Daughters and sons, don't give in to reality, as it may mold you according to its own image."[44] Here again, she uses an acceptable rhetoric, the role of a mother while giving a charge to students to defy social norms. The irony is that though the graduating class has more women—229 to 208 men[45]—the female graduates are the ones who will find that *reality* more difficult. For Qatari women sharing the same peninsula of land as Saudi women, they have legally been able to drive since the 1990s, but social convention means a male relative can discourage them from doing so; the law also requires the male guardian's permission in writing in order to obtain a driver's license. The sheikha's opening comments to a volume of conference proceedings organized by the Doha Family Policy Institute, another of the numerous centers of QF, demonstrate her public support for the nuclear, traditional family, even while advocating for cultural and social change. Her comments remind us she is a product of a conservative society: "all divine laws have blessed this sacred institution [the family], which forges a strong bond between males and females, a bond which conforms to human nature in bearing and raising new generations."[46] The situation facing students outside of QF is vastly different than the ones the sheikha rallies at commencement every year. The patriarchal nature of the family is reflected in social expectations for young women, which can include restrictions in career choices; for example, female engineers who wear a hijab do not wear the overalls required onsite, a decision that discourages some companies from hiring women.

In 2008, at Qatar University, the national university headed by the sheikha's aunt, Dr. Sheikha Al Misned, 75 percent of the students were women.[47] These higher numbers do not necessarily equal more women in the workforce. Women are often married while still in university and begin having children; motherhood becomes their chief occupation after graduation. This scholastic achievement is not mirrored by their male counterparts, as reported in the *Chronicle of Higher Education:*

> In the tiny emirates of the oil-rich Persian Gulf, women outperform men scholastically and are much more likely to attend and to graduate from university. When people speak of an educational "gender gap" here, increasingly they are referring to men's low enrollment and attainment.[48]

Males are hired into the workforce with often much less education than females; because of their position in the family as the primary breadwinner, they are eligible for additional allowances such as housing that women are ineligible for. The widening gender gap around education is rarely discussed in the public rhetoric around the importance of education:

> Guaranteed a job in the public sector, fewer men are motivated to attend university as compared to women; for example, at Qatar University 75 percent of students are female. According to a 2007 report by the government's Planning Council, Qatari female workers have 14.1 years of education compared to 10.7 for male workers. According to the report, overall Qataris remain woefully unprepared for the management of the country's ambitious development projects.[49]

The gender gap is what faces the female graduates of both the EC branch campuses and Qatar University. This is the harsh reality for women, which is often overlooked in commencement addresses that encourage graduates to go out into their community and be forces of change. Within the protected spaces of American universities with Western curriculum and social values, students escape traditional Qatari society, which does not permit non-relative males and females to mix socially, even in shopping malls or restaurants. The graduates Sheikha Moza addresses will come back to campus in order to see and spend time with their male friends, trying to recapture the vestiges of social freedoms they enjoyed as students, away from the disapproving public eye. The sheikha's chief project, the EC campus, continues to be a refuge even after graduation for this younger generation, straddling the modernization of a traditional culture. As their role model, and the official chairperson for nearly 15 years, she is an example of how to both fulfill conventional expectations for women, while simultaneously exerting a unique interpretation of that role that tests the limits of these conventions.

THE FUTURE FOR QATARI WOMEN: A YOUNGER GENERATION IN LEADERSHIP

Sheikha Moza, her aunt, Dr. Sheikha, and a handful of other women from prominent families, have established themselves in public roles and spaces, often representing Qatar abroad. Yet they are still in the minority, using the influence of their families for the good of the nation. For most Qatari women, conventional prohibitions about women's behavior in the Qatari public sphere persist.[50] In the 1999 central municipal elections, an historical moment in Qatar, none of the six female candidates garnered enough support to win their seats—this despite a population including 44 percent female voters.[51] The sheikha is aware of the social constraints facing women, as much as the female graduates she addresses, year after year: "People tend to believe that to be modern you have to disengage from your heritage, but it's not true. This is what we are trying to prove here," she explains.[52] The gap between the modern economy and traditional values of the society have several explanations which give Sheikha Moza's role in Qatari public life even more complexity. First, scholars including Fromherz, argue that oil economies by nature exclude women because of the menial physical labor required. Secondly, even white collar petroleum jobs, including engineering, require non-traditional feminine behavior such as wearing overalls or visiting oil rigs—tasks which would draw attention to women's bodies and take them away from their families, into the company of non-relative men. Thirdly, the small number of Qataris relative to the expatriate population means that there is pressure on Qatari women to produce more citizens for the state. The local, Arabic newspapers often publish articles about the negatives of the spinster problem. The inflexibility in attitudes toward men and women working closely together is an attitude widely held by the population, which will take some more time to change.

Instead, women are encouraged toward the humanities or traditionally accepted roles, including teaching young children, so much so that the number of available teachers vastly outweighs the demand.[53] A reported 53 percent of Qatari women in the workforce were in the educational sector in 2004.[54] In 2001, there were no female Qatari ministers; by 2004, there were two; one of them was Sheikha Moza, head of the Supreme Council for Family Affairs.[55] The sheikha mothers her own daughters with the ambitions she coaches for the graduates of the QF branch campuses; her eldest daughter, Sheikha Al Mayassa bint Hamad Al Thani, was named the most influential person in the art world by the *ArtReview* Power list.[56] The younger sheikha's influence as chair of the Qatar Museums Authority in establishing a network of numerous museums within Qatar also has an economic edge: purportedly the thirty-something-year-old has 600 million pounds a year at her spending discretion for the nation's galleries.[57] Sheikha Moza is the younger Sheikha Mayassa's maternal role model. Equally significantly, she is sister to the current emir, and continues to negotiate in both modern and traditional aspects of Qatari women's identity as the country enters its next stage of development. In addition to her role in the Museum's Authority, Sheikha Al Mayassa was also the chair of the Doha Tribecca Film Festival, an initiative to bring an appreciation of film and film making to Qatar. She quickly developed a reputation for being a supporter of the arts, a field not known for conservatism or tolerating religious restrictions.

However, Sheikha Al Mayassa's remarks during a Technology Education and Design (TED) talk exclusively for women, demonstrates her negotiation of the delicate balance between modernism and Islam:

> We are changing our culture from within, but at the same time we are reconnecting with our traditions. We know that modernization is happening. And yes, Qatar wants to be a modern nation. But at the same time we are reconnecting and reasserting our Arab heritage. It's important for us to grow organically. And we continuously make the conscious decision to reach that balance.[58]

Unlike her mother, the daughter exercises her family's freedom to appear unveiled in the press while abroad; she is photographed without her hijab or headscarf in Dados during the World Economic Forum and at the United Nations. Many of these photos caused quite a stir when they appeared in the local Qatari newspapers, as did photos of her younger sister, Hind, at her university graduation and at state events accompanying their father. This younger generation of Qatari female leaders, among whom the younger sheikha really has no peer, challenges the assumptions of proper female identity while at the same time upholding them. At the beginning of a TED talk, Sheikha Al Mayassa comments that her abaya, the black robe worn by Gulf women according to Islamic conventions for modest covering, " is not a religious garment, nor is it a religious statement. Instead, it's a diverse cultural statement that we choose to wear."[59] The younger sheikha demonstrates cultural dexterity modeled by her mother; she asserts her allegiance to traditional values while occupying a very non-traditional space in the history of the nation. Her presence in the public arena as a young woman respectful of Islamic tradition is an example of the agency Sheikha Moza has given younger Qatari women through her balancing of traditional values and modern behaviors.

QATARI WOMEN, THE ARAB WORLD, AND A NEW ERA

As Qatar's exposure in Western media grew, the position of these female leaders, particularly the sheikh and her elder daughter, also shifted. In 2011, the establishment of Hamad Bin Khalifa University (HBKU) surprised nearly everyone inside the country, including those involved in the Education City project.[60] HBKU is described as "an emerging research university building its foundation upon innovative and unique collaborations with local and international partners."[61] The establishment of an Arab identity for the now well-established collection of American branch campuses—and the addition of graduate programs—marked a transition from importing wholesale the best in foreign education, to instead imprinting bespoke programs like the Faculty of Islamic Studies, begun in September 2007. Along with this development, the sheikha's rhetoric in public speeches reflects a more purposeful alignment of Qatar with an Arab identity and the support of Arab intellectuals, as in the address to the annual research forum: "Here in Qatar, we will continue our long-standing commitment to attracting and supporting Arab expatriate scientists."[62] She positions Arab expatriate scientists among the "excellent centers" that QF also supports, highlighting their contribution but also the nation's role in serving the Middle East region: "We in Qatar have never been confined by our local geography. Rather, we have continuously placed our attention on the development needs of the Arab nations, as we set strategies and plans for scientific research."[63] Sheikha Moza is aligning the nation, her project, and herself with supporting the development of Arab intellectuals and thereby bolstering the Middle East region.

A change of rule in the summer of 2013, when Sheikh Hamad acceded his throne to the heir apparent, Sheikh Tamim, making him the youngest ruler in the Middle East at the age of 33, caused another ripple of conversation domestically. What would this mean for the powerbase of Sheikha Moza or the educational enterprise of Education City? The contemporary nature of these events makes any future predictions unclear. While the current Emir has two wives, neither seem inclined to take the limelight, and certainly not next to their most famous mother-in-law. Without another female spokesperson with the caliber and capability of Sheikha Moza, the public roles for Qatari woman may have lost their champion.

NOTES

1. Allen Fromherz, *Qatar: A Modern History* (Washington, DC: Georgetown University Press 2012), 5–10.
2. Rehenuma Asmi, "Language in the Mirror: Language Ideologies, Schooling and Islam in Qatar," (Ph.D. diss., Columbia University, 2013), 78.
3. Ibid.
4. General Secretariat for Development Planning, "Qatar National Vision 2030," Ministry of Development Planning and Statics, accessed January 18, 2014, www.gsdp.gov.qa/portal/page/portal/gsdp_en/qatar_national_vision/qnv_2030_document/QNV2030_English_v2.pdf.
5. Ibid.
6. miriam cooke, "Roundtable Discussion: Religion, Gender and the Muslim Woman," *Journal of Feminist Studies in Religion*, 24, no. 1 (2008), accessed March 1, 2014, www.jstor.org/discover/10.2307/20487917?uid=3739560&uid=2&uid=4&uid=3739256&sid=21103483748651.
7. Ibid.
8. Ibid.
9. Ibid.
10. Danna Harman, "Backstory: Qatar Reformed by a Modern Marriage," *Christian Science Monitor*, March 6, 2007, accessed March 1, 2014, www.csmonitor.com/2007/0306/p20s01-wome.html.
11. miriam cooke, "Roundtable Discussion: Religion, Gender and the Muslim Woman," *Journal of Feminist Studies in Religion*, 24, no. 1 (2008), accessed March 1, 2014, www.jstor.org/discover/10.2307/20487917?uid=3739560&uid=2&uid=4&uid=3739256&sid=21103483748651.
12. Julie Zeveloff, "Dubai Sets a World Record with the World's Largest Firework Display on New Year's Eve," *Business Insider*, Dec. 31, 2013, accessed March 1, 2014, www.businessinsider.com/dubai-record-fireworks-new-years-2013-12.
13. Kristian Coates Ulrichsen, "The Gulf States and the Rebalance of Regional Global Power." (working paper, James A. Baker III Institute for Public Policy, Rice University, Houston, TX, 2014), accessed December 19, 2013, bakerinstitute.org/media/files/Research/ec7b03d8/CME-Pub-GulfStates-010813.pdf.
14. Mansoor Moaddel, "The Study of Islamic Culture and Politics: An Overview and Assessment," *Annual Reviews* 28 (August 2002): 367, accessed December 19, 2013, DOI: 10.1146/annurev.soc.28.110601.140928.
15. Ida Lichter, *Muslim Women Reformers: Inspiring Voices Against Oppression* (New York: Prometheus Books, 2009), 275.
16. Hiba Khodr, "The Dynamics of International Education in Qatar: Exploring the Policy Drivers behind the Development of Education City," *Journal of Emerging Trends in Educational Research and Policy Studies* 2, no. 6 (2011): 518.
17. Peter Prengaman, "Qatar's First Lady Argues Islam not the Root of Extremism," *Free Republic*, May 16, 2007, accessed January 15, 2014, www.freerepublic.com/focus/f-news/1834553/posts.

18. Dominic J Brewer. et. al, *Education for a New Era: Design and Implementation of K-12 Education Reform in Qatar*, (working paper, RAND-Qatar Policy Institute, Santa Monica, CA, 2007), accessed January 16, 2014, www.rand.org/content/dam/rand/pubs/monographs/2007/RAND_MG548.pdf.

19. Sheikha Moza bint Nasser, "A Speech of Her Highness Sheikha Moza bint Nasser at the Second Education City Convocation Ceremony," *Her Highness Sheikha Moza bint Nasser,* May 5, 2009, accessed February 27, 2014, www.mozabintnasser.qa/en/Pages/ArticlePreview.aspx?ArticleGuid=31f7c347-690e-472a-92a0-38e412441165&Type=Speech.

20. Ibid.

21. Ibid.

22. Ibid.

23. Michael H. Romanowski and Ramzi Nasser, "Critical Thinking and Qatar's Education for a New Era: Negotiating Possibilities," *The International Journal of Critical Pedagogy* 4, no. 1 (2012): 120, accessed February 13, 2014, libjournal.uncg.edu/index.php/ijcp/article/view/300/262.

24. Sania Kelly, "Recent Gains and New Opportunities for Women's Rights in the Gulf Arab States," *Freedom House*, n.d., accessed December 19, 2013, www.freedomhouse.org/sites/default/files/Women's%20Rights%20in%20the%20Middle%20East%20and%20Noth%20Africa,%20Gulf%20Edition.pdf, (accessed December 19, 2013).

25. Sheika Moza bint Nasser Al Missned, "Speech of Her Highness Sheikha Moza bint Nasser, Chairperson of the Qatar Foundation," *Her Highness Sheikha Moza bint Nasser*, May 7, 2013, accessed December 19, 2014, www.mozabintnasser.qa/en/Pages/ArticlePreview.aspx?ArticleGuid=c779ab97-7f48-4324-b572-f29bd2ad4689&Type=Speech.

26. Tofol Jassim Al-Nasr, "Gulf Cooperation Council (GCC) Women and Misyar Marriage: Evolution and Progress in the Arabian Gulf," *Journal of International Women's Studies*, 12, no. 3 (2011), accessed February 27, 2014, vc.bridgew.edu/jiws/vol12/iss3/4.

27. Sheika Moza bint Nasser Al Missned, "Speech of Her Highness Sheikha Moza bint Nasser, Chairperson of the Qatar Foundation," *Her Highness Sheikha Moza bin Nasser*, May 7, 2013, accessed December 19, 2013, www.mozabintnasser.qa/en/Pages/ArticlePreview.aspx?ArticleGuid=c779ab97-7f48-4324-b572-f29bd2ad4689&Type=Speech (accessed December 19, 2013).

28. Ibid.

29. Ibid.

30. Harman, "Backstory."

31. Ibid.

32. Nassar, "Convocation Ceremony."

33. Harman, "Backstory."

34. Denna Harman, "The Royal Couple that Put Qatar on the Map," *Christian Science Monitor,* March 5, 2007, accessed March 1, 2014, www.csmonitor.com/2007/0305/p20s01-wome.html.

35. Lichter, *Muslim Women Reformers*, 276.

36. Ahmad Moussa, "Qatar's Sheikha Mozah Wins Chatham House Prize," *Business Intelligence Middle East*, September 25, 2007, accessed January 15, 2014, www.bi-me.com/main.php?id=13424&t=1.

37. Mozah bint Nasser Al Missned, "From Illusions of Clashes to an Awakening of Alliances: Constructing Understanding between 'Islam and the West.'" (Presentation to Chatham House, London, England, February 14, 2007), accessed January 17, 2014, www.unaoc.org/repository/chatham_published_version.pdf.

38. Moza Bint Nasser Al Missned, "The 'Woman's Issue' in Context: Deframing the Discourse on Middle Eastern Woman," (lecture, James A. Baker III Institute for Public Policy, Rice University, Houston, TX, May 21, 2007), accessed January 19, 2014, bakerinstitute.org/files/799.

39. Ibid.

40. Al Missned, "Speech of Her Highness."

41. Ibid.

42. Keli Goff, "Qatar's Jackie O," *The Daily Beast*, April 9, 2014, accessed April 12, 2013, news.yahoo.com/qatar-jackie-o-094500582--politics.html.

43. Mehran Kamrava, *Qatar: Small State, Big Politics*, (Ithaca: Cornell University Press, 2013), 82.

44. Al Missned, "Speech of Her Highness."

45. Qatar Foundation, "Qatar Foundation to Celebrate Convocation of 437 Graduates," *Qatar Foundation*, May 7, 2013, accessed January 16, 2014, www.qf.org.qa/news/293.

46. Maria Jakobsen, "Social Effects of the Educational Revolution in Qatar: A Gender Perspective," (master's thesis, The University of Bergen, 2010), 25.

47. Qatar Foundation, "Celebrate Convocation."

48. Kamrava, *Qatar: Small State, Big Politics*, 159.

49. Ursula Lindsey, "Arab Women Make Inroads in Higher Education, but Often Find Dead Ends," *Chronicle of Higher Education,* January 29, 2012, accessed January 30, 2014, chronicle.com/article/Arab-Women-Make-Inroads-in/130479/ur.

50. Hessa Saad Al Muhannadi, "The Role of Qatari Women: Between Tribalism and Modernity," (master's thesis, Lebanese American University, 2011), 30.

51. Lichter, *Muslim Women Reformers*, 273.

52. Ibid.

53. Harman, "Backstory."

54. Dell Felder and Mirka Vuollo, "Qatari Women in the Workforce," (working paper, Rand-Qatar Policy Institute Working Paper No. WR-612-Qatar, August 2008), 15, accessed January 30, 2014, www.rand.org/pubs/working_papers/WR612.html (accessed Janurary 30, 2014).

55. Ibid.

56. Ibid.

57. Mark Brown, "Qatar's Sheikha Mayassa Tops Power List," *The Guardian*, October 23, 2013, accessed March 1, 2014, www.theguardian.com/artanddesign/2013/oct/24/qatar-sheikha-mayassa-tops-art-power-list.

58. Ibid.

59. Al Mayassa bint Hamad bin Khalifa Al-Thani, *Globalizing the Local: Localizing the Global*, TED Talk, filmed December 2010, posted February 2012, accessed January 30, 2014, www.ted.com/talks/sheikha_al_mayassa_globalizing_the_local_localizing_the_global.html.

60. Ibid.

61. Hamad bin Khalifa University, "About HKU," accessed January 29, 2014, www.hbku.com/en/DynamicPages/index/70/AboutHBKU .

62. Ibid.

63. Moza Bint Nasser Al Missned, "Speech to the Annual Research Conference 2013," posted November 24, 2013, accessed March 1, 2014, www.mozabintnasser.qa/en/Pages/ArticlePreview.aspx?ArticleGuid=2a5282b7-a97b-4459-8bf1-b79fff90d2f1&Type=Speech.

Chapter Eight

Religiously Gendered

Online Political Discourse in the 2011 Egyptian Revolution

Nicole Khoury

Recent critical analyses of women's roles in the Egyptian revolution have sought to illustrate how Egyptian women have broken the oppressive silence, participated in the public sphere, and utilized religious references to make arguments that are embedded in the historical and cultural traditions while reflecting women's rights within Islam. The contemporary feminist movement in Egypt consists of several positions with different perceptions of universal concepts of feminism, such as gender equality, human rights, and choice/agency. Egyptian feminists, argues Anna Hellstrand, have used religion—both Christianity and Islam—to support their demands for equality and have strongly rejected any statement that religion is inherently anti-female and any automatic association between religion and misogyny and between "female religious devotion" and "victimhood."[1] Feminist groups criticize conservative political figures who oppose women's rights—both in Mubarak's regime and those following—as enforcing cultural patriarchy and misogyny. Hellstrand further argues that women in the Egyptian revolution have broken with the stereotype depicting them as helpless and devoid of agency. They fought for change on par with men and looked to reform the misogynistic culture, knowing that laws on their own would not enforce and guarantee their rights, especially considering the gap between the law and its implementation and the startling rise in violence against women. Women relied on individual activists and collectives to promote the struggle for equality but also violated social and patriarchal codes of behavior in order to achieve public agency during the revolution.[2] Though their gains were limited after the revolution, following a trend of women's movements being resisted as an independent cause, the 2011 revolution may have provided a new opportunity for their struggles by opening a political path for them.

Consequently, Victoria Newsom and Lara Lengel in "Arab Women, Social Media, and the Arab Spring: Applying the Framework of Digital Reflexivity to Analyze Gender and Online Activism," claim social media and online activism provides what they call a "third space" of contained empowerment "between concepts and experiences of power . . . where traditional rules governing society can be set aside," and in these spaces women are able to articulate alternative discourses that challenge those on the ground.[3] These online feminist activist spaces attempt to provide a means for rethinking gendered discourse and for engaging with constructions of gendered citizenship. However, since the majority of women with access to the Internet are female academics and other privileged women, and since a large portion of the population exercise self-censorship, the ability for these spaces to empower marginalized voices remains to be seen.[4] Furthermore, Newsom and Lengel argue that information is produced locally but is transformed through various stages of dissemination. The "citizen journalism" produced by activists on the ground is manipulated and altered within both the political scene and the larger global Western media.[5] The message is often reframed to suit the purposes of local governments and global media audiences. However, the use of online third space has contributed in significant ways to the Egyptian revolution.

Initially involved in the April 6 Youth Movement, Asmaa Mahfouz is known as one of the protagonists in what has become known as the Arab Spring in Egypt as a result of her YouTube video blog calling for action against the Mubarak regime.[6] Her YouTube video was prepared on January 18, 2011 and posted to her Facebook page, garnering a relatively huge amount of hits and views.[7] Later that same year, she was awarded the Sakharov Prize for Freedom of Thought with four other Arab Spring activists.[8] Her speech is a very well-articulated call for action in both Egyptian and international contexts. She draws from essentialist notions of gender ideology embedded in Middle Eastern culture to challenge the dominant patriarchal constructions of gender. Her argument for political participation is embedded in religious and cultural references that historically have been used to keep women out of the public sphere. Her careful negotiation of the cultural elements that restrict gender roles and the human rights concepts of freedom and justice to liberate gender roles is an important alternative narrative that challenges dominant concepts and the binary between religious and secular. Her speech provides us an integral understanding of the many challenges and negotiations of contemporary transnational feminist rhetorics.

This chapter rhetorically analyzes Mahfouz's call for action, addressing the Egyptian context in which political calls for action are made. First, I provide an historical overview of early Egyptian feminist discourses and the parallels between them as arguments for women's rights are grounded within the

Islamic religion, drawing on both secular and religious discourses. Second, I address the April 6 Youth Movement Mahfouz helped establish and the role of the Internet in dissipating information during the 2011 Egyptian revolution and the concept of "online third space" that provides opportunities for women to share alternative narratives. Finally, I rhetorically analyze Asmaa Mahfouz's YouTube speech using Kenneth Burke's theory of identification by locating her use of rhetorical appeals in both religious discourse and international human rights discourse. By performing her speech online, in a space outside the dominant discourse, Mahfouz is able to draw from secular and religious discourses, which are often seen as antithetical to one another, to disrupt this binary.

EARLY EGYPTIAN FEMINIST DISCOURSES

Much of the analysis of gender roles in the revolution failed to acknowledge that women have been organizing, mobilizing, and vocalizing their gendered positions for many years, often within the Islamic framework.[9] Egypt's feminist movements have been significantly shaped by its history of colonial occupation.[10] Feminist arguments within an Islamic framework began surfacing in early nineteenth-century Egypt. Arguments for women's education and for eradicating polygamy were voiced in the 1870s and 1880s by Muslim intellectuals such as Rifa'ah Rafi al-Tahtawi and Muhammad 'Abdu, an intellectual and influential figure who taught that Islam is compatible with modernity.[11] He championed the education of women "in the obligations and rights established for them by their religion."[12] 'Abduh was specifically concerned, however, with women's rights insofar as they strengthened the Islamic order. He was not concerned with the liberation of women for their benefit, but "as an essential precondition for the building of a virtuous society."[13] Similarly, Qasim Amin's *The Liberation of Women* is one of the first controversial texts arguing for women's equality, published in 1899. However, its controversial reception was not due to the argument for women's liberation, but for its glorification of Western culture and a readiness to imitate European standards in an attempt to become modernized. His arguments were grounded in the assumption that veiling and seclusion were backward and represented an internalized notion of the Western civilization as modern and worthy of imitation.[14] The imposition of feminist arguments for the liberation of women in the Arab and Egyptian culture is defined as "colonial feminism": "using the argument that the cultures of the colonized peoples degraded women in order to legitimize Western domination and justify colonial policies of actively trying to subvert the cultures and regions of the colonized peoples."[15]

The "liberation" of women from the Islamic veil was the focus of the debate. The practice of veiling was targeted as the indication of the Islamic degradation of women, and "stood in the way, according to the imperialist thesis, of the 'progress' and 'civilization' of Muslim societies and of their populaces being 'persuaded or forced' into imbibing 'the true spirit of Western civilization.'"[16] The 1920s in Egypt marked the rise of women's public movements organized by women such as Huda Shaarawi, who founded The Intellectual Association of Egyptian Women in 1914 later followed by the Egyptian Feminist Union (EFU) in 1923.[17] The Arab Feminist Union (AFU) was later founded in Cairo in 1944 and produced fifty resolutions addressing political, social, and economic issues as well as gender equality, during their first conference for women.[18] These public organizations provided opportunities to articulate arguments for gender equality in a public forum.

Leila Ahmed, in *Women and Gender in Islam*, traces critical tensions between two strains of Arab feminism in the early 1920s in Egypt. While both discourses stood against British dominance and occupation of Egypt, they diverged in their attitude toward Western political institutions and culture. The dominant strain, which supported reforms toward a more Western political institution of secular governance, was represented by Huda Shaarawi; the alternative strain, which remained critical of adopting Western customs and stood for less radical reforms of Egyptian governance, was represented by Malak Hifni Nassef, whose pen name was Bahithat al-Badiya.[19] Both the dominant and alternative strains articulate arguments outside of Western feminist discourse and, I believe, do so purposefully to provide means for maintaining identification with local religious and cultural traditions. Their discourse is instead grounded in religion—Islam—in an attempt to remain within the local context and maintain a shared goal with their audience while articulating alternative constructions of citizenship.

Early Arab feminists thus articulate a discourse that draws from local traditions. Shaarawi, representing the dominant strain of feminism in early twentieth-century Egypt, articulates her arguments for gender equality by remaining within the dominant Islamic discourse and finding support within the *Qur'an*. In her opening speech to the AFU conference in 1944, she states: "Islam has given her the right to vote for the ruler and has allowed her to give opinions on questions of jurisprudence and religion. . . . The Shari'a [Islamic Law] gave her the right to education. . . . [Women] will not agree to be chained in slavery or pay for the consequences of men's mistakes."[20] In Sharaawi's opening speech, she refers to Islam and Islamic law to support her arguments; her decision to ground her argument within Islam is a rhetorical move of identification with the audience meant to appease fears that women's equality is an imported Western concept that corrupts the indigenous beliefs.

She is then able to argue for more liberal and secular democratic reforms, because she has identified the common goal of freedom from British cultural imposition and shared values of the Islamic religion with her audience.

Nassef best represents the alternative strain of feminism in early Egypt in her arguments to reform cultural, social, and political measures and resist foreign influence while retaining an authentic position within the culture and the religion. In her lecture in 1909 for the Umma Party club, a secular liberal club, she argues for reforming education, veiling, and marriage practices, but is clear about not advocating European standards.[21] She states, "Customs should not be abandoned except when they are harmful. European customs should not be taken up by Egyptians except when they are appropriate and practical."[22] Nassef advocates reforming harmful cultural traditions, but maintains a clear sense of identification with the Egyptian culture, and emphasizes women's roles within the Egyptian nation, questioning the imitation of European standards.

The organizations to which these women belonged, the Umma Party club and the Arab Feminist Union, positioned them in public spaces and national movements by allowing for a space in which female rhetors were able to respond to national concerns and articulate constructions of citizenship in their local communities in ways that identified with the values and beliefs of their audience. Although the cultural divide and attitudes toward Westernization fostered various articulations for women's positions, the arguments remained grounded in Islamic discourse. As Shaarawi and Nassef were speaking in public organizations to a group of conservative Muslim women, they were also addressing the larger social and national implications of modernizing Egypt and responding to the European modernizing influence on the country. Consequently, Mahfouz's speech mirrors those of her predecessors; while she is speaking to local Egyptians, she is also addressing the larger social and national implications of the Egyptian state and the role of religion in the public sphere. Similarly, the "online third space" positions Mahfouz in a public space that remains grounded in the dominant discourse persuade her audience, which I will further elaborate on in the next section.

APRIL 6 YOUTH MOVEMENT AND THE FACEBOOK REVOLUTION

Asmaa Mahfouz, along with a number of other activists—including Esraa Abdel Fattah, Ahmed Rashid, and Ahmed Maher—helped form the April 6 Youth Movement in spring 2008 to support the workers in the industrial town of El-Mahalla El-Kubra. The April 6 Youth Movement planned a strike on

April 6, 2008 by calling on participants to wear black and stay home,[23] which was initially known as the "Facebook strike."[24] A few years later, inspired by the Tunisian revolutions in December 2010, the April 6 Youth Movement played a role in the early days of the 2011 Egyptian revolution.[25] "Although there are countless political Facebook groups in Egypt, many of which flare up and fall into disuse in a matter of days, the one with the most dynamic debates is that of the April 6 Youth Movement, a group of 70,000 mostly young and educated Egyptians, most of whom had never been involved with politics before joining the group."[26] The organization's core concerns include fostering an environment of free speech, addressing the corruption in government, and addressing the country's stagnant economy.

Rodolfo Diaz, in "From Lambs to Lions: Self-Liberation and Social Media in Egypt," says of the April 6 Youth Movement: "What started as a Facebook group to support a worker's protest in the spring of 2008 evolved into a powerful pressure group with around 70,000 members as of January 2009 mainly concerned with restrictions on freedom of speech, nepotism, and the country's economic stagnation."[27] He maintains that the role of the Internet in the later 2011 Egyptian revolution allowed for a decentralization of the dissipation of information, including the propagation of photos, forums, and blogs that critically address the brutality of the Mubarak regime.[28] The Internet has also allowed for the mobilization of activists and organizations across the country. For example, bloggers and citizen journalists used Facebook, Twitter, Flickr, and blogs to report on the strike, alert their networks about police activity, organize legal protection, and draw attention to their efforts.[29] Diaz highlights the April 6 Youth Movement as an example of the power of social media and mobilization, also crediting the Facebook group for mobilizing the march of one million participants on February 1, 2011. The group continues to maintain its online presence and network.

The April 6 Youth Movement played an important role in the organization of the 2011 Egyptian revolution through various activities, including the online distribution of Mahfouz's YouTube video. The movement established itself as a threat to the Mubarak regime early on. Esraa Rashid was arrested and imprisoned for more than two weeks before the revolution protest broke out, and Ahmed Maher was later detained, questioned, and beaten.[30] These incidents were just the first two of a series of arrests that would further divide the country, the government, and the police. Asmaa Mahfouz was also arrested in 2011 for allegedly insulting the Supreme Council of Armed Forces (SCAF) by referring to them as a "council of dogs"[31] and for inciting violence by tweeting: "If the judiciary doesn't give us our rights, nobody should be surprised if militant groups appear and conduct a series of assassinations, because there is no law and there is no judiciary."[32] In response to the publication of a report documenting 1,000 casualties of the revolution by the Egyptian Organization for Human Rights, civilians, including Asmaa Mahfouz, began being referred to military courts, violating their rights to a fair trial. Presidential candidate Ayman Nour denounced her arrest and referral to a military court:[33] "The referral of Mahfouz to the military prosecution sparked a barrage of criticism of the Supreme Council of the Armed Forces (SCAF), which has ruled Egypt since the ouster of former President Hosni Mubarak."[34] She was later released on bail and the charges against her were dropped.[35] As soon as she was out of jail, Mahfouz tweeted "May the government fall!"[36] The containment and cessation of such critical activities proved to be difficult for the Mubarak regime and its successors because of their viral nature. The Mubarak regime used its authority under the emergency law to shut down the Internet a few days after the initial organized protest on January 25 in an effort to deter the mass organizing.[37] This effort did not have the desired effect because the organizing and networking was already established and other means of communicating, such as text messages, were then used to update information. Furthermore, shutting down the Internet infuriated many who were prompted to join the protest, thus failing to halt the mobilization of activists.[38]

The April 6 Youth Movement summoned all types of movements—labor, feminist, Islamist—to participate in the revolution against the regime, citing common political, economic, and social grievances.[39] The demand for dignity—that the state must respect the integrity, safety, and autonomy of the body—resonated with women because they could demand a safe space in the public realm, request public services, and call for freedom of expression and choice. Despite the regime change, women in Egypt are currently still subjected to violations of their dignity, politically challenged by patriarchal liberals and conservative Islamists, and consistently excluded from political participation.[40] On February 6, 2011, they released a statement to the media outlining six demands: Mubarak's resignation, dissolution of the national assembly, establishment of a "national salvation group" constituting public personalities and organizers of the revolution, a new constitution, prosecuting those that killed the Tahrir Square martyrs, and the release of detainees.[41] The April 6 Youth Movement remained visible in the public sphere after toppling the Mubarak regime on February 11, 2011.

The slogan of the January 25th revolution, "Freedom, Dignity, Social Justice," is further reiterated in the document issued by the Cairo Institute for Human Rights Studies and human rights organizations, the Egyptian Human Rights NGOs Papyrus, so named in "appreciation of ancient Egyptian civilization and the great cultural heritage of cultural, social, ethnic, and religious diversity that has shaped Egyptian's character and identity."[42] The Papyrus proposes the need for a constitution that is based on human rights principles, but refrains from advocating one type of governance over another. It simply states constitutional provisions that should be taken into account in any democratic government. The first article of the document states: "Egyptian identity is multidimensional and has roots in multiple civilizations. This diversity is the most significant source of the richness and distinction of Egyptian identity. Historically and practically it cannot be reduced to one dimension without destroying Egyptians' national unity or depriving the country of its independence."[43] This multicultural and multi-religious context is important to understanding how human rights activists structure arguments for reform and democracy using both religious and secular discourse.

Similarly, in her speech, Mahfouz draws on political, cultural, and religious references in order to compose an alternative vision for the future of the nation in an online space. Her alternative vision includes not only her understanding of women's roles in the public sphere, but illustrates her rhetorical positioning within the local context and the global discourse. Her speech further highlights an argument for her vision of the political state, one that includes fundamental human rights reflecting a secular political vision and simultaneously provides articulations of religious ideology in the public sphere. Using Burke's theory of identification, I first analyze how Mahfouz's text draws from Islam and religious ideology to establish a shared and common goal among her audience. I then explore how her use of human rights discourse disrupts the binary between religious and secular ideologies, and I finally discuss how she incorporates religious and secular ideology within her speech for a democratic state. Celeste Condit's concept of gender diversity[44] is essential to my analysis in order to provide an accurate understanding of the ways Mahfouz utilizes discursive rhetorical strategies that may often be attributed to masculine patriarchal rhetorical tradition but, I argue, that forward a feminist goal of inclusion and egalitarianism.

ASMAA MAHFOUZ'S YOUTUBE SPEECH

Twenty-five-year-old Asmaa Mahfouz uploaded a YouTube video to her Facebook page[45] on January 18, 2011 urging Egyptians to join her in protesting against the Mubarak regime in Tahrir Square on January 25, 2011.[46] In this section, I provide a rhetorical analysis of the speech in the YouTube video to argue that Mahfouz's articulation of both religious and secular ideologies in the public sphere is an argument for the reevaluation of the governing state and an example of a rethinking of the role of religion in a secular democratic state. Mahfouz uses discourse grounded in Islam, cultural traditions, and secular ideology to forward a call to action that is situated locally, as the call is specifically addressed to "men" for the protection and honor of the female citizens.[47] She also references secular and human rights discourse to locate her call internationally.

It has been argued that traditional rhetorical strategies for persuasion are gender-biased in that they reflect masculine strategies. Rhetorical persuasion is associated with the public sphere, a traditionally male-dominated space in which women's roles as rhetors is marginalized to adopting masculine strategies.[48] Rhetorical scholars Sonja Foss and Cindy Griffin, in "Beyond Persuasion: A Proposal for Invitational Rhetoric," maintain that persuasion is inherently masculine because the goal is to change the audience's perspective; they attempt to expand rhetorical studies by introducing the term "invitational rhetoric" as a mode of communication more aligned with feminist principles, utilizing strategies such as offering and yielding, which is to express a perspective with the goal of a free exchange of ideas.[49] Scholar Celeste Condit, in her article "In Praise of Eloquent Diversity: Gender and Rhetoric as Public Persuasion," further addresses the dichotomous relationship between what Foss and Griffin frame as masculine and feminine communication styles, arguing that this gender dichotomy perpetuates gender binaries.[50] Condit forwards an interpretation of persuasion styles as gender diversity, a perspective that seeks to address various persuasion styles that can be adopted by various genders, providing the rhetor with agency as the "constructor of gender rather than as constructed by gender."[51] Condit's concept of gender diversity is important to understanding Mahfouz's speech. While she may utilize patriarchal rhetoric by attempting to persuade her audience to action, she also shares an alternative feminist vision of the future by exposing oppressive systems of domination and injustice and calling on a shared vision of hope and political participation.

In the first sentence of her speech, Mahfouz begins by referring to the four Egyptians who set themselves on fire.[52] She speculates that perhaps they set themselves on fire because they wanted a revolution like the one that had just occurred in Tunisia: "maybe we can have freedom, justice, honor and human dignity."[53] Her initial reference to secular ideology—freedom, justice, human dignity—and a more traditional cultural concept—honor—sets the tone for the rest of her speech. She uses human rights discourse as an important reference to mobilize her audience against the Mubarak regime, whose human rights violations caused the principle sparks of the Egyptian revolution.[54] However, in order to create a sense of a common goal, Mahfouz further uses the traditional cultural concepts of honor and shame. When people reacted to the four Egyptians who set themselves on fire by saying they died for nothing, she responds directly by using the cultural concepts embedded in local traditions: "People, have some shame."⁵⁵ She then states: "I posted that I, a girl, am going down to Tahrir Square, and I will stand alone."⁵⁶ Her reference to herself as a girl standing alone in a public space can only be understood within the local context, as I will further explain.

The concept of honor is deeply embedded within the cultural traditions in the Middle East, often utilized for rhetorical purposes to move audiences to action or inaction. Bringing honor or shame to one's family is a concept deeply embedded in the cultural and social traditions and is particularly gendered. Suad Joseph, in "Brother/Sister Relationships: Connectivity, Love, and Power in the Reproduction of Arab Patriarchy," argues that patriarchy operates effectively because of the social constructions of men and women in Arab society as relational: "Connectivity held families together in part because women and men, adults and children internalized the psychological demands of compliance with gendered and aged hierarchies. Intertwined, patriarchy and connectivity underwrote the crafting of relationally oriented selves, socialized to negotiate gendered and aged hierarchies, and locally recognized as healthy, mature, and responsible."⁵⁷ It is because of this dynamic, she argues, that families have such a strong hold on their members and that "honor and shame could moralize and energize Arab families."⁵⁸ The social construction of gender as relational extends not only to nuclear families, but also to the relations between genders in society and networks extending well beyond the immediate family.⁵⁹ Thus, honor and shame are concepts extended to describe the social gendered relationships between Egyptian citizens.⁶⁰ As Forouz Jawkar observes, "Patriarchy has often been utilized as a central concept in analyses of the nature of women's oppression. Management of sexuality as expressed in lexicons of morality, and the code of honor and shame as the encapsulation of societal sexual norms are the dominant expressions of patriarchal ideology in the Mediterranean region."⁶¹ Thus, the limits of activities available to men and women in social life is meant to regulate gendered roles and sexual norms, including the limitation of women in the public sphere.

Mahfouz's reference to herself as a "girl," emphasizes her single, young, unmarried, and virginal status and reflects the larger cultural concepts of honor and shame within public discourse in the Middle East. Jawkar also refers to veiling "as a primary urban practice maintains the segregated nature of social life and provides further grounds for the reproduction of *ird* [honor]" (emphasis in original).⁶² Thus, her unmarried status coupled with her public presence standing alone in Tahrir Square positions Mahfouz as a vulnerable woman whose honor needs to be protected. She draws a parallel between her status as an unmarried girl within the family and implicitly refers to the larger Egyptian nation as the family, suggesting her honor can be saved by the male

Egyptian citizens—her male brothers. She later calls on men to come down to the square to protect her: "If you think yourself a man, come with me on January 25th. Whoever says women shouldn't go to protests because they will get beaten, let him have some honor and manhood and come with me on January 25th."[63] She draws on traditional essentialist gender constructions, shared with her Egyptian male audience, to motivate her audience to stand with her against the Mubarak regime. By implicitly referring to herself as virginal and unmarried whose honor needs to be protected, she draws on the very same concepts of gender she wishes to subvert. She uses the concepts of honor and shame, traditionally employed to argue against women's participating in the public sphere, to instead argue for women's participation in the public sphere.

Burke's theory of identification may provide us with a lens with which to analyze Mahfouz's speech, as she constructs identifications among several intersections to establish a shared goal with her audience. Kenneth Burke's rhetorical theory of identification states: "A is not identical with his colleague, B. But insofar as their interests are joined, A is identified with B. Or he may identify himself with B even when their interests are not joined, if he assumes that they are, or is persuaded to believe so."[64] According to Burke, interests do not define identification, but the act of identifying is a persuasive act. He continues, "In being identified with B, A is 'substantially one' with a person other than himself. Yet at the same time he remains unique, an individual locus of motives. Thus he is both joined and separate, at once a distinct substance and consubstantial with another."[65] For example, through consubstantiality, Mahfouz is able to persuade her Egyptian male audience to meet her down in Tahrir Square by creating a willing act on the part of the recipient to identify with her as a young girl in their family whose honor needs protection. Our understanding of Egyptian commonplaces and their everyday use, such as the concept of family honor and shame, further illustrates how the local audience is able to strengthen their identification with Mahfouz, who they see as having shared motives, goals, and beliefs.

Mahfouz further uses both religious connotations, referring to Allah, and the need for religion to be represented in the state through the people: "Don't be afraid of the government. Fear none but God. God says He will not change the condition of a people until they change what is in themselves. Don't think you can be safe anymore."[66] Mahfouz makes the distinction between God and the state, which she believes people have conflated. She claims that the people should fear only God and this reference to religion as the ultimate power instead of the state serves to instigate a rethinking of the nature of religion in the public sphere and in the governing system.[67] She is also referring to fear of God, drawing from religious discourse to establish fear as religious and not political. Fear of the state, she insists, is misplaced fear.[68] Religion and secularism have been traditionally viewed as antithetical, with secularism representing rationality and religion representing irrationality.[69] Rethinking this binary is in fact a rethinking of the public sphere and religion's role in a democratic state, one that Mahfouz articulates in her alternative discourse.

In order to further understand the rhetorical context, it is important to address the medium of the speech. In this particular case, the visual set-up of the YouTube video adds to the private/public context. Mahfouz speaks to the camera while sitting in what appears to be a private space. However, she is wearing her hijab, which also indicates she is within a public space, the online space. She alludes to the fact that on January 25, the date of the revolution, she will be in Tahrir Square, a public historically political space vulnerable to attack from the Mubarak regime and security forces. When the audience clicks on the play button on YouTube, they have accepted the invitation to engage in discourse with Mahfouz and hear her speech. Their response is either action or inaction: They will either choose to go down to Tahrir Square on January 25 or not.[70] She frames their options as such: "If you stay at home, then you deserve all that is being done, and you will be guilty before your nation and your people."[71] She urges her audience, "come and protect me and other girls in the protest."[72] By not coming down to Tahrir Square, she insists, the audience is rendered guilty of allowing the oppressive government regime to attack the nation. She continues to maintain the sense of identification with her audience by implying that she and the audience share the same feelings of frustration and disappointment with the Mubarak regime.[73] She instead plays on their sense of shame and honor to her and the nation to persuade them to action.

Mahfouz further addresses the larger global audience by drawing on human rights discourse as referenced throughout her speech using terminology such as "freedom," "justice," and "human rights."[74] Since the scene of the rhetorical act is in an online space, it is not only viewed by the local Egyptian people to whom she speaks, but also by the wider audience on whom she calls to address the oppression of the Mubarak regime. By articulating a call to fundamental human rights, Mahfouz is drawing international attention to the corruption of the state and to the need for a revolutionary movement and international support for such a movement. She is also stating that the revolution is not an Islamic revolution. She is careful to make this distinction in her speech and also in an interview conducted one year after the revolution. Mahfouz explains that her relationship with journalists in the United States is one in which she provides them with accurate information in order to show that "this is not a war between Islam and the U.S."[75] She is clear to indicate that the focus should be on developing a constitution in Egypt.[76] Her use of the term fundamental human rights further disrupts the binary between religious and secular, instead drawing on both ideologies to construct an alternative narrative of the possibilities of the public sphere in Egypt.

CONCLUSION

Her rhetorical positioning within religion and references to international norms articulate a constructed position in which Mahfouz is able to speak to Egyptian people and speak to an international audience simultaneously. Her political discourse uses both Islam and human rights ideological concepts to break down the current existing dichotomy between the religious and the secular and to establish a call that transcends the limitations of both. By remaining grounded in her cultural and social context, however, Mahfouz's political cry is gendered. She draws from essentialist notions of gender in patriarchal structure in order to challenge them. She paints herself as a young unmarried woman who needs protection in order to subvert this very gendered limited concept, to allow women to fight alongside men against the state. She argues for human rights as a fundamental concept of democracy while also drawing on religious ideology that shapes the local culture.

As Mahfouz's calculated and well-articulated call for a revolution is heard by her viewers in an online third space, she reaches a wider audience, mobilizing individuals and organizations through alternative means[77] to instigate what is now known as the Egyptian revolution. Her references to the inherent structural inequalities of gender relationships and the use of notions of honor and shame to articulate an alternative construction of gender may be limited in that it does not allow for a thorough investigation of the system of oppression, but instead works from within its framework. However, her articulation of an alternative vision attempts to draw from concepts embedded in the cultural values in order to produce an indigenous framework that incorporates democratic values and traditional cultural values in order to remain relevant to the lives of the Egyptian people in specific. Her hope is that the Egyptian nation is able to generate a constitution that reflects the lives of the people, while maintaining a vision for the future.[78] While this may seem like an immensely difficult task, as Mahfouz states in her speech, "Never say there's no hope. Hope disappears only when you say there's none."[79]

NOTES

1. Anna Hellstrand, "Feminist Perspectives on the Egyptian Revolution" (Ph.D. diss, Uppsala University, 2012).
2. Ibid.

3. Victoria Newsom and Lara Lengel, "Arab Women, Social Media, and the Arab Spring: Applying the Framework of Digital Reflexivity to Analyze Gender and Online Activism," *Journal of International Women's Studies* 13, no. 4 (2012): 32.

4. Ibid., 33.

5. Ibid., 34.

6. "Asmaa Mahfouz & the YouTube Video that Helped Spark the Egyptian Uprising," *Democracy Now!*, February 8, 2011, accessed March 13, 2014.

7. Ibid.

8. "European Parliament," accessed April 29, 2014. www.europarl.europa.eu/aboutparliament/en/00f3dd2249/Sakharov-Prize-for-Freedom-of-Thought.html.

9. For a reference book to a range of Arab and Egyptian women's public arguments, see Margot Badran and miriam cooke, *Opening the Gates: An Anthology of Arab Feminist Writing*, 2nd edition (Indiana: Indiana University Press, 2004).

10. In this section, I briefly discuss the two feminist discourses that dominated the early twentieth century. While this is not a comprehensive overview of early Egyptian feminist discourses and voices, it is a short summary of feminist arguments in order to contextualize the references in Mahfouz's YouTube speech. It is essential that we acknowledge that Egyptian women have been arguing for women's rights in the public sphere long before January 2011.

11. Leila Ahmed, *Women and Gender in Islam: Historical Roots of a Modern Debate* (Yale University Press, 1993), 144.

12. Barbara Stowasser, "Women's Issues in Modern Islamic Thought," in *Arab Women: Old Boundaries, New Frontiers*, ed. Judith E. Tucker (Bloomington: Indiana University Press, 1993). 8.

13. Stowasser, 10.

14. Leila Ahmed, *Women and Gender in Islam: Historical Roots of a Modern Debate* (London: Yale University Press, 1993), 160.

15. Ibid., 245.

16. Ibid.

17. Margot Badran and miriam cooke, *Second Edition*: *Opening the Gate, Second Edition: An Anthology of Arab Feminist Writing* (Indiana: Indiana University Press, 2004), 337.

18. Ibid.

19. Ahmed, 174.

20. Badran and cooke, 338.

21. Ahmed, 175.

22. Badran and cooke, 234.

23. Rodolfo Diaz, "From Lambs to Lions: Self-Liberation and Social Media in Egypt," *Harvard International Review* 33, no. 1 (2011): 6.

24. Daly, Sunny, "Young Women as Activists in Contemporary Egypt: Anxiety, Leadership, and the Next Generation," *Journal of Middle East Women's Studies*, 6, no. 2 (2010): 71.

25. Michele Dunne and Tarek Radwan, "Egypt: Why Liberalism Still Matters," *Journal of Democracy* 24, no.1 (2013): 86–100.

26. Samantha M. Shapiro, "Revolution, Facebook-Style," *The New York Times*, January 22, 2009, accessed December 28, 2013. www.nytimes.com/2009/01/25/magazine/25bloggers-t.html?_r=0.

27. Rodolfo Diaz, "From Lambs to Lions: Self-Liberation and Social Media in Egypt," *Harvard International Review* 33, no. 1 (2011): 6.

28. Ibid., 6–7.

29. Ibid.

30. "Frontline: Revolution in Cairo, April 6 Youth Movement," *Public Broadcasting System*, accessed March 13, 2014, www.pbs.org/wgbh/pages/frontline/revolution-in-cairo/inside-april6-movement/.

31. Ahmad Zaki Osman, "Activists and Presidential Hopefuls Condemn Asmaa Mahfouz Arrest," *Egypt Independent*, August 14, 2011, accessed March 13, 2014, www.egyptindependent.com/news/activists-and-presidential-hopefuls-condemn-asmaa-mahfouz-arrest.

32. Ibid.

33. Mohamed Hussein el Naggar, "Human Rights Organizations and the Egyptian Revolution," *IDS Bulletin*, 43, no. 1 (January 2012): 83.

34. Ibid.

35. Leila Fadel, "Egypt's Military Rulers Drop Charges Against 2 Activists for Criticizing Military," *The Washington Post*, August 8, 2011, accessed March 13, 2014, www.cleveland.com/world/index.ssf/2011/08/egypts_military_rulers_drop_ch.html.

36. Juan Cole, "Egypt's New Left versus the Military Junta," Egypt in Transition. *Social Research* 79, no. 2 (2012): 487–510, 551.

37. Miriyam Aouragh and Anna Alexander, "The Egyptian Experience: Sense and Nonsense of the Internet Revolution," *International Journal of Communication* 5 (2011), 1350.

38. Ibid.

39. Diane Singerman, "Youth, Gender, and Dignity in the Egyptian Uprising," *Journal of Middle East Women's Studies* 9.3 (2013): 1–27.

40. Ibid.

41. Translation by Fida Adely and Aiman Haddad. "Statement of the April 6 Movement Regarding the Demands of the Youth and the Refusal to Negotiate with Any Side," *Jadaliyya*, 8 February 2011, accessed December 28, 2013, www.jadaliyya.com/pages/index/579/statement-of-the-april-6-movement-regarding-the-demands-of-the-youth-and-the-refusal-to-negotiate-with-any-side.

42. Mohamed Hussein El Naggar, "Human Rights Organizations and the Egyptian Revolution," *IDS Bulletin* 43, no.1 (January 2012): 83.

43. "Basic Provisions in the Constitution: Egyptian Human Rights NGOs Papyrus," accessed May 9, 2014, www.cihrs.org/wp-content/uploads/2011/12/659.pdf.

44. Celest Condit, "In Praise of Eloquent Diversity: Gender and Rhetoric as Public Persuasion," *Women's Studies in Communication* 20, no. 2 (1997), 91–116.

45. Mahfouz's YouTube video was initially published on her Facebook page, but the video on the website YouTube was eventually dissipated widely. I base my

analysis on the version available on YouTube. "Meet Asmaa Mahfouz and the Vlog that Helped Spark the Revolution," February 1, 2011, video clip, accessed October 1, 2013, YouTube, www.youtube.com/watch?v=SgjIgMdsEuk.

46. "Asmaa Mahfouz and the YouTube Video that Helped Spark the Egyptian Uprising," *Democracy Now!* February 2, 2011, accessed December 28, 2013, www.democracynow.org/2011/2/8/asmaa_mahfouz_the_youtube_video_that.

47. Asmaa Mahfouz, "Asmaa Mahfouz and the YouTube Video that Helped Spark the Egyptian Uprising," (speech, YouTube Egypt, Jan. 18, 2011), *Democracy Now!*, www.democracynow.org/2011/2/8/asmaa_mahfouz_the_youtube_video_that. ASMAA MAHFOUZ: [translated]

> Four Egyptians have set themselves on fire to protest humiliation and hunger and poverty and degradation they had to live with for 30 years. Four Egyptians have set themselves on fire thinking maybe we can have a revolution like Tunisia, maybe we can have freedom, justice, honor and human dignity. Today, one of these four has died, and I saw people commenting and saying, "May God forgive him. He committed a sin and killed himself for nothing."
>
> People, have some shame.
>
> I posted that I, a girl, am going down to Tahrir Square, and I will stand alone. And I'll hold up a banner. Perhaps people will show some honor. I even wrote my number so maybe people will come down with me. No one came except three guys—three guys and three armored cars of riot police. And tens of hired thugs and officers came to terrorize us. They shoved us roughly away from the people. But as soon as we were alone with them, they started to talk to us. They said, "Enough! These guys who burned themselves were psychopaths." Of course, on all national media, whoever dies in protest is a psychopath. If they were psychopaths, why did they burn themselves at the parliament building?
>
> I'm making this video to give you one simple message: we want to go down to Tahrir Square on January 25th. If we still have honor and want to live in dignity on this land, we have to go down on January 25th. We'll go down and demand our rights, our fundamental human rights. I won't even talk about any political rights. We just want our human rights and nothing else.
>
> This entire government is corrupt—a corrupt president and a corrupt security force. These self-immolaters were not afraid of death but were afraid of security forces. Can you imagine that? Are you going to kill yourselves, too, or are you completely clueless? I'm going down on January 25th, and from now 'til then I'm going to distribute fliers in the streets. I will not set myself on fire. If the security forces want to set me on fire, let them come and do it.
>
> If you think yourself a man, come with me on January 25. Whoever says women shouldn't go to protests because they will get beaten, let him have some honor and manhood and come with me on January 25. Whoever says it is not worth it because there will only be a handful of people, I want to tell him, "You are the reason behind this, and you are a traitor, just like the president or any security cop who beats us in the streets." Your presence with us will make a difference, a big difference. Talk to your neighbors, your colleagues, friends and family, and tell them to come. They don't have to come to Tahrir Square. Just go down anywhere and say it, that we are free human beings. Sitting at home and just following us on news or Facebook leads to our humiliation, leads to my own humiliation. If you have honor and dignity as a man, come. Come and protect me and

other girls in the protest. If you stay at home, then you deserve all that is being done, and you will be guilty before your nation and your people. And you'll be responsible for what happens to us on the streets while you sit at home.

Go down to the street. Send SMSes. Post it on the net. Make people aware. You know your own social circle, your building, your family, your friends. Tell them to come with us. Bring five people or 10 people. If each one of us manages to bring five or 10 to Tahrir Square and talk to people and tell them, "This is enough. Instead of setting ourselves on fire, let us do something positive," it will make a difference, a big difference.

Never say there's no hope. Hope disappears only when you say there's none. So long as you come down with us, there will be hope. Don't be afraid of the government. Fear none but God. God says He will not change the condition of a people until they change what is in themselves. Don't think you can be safe anymore. None of us are. Come down with us and demand your rights, my rights, your family's rights. I am going down on January 25, and I will say no to corruption, no to this regime.

48. Samuel R. Evans, "Debate the Aims of Discourse: Persuasive Versus Invitational Rhetoric," in *Walking and Talking Feminist Rhetorics: Landmark Essays and Controversies*, ed. Lindal Buchanan and Kathleen J. Ryan (West Lafayette: Parlor Press, 2010), 360–61.

49. Sonja Foss and Cindy Griffin, "Beyond Persuasion: A Proposal for Invitational Rhetoric," *Communication Monographs* 62 (1995), 2–18.

50. Condit, 110.

51. Ibid.

52. Mahfouz, "YouTube Vlog," par. 1.

53. Ibid., par. 1.

54. Mohamed Hussein El Naggar, "Human Rights Organizations and the Egyptian Revolution," *IDS Bulletin* 43, no.1 (January 2012): 78.

55. Mahfouz, "YouTube Vlog," par. 2.

56. Ibid., par. 3.

57. Suad Joseph, "Brother/Sister Relationships: Connectivity, Love, and Power in the Reproduction of Patriarchy in Lebanon," *America Ethnologist* 21, no. 1 (1994), 50–73.

58. Ibid.

59. For further discussion, see Suad Joseph's *Gender and Citizenship in the Middle East* (2000).

60. For a review of the honor/shame complex literature, see Forouz Jowkar, "Honor and Shame: A Feminist View from Within," *Feminist Issues* 6 (1986), 45–63.

61. Jowkar, 59.

62. Ibid., 55.

63. Mahfouz, "YouTube Vlog," par. 6.

64. Kenneth Burke, *Rhetoric of Motives* (Los Angeles: University of California Press, 1969), 20.

65. Burke, 21.

66. Mahfouz, "YouTube Blog," par. 8.

67. Ibid.

68. Ibid.

69. Charles Taylor, "Why We Need a Radical Redefinition of Secularism," in *Power of Religion in the Public Sphere*, ed. Eduardo Mendieta and Jonathan VanAntwerpen (New York: Columbia University Press, 2011), 34–59.

70. Mahfouz, "YouTube Vlog," par. 4.

71. Mahfouz, "YouTube Vlog," par. 6.

72. Ibid.

73. Ibid., par. 5.

74. Ibid., par. 1 and par. 3.

75. Nina zu Fürstenberg, "Interview with Asmaa Mahfouz," Qantara.de. November 15, 2012, accessed March 13, 2014. en.qantara.de/content/interview-with-the-egyptian-muslim-activist-asmaa-mahfouz-there-is-no-war-between-islam-and.

76. Ibid.

77. Mahfouz, "YouTube Vlog," par. 7.

78. Fürstenberg, "Interview with Asmaa Mahfouz," Quantara.de.

79. Mahfouz, "YouTube Vlog," par. 8.

Bibliography

Adely, Fida and Aiman Haddad. "Statement of the April 6 Movement Regarding the Demands of the Youth and the Refusal to Negotiate with Any Side." *Jadaliyy* February 8, 2011. Accessed December 28, 2013. www.jadaliyya.com/pages/index/579/statement-of-the-april-6-movement-regarding-the-demands-of-the-youth-and-the-refusal-to-negotiate-with-any-side.

Ahmed, Leila. *Women and Gender in Islam: Historical Roots of a Modern Debate.* London: Yale University Press, 1993.

Al Missned, Mozah bint Nasser. "From Illusions of Clashes to an Awakening of Alliances: Constructing Understanding between 'Islam and the West.'" Presentation to Chatham House, London, England, February 14, 2007. Accessed January 17, 2014. www.unaoc.org/repository/chatham_published_version.pdf.

———. "The 'Woman's Issue' in Context: Deframing the Discourse on Middle Eastern Women." Lecture, James A. Baker III Institute for Public Policy, Rice University, Houston, TX. May 21, 2007. Accessed January 19, 2014. bakerinstitute.org/files/799/.

———. "Speech of Her Highness Sheikha Moza bint Nasser, Chairperson of the Qatar Foundation Convocation 2013." Posted May 7, 2013. Accessed December 19, 2013. www.mozabintnasser.qa/en/Pages/ArticlePreview.aspx?ArticleGuid=c779ab97-7f48-4324-b572-f29bd2ad4689&Type=Speech.

———. "Speech of Her Highness Sheikha Moza Speech to the Annual Research Conference 2013." Posted November 24, 2013. Accessed March 1, 2014. www.mozabintnasser.qa/en/Pages/ArticlePreview.aspx?ArticleGuid=2a5282b7-a97b-4459-8bf1-b79fff90d2f1&Type=Speech.

———. "Speech of Her Highness Sheikha Moza at the Second Education City Convocation Ceremony." Posted May 5, 2009. Accessed February 27, 2014. www.mozabintnasser.qa/en/Pages/ArticlePreview.aspx?ArticleGuid=31f7c347-690e-472a-92a0-38e412441165&Type=Speech.

Al Muhannadi, Hessa Saad. "The Role of Qatari Women: Between Tribalism and Modernity." Master's Thesis, Lebanese American University, 2011.

Al-Nasr, Tofol Jassim. "Gulf Cooperation Council (GCC) Women and Misyar Marriage: Evolution and Progress in the Arabian Gulf." *Journal of International Women's Studies* 12, no. 3 (2006). Accessed February 27, 2014. vc.bridgew.edu/jiws/vol12/iss3/4.

Al Thani, Al-Mayassa bint Hamad bin Khalifa. *Globalizing the Local: Localizing the Global*. TED Talk. Filmed December 2010, posted February 2012. Accessed January 30, 2014. www.ted.com/talks/sheikha_al_mayassa_globalizing_the_local_localizing_the_global.html.

Annan, Kofi. *We the Peoples: The Role of the United Nations in the Twenty-First Century*. New York: United Nations Department of Public Information, 2000.

Aouragh, Miriyam and Anna Alexander. "The Egyptian Experience: Sense and Nonsense of the Internet Revolution." *International Journal of Communication* 5 (2011): 1350.

Aristotle. *The "Art" of Rhetoric*. Trans. John Henry Freese Cambridge: Harvard University Press, 1926.

Aseka, Eric Masinde. *Jomo Kenyatta: A Biography*. Nairobi: East African Educational Publishers, 1992.

"Asmaa Mahfouz and the YouTube Video that Helped Spark the Egyptian Uprising." *Democracy Now!* February 8, 2011. Accessed March 13, 2014. www.democracynow.org/2011/2/8/asmaa_mahfouz_the_youtube_video_that

Asmi, Rehenuma. "Language in the Mirror: Language Ideologies, Schooling and Islam in Qatar." Ph.D. diss. Columbia University, 2013.

Badran, Margot and miriam cooke. *Opening the Gates: An Anthology of Arab Feminist Writing*. 2nd ed. Bloomington: Indiana University Press, 2004.

Banda, Joyce H. M. Address to the United Nations General Assembly. New York, NY, September 26, 2012.

Bassnett, Susan. *Elizabeth I: A Feminist Perspective,* Oxford: Berg, 1988.

"Basic Provisions in the Constitution: Egyptian Human Rights NGOs Papyrus." Accessed May 9, 2014. www.cihrs.org/wp-content/uploads/2011/12/659.pdf.

Basu, Amrita ed. *The Challenge of Local Feminisms: Women's Movements in Global Perspectives*. With C. Elizabeth McGrory. Boulder: Westview Press, 1995.

Beemer, Cristy. "The Female Monarchy: A Rhetorical Strategy of Early Modern Rule." *Rhetoric Review* 30, no. 3 (July 2011): 258–74.

Belsky, Jill, "Beyond the Natural Resource and Environmental Sociology Divide: Insights from a Transdisciplinary Perspective." *Society and Natural Resources* 15 (2002): 269–280.

Bethel, Paulette. Speech to the United Nations General Assembly. New York, NY, October 17, 2012.

"Biography of Grace Ogot." *African Success: People Changing the Face of Africa.* Accessed December 26, 2013. Africansuccess.org.

Bogonko, Sorobea N. *Kenya 1945–1963: A Study in African National Movements*. Nairobi: Kenya Literature Bureau, 1980.

Bohlen, Celestine. "On a Mission to Shine a Spotlight on Genocide; Samantha Power's Mind Leaps from Bosnia to Iraq." *New York Times*, February 5, 2003. Accessed October 3, 2013. www.nytimes.com/2003/02/05/books/mission-shine-spotlight-genocide-samantha-power-s-mind-leaps-bosnia-iraq.html?pagewanted.

Brewer, Dominic J., Catherine H. Augustine, Gail L. Zellman, Gery Ryan, Charles A. Goldman, Cathleen Stas, and Louay Constant. *Education for a New Era: Design and Implementation of K-12 Education Reform in Qatar*. RAND Corporation. 2007. Working paper, RAND-Qatar Policy Institute, Santa Monica, CA, 2007. Accessed January 16, 2014. www.rand.org/content/dam/rand/pubs/monographs/2007/RAND_MG548.pdf.

Brown, Mark. "Qatar's Sheikha Mayassa Tops Power List." *The Guardian*. October 23, 2013. Accessed March 1, 2014. www.theguardian.com/artanddesign/2013/oct/24/qatar-sheikha-mayassa-tops-art-power-list.

Burke, Kenneth. *A Rhetoric of Motives*. Berkeley: University of California Press, 1969.

Campbell, Karlyn Kohrs. *Man Cannot Speak for Her: A Critical Study of Early Feminist Rhetoric*. New York: Greenwood, 1989.

———. *Presidents Creating the Presidency: Deeds Done in Words*. Chicago and London: The University of Chicago Press, 2008.

———. "The Discursive Performance of Femininity: Hating Hillary." *Rhetoric & Public Affairs* 1, no. 1 (1998): 1–19.

Ceaser, James W., Thurow, Glen E., Tulis, Jeffrey, and Joseph M. Bessette. "The Rise of the Rhetorical Presidency." *Presidential Studies Quarterly* 11, no. 2 Presidential Power and Democratic Constraints: A Prospective and Retrospective Analysis (1981): 158–71.

Checkel, Jeffery, "Social Constructivisms in Global and European Politics a Review Essay." *Review of International Studies* 30 (2004): 229–44.

Chege, Njoki. Interview. "Charity Ngilu: Back with a Band." *My Turn Blog*. October 9, 2012. Accessed January 3, 2014, njokichege.wordpress.com/tag/charity-ngilu/.

"Christmas Broadcast 1953." *The Official Website of the British Monarchy*. Last modified 2009. Accessed on November 30, 2013. www.royal.gov.uk/ImagesandBroadcasts/TheQueensChristmasBroadcasts/ChristmasBroadcasts/Christmasbroadcast1953.aspx.

Clinton, Hillary. "First Lady Hillary Rodham Clinton Remarks for the United Nations Fourth World Conference on Women." Fourth World Conference on Women by the United Nations Development Programme (UNDP). September 5, 1995. Accessed January 4, 2014. www.un.org/esa/gopher-data/conf/fwcw/conf/gov/950905175653.txt.

Cole, Juan. "Egypt's New Left versus the Military Junta." *Social Research* 79, no. 2 (2012): 487–510.

Condit, Celeste. "In Praise of Eloquent Diversity: Gender and Rhetoric as Public Persuasion." *Women's Studies in Communication* 20, no. 2 (1997): 91–116.

cooke, miriam. "Roundtable Discussion: Religion, Gender and the Muslim Woman." *Journal of Feminist Studies in Religion* 24, no. 1 (Spring, 2008). Accessed March

1, 2014. www.jstor.org/discover/10.2307/20487917?uid=3739560&uid=2&uid=4&uid=3739256&sid=21103483748651.

Cox, Ramsey. "Samantha Power Confirmed as Obama's UN Ambassador." *The Hill*, August 1, 2013. Accessed November 29, 2013. thehill.com/blogs/floor-action/senate/315137-senate-votes-to-confirm-power-as-un-ambassador.

Daly, Sunny. "Young Women as Activists in Contemporary Egypt: Anxiety, Leadership, and the Next Generation," *Journal of Middle East Women's Studies* 6, no. 2 (2010): 59–85.

Deeb, Lara. *An Enchanted Modern: Gender and Public Piety in Shi'i Lebanon*. Princeton, NJ: Princeton University Press, 2006.

Demeritt, David, "What is the 'Social Construction of Nature'? A Typology and Sympathetic Critique." *Progress in Human Geography* 26, no. 6 (2000): 766–89.

Diaz, Rodolfo. "From Lambs to Lions: Self-Liberation and Social Media in Egypt." *Harvard International Review* 33, no.1 (2011): 6–7.

Doran, Susan. "Elizabeth I: Gender, Power, & Politics." *History Today* 53, no. 5 (May 2003).

Dorsey, Leroy. G. *The Presidency and Rhetorical Leadership*. College Station: Texas A&M University Press, 2008.

Eagly, Alice H., and Linda L. Carli. "Are Men Natural Leaders?" In *Through the Labyrinth: The Truth About How Women Become Leaders*, 29–48. Boston, MA: Harvard Business School Publishing, 2007.

East African Standard. "Women May Lead the Way Back." June 24, 1955.

———. "Women Main Supports of Gangs in Reserves: Rehabilitation." June 26, 1955.

El Naggar, Mohamed Hussein. "Human Rights Organizations and the Egyptian Revolution." *IDS Bulletin* 43 (2012): 78–86.

Elton, G.R. *Tudor England*. London: The Folio Society, 1997.

Eshbaugh-Soha, Matthew, and Jeffrey S. Peake. *Breaking through the Noise: Presidential Leadership, Public Opinion, and the News Media*. Stanford: Stanford University Press, 2011.

"European Parliament." Accessed April 29, 2014. www.europarl.europa.eu/aboutparliament/en/00f3dd2249/Sakharov-Prize-for-Freedom-of-Thought.html.

Evans, Samuel R. "Debate the Aims of Discourse: Persuasive Versus Invitational Rhetoric." In *Walking and Talking Feminist Rhetorics: Landmark Essays and Controversies*, edited by Lindal Buchanan and Kathleen J. Ryan, 360–61. West Lafayette: Parlor Press, 2010.

Every Woman Every Child. "About Every Woman Every Child: An Unprecedented Effort to Save Lives." Accessed December 29, 2013. www.everywomaneverychild.org/about.

Fadel, Leila. "Egypt's Military Rulers Drop Charges Against 2 Activists for Criticizing Military." *The Washington Post*. August 8, 2011. Accessed March 13, 2014. www.cleveland.com/world/index.ssf/2011/08/egypts_military_rulers_drop_ch.html.

Fellder, Dell and Mirka Vuollo. "Qatari Women in the Workforce." Rand-Qatar Policy Institute Working Paper No. WR-612-Qatar. Accessed January 30, 2014. www.rand.org/pubs/working_papers/WR612.html.

Fernández, Cristina. Address to the United Nations General Assembly. New York, NY, September 25, 2012.

Finnemore, Martha and Kathryn Sikkink, "Taking Stock: The Constructivist Research Program in International Relations and Comparative Politics." *Annual Review of Political Science*. 4 (2000): 391–416.

Fisher, Max. "What Do Susan Rice and Samantha Power Promotions Mean for Syria Policy? Probably Not Much." *The Washington Post*, June 5, 2013. Accessed November 30, 2013. www.washingtonpost.com/blogs/worldviews/wp/2013/06/05/what-do-susan-rice-and-samantha-power-promotions-mean-for-syria-policy-probably-not-much.

Fridkin, Kim L., Jill Carle and Gina S. Woodall. "The Vice Presidency as the New Glass Ceiling: Media Coverage of Sarah Palin." In *Women and Executive Office: Pathways and Performance*, edited by Melody Rose, 33–52. Boulder, CO: Lynne Rienner Publishers, 2012.

Foss, Sonja and Cindy Griffin. "Beyond Persuasion: A Proposal for Invitational Rhetoric." *Communication Monographs* 62 (1995), 2–18.

Fromherz, Allen J. *Qatar: A Modern History*. Washington, DC: Georgetown University Press 2012.

"Frontline: Revolution in Cairo, April 6 Youth Movement." *Public Broadcasting System*. Accessed March 13, 2014. www.pbs.org/wgbh/pages/frontline/revolution-in-cairo/inside-april6-movement/.

Fürstenberg, Nina zu. "Interview with Asmaa Mahfouz." *Qantara.de*. November 15, 2012. Accessed March 13, 2014. en.qantara.de/content/interview-with-the-egyptian-muslim-activist-asmaa-mahfouz-there-is-no-war-between-islam-and.

Gaffney, Frank. "Samantha Power Will Concede US Self-Determination to the UN." Last modified June 14, 2013. www.centerforsecuritypolicy.org/2013/06/14/samantha-power-will-concede-us-self-determination-to-the-un.

General Assembly of the United Nations. Last modified December 2013. www.un.org/en/ga/.

General Secretariat for Development Planning. "Qatar National Vision 2030." Ministry of Development Planning and Statics. Accessed January 18, 2014. www.gsdp.gov.qa/portal/page/portal/gsdp_en/qatar_national_vision.

Gillard, Julia. Address to the United Nations General Assembly. New York, NY, September 26, 2012.

Gladstone, Rick. "New U.S. Envoy to U.N. Strongly Condemns Russia." *New York Times*, September 5, 2013. Accessed December 20, 2013. www.nytimes.com/2013/09/06/world/middleeast/new-us-envoy-to-un-strongly-condemns-russia.html?_r=0.

Goff, Keli. "Qatar's Jackie O." *The Daily Beast*. April 9, 2014. Accessed April 12, 2014. news.yahoo.com/qatar-jackie-o-094500582--politics.html.

Graegaer, Nina, "Environmental Security." *Journal of Peace Research* 33, no. 1 (1996): 109–116.

Green Belt Movement, "Wangari Maathai Biography." 2013. Accessed September 24, 2013. www.greenbeltmovement.org/wangari-maathai/biography.

Green, Janet M. "'I My Self': Queen Elizabeth I's Oration at Tilbury Camp." *Sixteenth Century Journal* 28, no. 2 (1997): 421.

Grint, Keith, "Problems, Problems, Problems: The Social Construction of 'Leadership.'" *Human Relations* 58, no.11 (2005): 1467–1494.

Gromada, Tadeusz; Halecki, Oskar, *Jadwiga of Anjou and the Rise of East Central Europe*, New York: Social Science Monographs, 1991.

Guerrero, Amadís M. "War and Peace–and Literature." *Philippines Daily Inquirer*, December 19, 2013. Accessed February 22, 2014, lifestyle.inquirer.net/141545/war-and-peace-literature.

Habermas, Jürgen. *The Structural Transformation of the Public Sphere.* Cambridge: MIT Press, 1991.

Hackett, Helen. "Rediscovering Shock: Elizabeth I and the Cult of the Virgin Mary." *Critical Quarterly* 35, no. 3 (September 1993).

Hamad bin Khalafi University. "About HBKU." Accessed January 29, 2014. www.hbku.edu.qa/en/DynamicPages/index/70/AboutHBKU.

Hannigan, John, *Environmental Sociology: A Social Constructionist Perspective.* London: Routledge, 1995.

Hardman, Robert. *Her Majesty: Queen Elizabeth II and Her Court*. New York: Penguin Books, 2012.

Harman, Danna. "Qatar Reformed by a Modern Marriage." *Christian Science Monitor,* March 6, 2007. Accessed March 1, 2014. www.csmonitor.com/2007/0306/p20s01-wome.html.

———. "The Royal Couple that Put Qatar on the Map." *Christian Science Monitor,* March 5, 2007. Accessed March 2, 2014. www.csmonitor.com/2007/0305/p20s01-wome.html.

Hauge, Wenche and Tanja Ellingsen, "Beyond Environmental Scarcity: Causal Pathways to Conflict." *Journal of Peace Research*. 35, no. 3 (1998): 299–317.

Hauser, Christine, and Robert Mackey. "Video of Samantha Power's 2002 Remarks on Imposing Peace on Israel Could Haunt Her, Israeli Paper Says." *New York Times*, June 5, 2013. Accessed November 29, 2013. thelede.blogs.nytimes.com/2013/06/05/israeli-newspaper-focuses-on-samantha-powers-remarks-in-2002/?ref=samanthapower.

Hellstrand, Anna. "Feminist Perspectives on the Egyptian Revolution." Ph.D. diss, Uppsala University, 2012.

Herman, Edward S., and David Peterson. "The Dismantling of Yugoslavia, Part IV." *Monthly Review* 59 (2007). Accessed November 29, 2013. monthlyreview.org/2007/10/01/the-dismantling-of-yugoslavia-part-iv.

"Historical Speeches and Writing." *The Official Website of the British Monarchy.* Last modified 2009. Accessed December 18, 2013. www.royal.gov.uk/pdf/edwardviii.pdf.

Homer-Dixon, Thomas, "Environmental Scarcities and Violent Conflict: Evidence from Cases." *International Security* 19, no.1 (1994): 5–40.

Hopkins, Lisa. *Writing Renaissance Queens: Texts by and about Elizabeth and Mary, Queen of Scots,* Newark, DE: University of Delaware Press, 2002.

Howe, Florence and Tobe Levin, eds. "Beijing and Beyond: Toward the Twenty-first Century of Women: Includes the Complete Text of the Platform for Action." *Women's Studies Quarterly* 25, nos. 1 & 2 (1996).

Jad, Islah. "Between Religion and Secularism: Islamist Women of Hamas." In *On Shifting Ground: Muslim Women in the Global Era*, edited by Fereshteh Nouraie-Simone, 172–98. New York: The Feminist Press, 2005.

Jakobsen, Maria. "Social Effects of the Educational Revolution in Qatar: A Gender Perspective." Master's thesis, The University of Bergen, 2010.

Joseph, Suad. "Brother/Sister Relationships: Connectivity, Love, and Power in the Reproduction of Patriarchy in Lebanon." *America Ethnologist* 21, no.1 (1994): 50–73.

Jowkar, Forouz. "Honor and Shame: A Feminist View from Within," *Feminist Issues* 6 (1986): 45–63.

Kahn, Kim Fridkin. *The Political Consequences of Being a Woman: How Stereotypes Influence the Conduct and Consequences of Political Campaigns.* New York, NY: Columbia University Press, 1996.

Kamrava, Mehran. *Qatar: Small State, Big Politics.* Ithaca: Cornell University Press, 2013.

Kanina, Wangui and Andrew Cawthorne. "Charity Ngilu Gets Sacked from the Cabinet." (Nairobi) Reuters, October 6, 2007. Accessed March 1, 2014. wanjuna.blogspot.com/2007/10/charity-ngilu-gets-sacked-from-cabinent.html.

Kaur, Preneet. Speech to the United Nations General Assembly. New York, NY, October 17, 2012.

Kelly, Sanja. "Recent Gains and New Opportunities for Women's Rights in the Gulf Arab States." *Freedom House.* n.d. Accessed December 19, 2013. www.freedomhouse.org/sites/default/files/Women's%20Rights%20in%20the%20Middle%20East%20and%20Noth%20Africa,%20Gulf%20Edition.pdf.

Khaled, Dania N. "Architecture in a Quiet Revolution." Master's thesis, McMaster University, 2010.

Khodr, Hiba. "The Dynamics of International Education in Qatar: Exploring the Policy Drivers behind the Development of Education City." *Journal of Emerging Trends in Educational Research and Policy Studies* 2, no. 6 (2011): 514–25.

Kingsley, Patrick. "80 Sexual Assaults in One Day—The Other Story of Tahrir Square." *The Guardian*, July 5, 2013. Accessed March 13, 2014. www.theguardian.com/world/2013/jul/05/egypt-women-rape-sexual-assault-tahrir-square.

Kittilson, Miki Caul and Kim Fridkin. "Gender, Candidate Portrayals, and Election Campaigns: A Comparative Perspective." *Politics & Gender* 4, no. 3 (2008): 371–92.

Klenke, Karin. *Women in Leadership: Contextual Dynamics and Boundaries.* Bingley, UK: Emerald Publishing, 2011.

Koinange, Jeff. "Capital Talk," *K24TV*, YouTube. Accessed December 28, 2013.

Koenigsberger, H.G., Mosse, George L., and Bowler, G.Q., *Europe in the Sixteenth Century,* Essex: Pearson Education Limited, 1989.

Knox, John. "The First Blast of the Trumpet Against the Monstrous Regiment of Women 1558," *Selected Writings of John Knox: Public Epistles, Treatise, and*

Expositions to the Year 1559, Presbyterian Heritage Publications, 1995. Accessed December 15, 2013. www.swrb.com/newslett/actualNLs/firblast.htm.

Kuria, Mike, ed. "Grace Ogot: Introduction" *Talking Gender: Conversations with Kenyan Women Writers*. Nairobi: PJ-Kenya, 2003.

Lacey, Robert. *Majesty*. New York: Harcourt, Brace, Jovanovich, 1977.

Laird, Dorothy. *How the Queen Reigns: An Authentic Study of the Queen's Personality and LifeWork*. Cleveland and New York: The World Publishing Co., 1959.

Lawless, Jennifer. "Women, War, and Winning Elections: Gender Stereotyping in the Post September 11th Era." *Political Research Quarterly* 53, no. 3 (2004): 479–90.

Levine, Mortimer, "The Place of Women in Tudor Government," in *Tudor Rule and Revolution*, ed. Delloyd J. Guth and John W. McKenna, New York: Cambridge University Press, 1982.

Lichter, Ida. *Muslim Women Reformers: Inspiring Voices Against Oppression*. New York: Prometheus Books, 2009.

Liftin, Karen, "Constructing Environmental Security and Ecological Interdependence." *Global Governance*. 5 (1999): 359–77.

Likimani, Muthoni. *Passbook Number F.47927L: Women and Mau Mau in Kenya*. London: Macmillan Publishers, Ltd. 1985.

Lindsey, Ursula. "Arab Women Make Inroads in Higher Education, but Often Find Dead Ends." *Chronicle of Higher Education*. Last modified January 29, 2012. Accessed January 30, 2014. chronicle.com/article/Arab-Women-Make-Inroads-in/130479/ur.

Loveless, A. Scott and Thomas B. Holman, eds. *The Family in the New Millennium: World Voices Supporting the "Natural" Clan, Vol 1: The Place of Family in Human Society*. Westport, CT, US: Praeger Publishers/Greenwood Publishing Group, 2007.

Lowe, Will. "Yoshikoder: An Open Source Multilingual Content Analysis Tool for Social Scientists." Presentation at the Annual Meeting of the American Political Science Association, Philadelphia, PA, August 31–September 3, 2006.

Lucas Stephen, *The Art of Public Speaking*. 7th ed. Boston: McGraw-Hill, 2001.

Marcus, Leah S., Mueller, Janel, and Rose, Mary Beth, eds, *Elizabeth I: Collected Works*, Chicago: University of Chicago, 2002, Kindle Edition.

Maathai, Wangari, "Nobel Lecture." Oslo, December 10, 2004. Accessed September 23, 2013. ogiek.com/indepth/NobelPeacePrizeAcceptanceSpeech.pdf

———. "Inaugural World Food Law Distinguished Lecture." Howard University, Washington, DC, May 10, 2005. Accessed September 23, 2013. www.green beltmovement.org/wangari-maathai/key-speeches-and-articles/inaugural-world-food-law-distinguished-lecture.

———. "Sustained Development, Democracy, and Peace in Africa." Gwangju, South Korea, June 16, 2006. Accessed September 23, 2013. www.greenbelt movement.org/wangari-maathai/key-speeches-and-articles/sustained-develop ment-democracy-and-peace.

———. *Unbowed: A Memoir*. New York: Alfred A. Knopf, 2006.

"Meet Asmaa Mahfouz and the Vlog That Helped Spark the Revolution." February 1, 2011. Video clip. Accessed October 1, 2013. *YouTube*. www.Youtube.com, www.youtube.com/watch?v=SgjIgMdsEuk.

Migiro, Katy. "Factbox: Women in Kenyan Politics by the Numbers." Thomas Reuters Foundation. Accessed December 6, 2013. www.trust.org.

Moaddel, Mansoor. "The Study of Islamic Culture and Politics: An Overview and Assessment." *Annual Reviews* 28 (August 2002): 359–86. Accessed December 19, 2013. doi: 10.1146/annurev.soc.28.110601.140928.

Mohanty, Chandra Talpade, Ann Russo, and Lourdes Torres, eds. *Third World Women and the Politics of Feminism*. Bloomington: Indiana University Press, 1997.

Moussa, Ahamd. "Qatar's Sheikha Mozah Wins Chatham House Prize." *Business Intelligence Middle East,* September 25, 2007. Accessed January 15, 2014. www.bi-me.com/main.php?id=13424&t=1.

Mupuchi, Speedwell. "Zambia: 'Twenty-First Century Must Be a Century of Women.'" *AllAfrica.com*. Originally from The Post (Zambia). October 19, 2001. Accessed February 22, 2014. allafrica.com/stories/200110190422.html.

Mwangi, Catherine, "A Rhetorical Analysis of African Unification Oratory" (Ph.D. thesis, National University of Lesotho, 2009).

Mwangi, Oscar, "Environmental Change and Human Security in Lesotho: The Role of the Lesotho Highlands Water Project in Environmental Degradation." *African Security Review*.17, no. 3 (2008): 58–70.

National Democratic Institution, Final Report, Kenya: Supporting Women's Political Participation, October 1997. Accessed February 28, 2014.

NBC Today. "Tom Brokaw: Welcome to the Century of Women." Aired May 2, 2013. Accessed February 22, 2014. www.today.com/video/today/51745555#51745555.

Neuendorf, Kimberly A. *The Content Analysis Handbook*. Thousand Oaks, CA: SAGE Publications, 2002.

Nevins, Joseph. "On Justifying Intervention." *The Nation*, May 20, 2002. Accessed November 30, 2013. www.thenation.com/article/justifying-intervention#.

Newsom, Victoria and Lara Lengel. "Arab Women, Social Media, and the Arab Spring: Applying the Framework of Digital Reflexivity to analyze Gender and Online Activism." *Journal of International Women's Studies* 13, no. 4 (2012): 32.

Nguli, Peter Ngangi. "Grace Ogot Took the African Story to the World." *Kenya National Standard*. September 11, 2013. Accessed December 3, 2013. www.standardmedia.co.ke/mobile/?articleID=2000093261&story_title=grace-ogot-took-the-african-story-to-the-world.

Njiro, E.I. *The Women's Movement in Kenya*. Nairobi: Association of African Women for Research and Development, 1993.

Nikkah, Roya, "Princess Margaret: Recently Unearthed Letter Sheds New Light on Decision Not to Marry." *The Telegraph*. Accessed December 3, 2013. www.telegraph.co.uk/news/uknews/theroyalfamily/6520837/Princess-Margaret-recently-unearthed-letter-sheds-new-light-on-decision-not-to-marry.html.

Nnaemeka, Obioma, ed. *Sisterhood, Feminisms and Power: From Africa to the Diaspora*. Asmara: Africa World Press, Inc., 1998.

Nzomo, Maria. *Empowering Kenya Women*. Nairobi: National Committee on the Status of Women, 1993.

Obi, Cyril, "Globalised Images of Environmental Security in Africa." *Review of African Political Economy* 27, no 83 (2000): 47–62.

Okeke, Philomina E. "Postmodern Feminism and Knowledge Production: The African Context." *Africa Today*, 43 (1996): 223–34.
Osman, Ahmad Zaki. "Activists and Presidential Hopefuls Condemn Asmaa Mahfouz Arrest." *Egypt Independent*, August 14, 2011. Accessed March 13, 2014. www.egyptindependent.com/news/activists-and-presidential-hopefuls-condemn-asmaa-mahfouz-arrest.
Otieno, Wambui. *Mau Mau's Daughter: The Life History of Wambui Otieno*. Edited and with an introduction by Cora Ann Presley. Boulder: Lynne Rienner, Publishers, 1998.
Oyewumi, Oyeronke. *The Invention of Women: Making an African Sense of Western Gender Discourses*. Minneapolis: University of Minnesota Press, 1997.
Pan American Health Organization. "History of the MDGs." Last modified 2010. www.paho.org/mdg/index.php?option=com_content&view=article&id=77&Itemid=60&lang=en.
Panton, J, "Matilda," *Historical Dictionary of the British Monarchy*, Plymouth: Scarecrow Press, 2011.
Peev, Gerri. "'Hillary Clinton's a Monster': Obama Aide Blurts Out Attack in Scotsman Interview." *The Scotsman*, June 3, 2008. Accessed November 30, 2013. www.scotsman.com/news/hillary-clinton-s-a-monster-obama-aide-blurts-out-attack-in-scotsman-interview-1-1158300.
Pimlott, Ben. *The Queen: A Biography of Elizabeth II*. New York: John Wiley and Sons, Inc., 1996.
Pittinsky, Todd L., Bacon, Laura M., and Brian Welle. "The Great Women Theory of Leadership? Perils of Positive Stereotypes and Precarious Pedestals." In *Women and Leadership: The State of Play and Strategies for Change*, edited by Barbara Kellerman and Deborah Rhode, 93–116. San Francisco, CA: Jossey-Bass, 2007.
Pollard, A.F. *The Political History of England: From the Accession of Edward VI to the Death of Elizabeth (1547–1603)*. London: Longmans, Green and Co, 1910.
Prengaman, Peter. "Qatar's First Lady Argues Islam not the Root of Extremism." *Free Republic*, May 16, 2007. Accessed January 15, 2014. www.freerepublic.com/focus/f-news/1834553/posts.
Power, Samantha. *A Problem from Hell: America and the Age of Genocide*. New York: Harper-Collins, 2002.
———. "Bystanders to Genocide." *The Atlantic Monthly*, September 2001. Accessed December 1, 2013. www.theatlantic.com/magazine/archive/2001/09/bystanders-to-genocide/304571/2.
———. "Once Upon A Nomar." *Boston Globe*, June 5, 2013. Accessed December 20, 2013. www.bostonglobe.com/opinion/columns/2013/06/05/once-upon-nomar/uXl3d0AiplZj1IwaD9PRfK/story.html.
———. "Raising the Cost of Genocide." *Dissent* (Spring 2002): 85–96.
———. "The Democrats and National Security." *The New York Review of Books* 55 (2008). Accessed December 20, 2013. www.nybooks.com/issues/2008/aug/14.
———. "US Leadership to Advance Equality for LGBT People Abroad." *The White House Blog*, December 13, 2012. Accessed December 20, 2013. www.whitehouse.gov/blog/2012/12/13/us-leadership-advance-equality-lgbt-people-abroad.

Power, Samantha, and Graham Allison. *Realizing Human Rights: Moving From Inspiration to Impact*. New York: Palgrave, 2000.
Presley, Cora Ann. *Kikuyu Women, the Mau Mau Rebellion, and Social Change in Kenya*. Boulder: Westview Press, 1992.
Price Richard, "Moral Limit and Possibility in World Politics." *International Organization*. 62, no. 2 (2008): 191–220.
Qatar Foundation. "Qatar Foundation to Celebrate Convocation of 437 Graduates." *Qatar Foundation*, May 7, 2013. Accessed January 16, 2014. www.qf.org.qa/news/293.
Riffe, Daniel, Lacy, Stephen, and Frederick G. Fico. *Analyzing Media Messages: Using Quantitative Content Analysis in Research*, 2nd edition. Mahwah, NJ: Lawrence Erlbaum Associates Inc., 2005.
Risse, Thomas, "'Let's Argue!': Communicative Action in World Politics." *International Organization*. 54, no. 1 (2000): 1–37.
Romanowski, Michael H. and Ramzi Nasser. "Critical Thinking and Qatar's Education for a New Era: Negotiating Possibilities." *The International Journal of Critical Pedagogy* 4, no. 1 (2012): 118–134. Accessed February 13, 2014. libjournal.uncg.edu/index.php/ijcp/article/view/300/262.
Rose, Mary Beth. "The Gendering of Authority in the Public Speeches of Elizabeth I." *PMLA: Publications Of The Modern Language Association Of America* 115, no. 5 (October 2000): 1077–82.
Saban, Cheryl. Speech to the United Nations General Assembly. New York, NY, October 17, 2012.
Santoru, Marina. "The Colonial Idea of Women and Direct Intervention: The Mau Mau Case," *African Affairs* 95 (1996): 253–267.
Schnall, Marianne. "Conversations with Wangari Maathai," December 9, 2008. Accessed January 3, 2013. www.Feminist.com.
Sengupta, Somini. "U.N. Ambassador, in Central Africa, Vows Aid and Hears of a Unity Shattered." *New York Times*, December 19, 2013. Accessed December 20, 2013. www.nytimes.com/2013/12/20/world/africa/us-ambassador-visits-central-african-republic-amid-bloodshed.html.
Shapiro, Samantha M. "Revolution, Facebook-Style." *New York Times*, January 22, 2009. Accessed December 28, 2013. www.nytimes.com/2009/01/25magazine/25bloggers-t.html?_r=0.
Singerman, Diane. "Youth, Gender, and Dignity in the Egyptian Uprising," *Journal of Middle East Women's Studies* 9, no. 3 (2013): 1–27.
Smith, Sally Bedell. *Queen Elizabeth II: The Life of a Modern Monarch*. New York: Random House, 2012.
"Speech Following the Death of Diana, Princess of Wales." *The Official Website of the British Monarchy*. Accessed on December 13, 2013. www.royal.gov.uk.
Stead, Valerie, and Carole Elliott. "Common Understandings: Leadership and Leadership Development." In *Women's Leadership*, 15–39. New York, NY: Palgrave Macmillan, 2009.
———. "Visualising Women's Leadership: Stereotypes and Metaphors." In *Women's Leadership*, 40–59. New York, NY: Palgrave Macmillan, 2009.

Steady, Filomina Chioma. "African Feminism: A Worldwide Perspective." In *Women in Africa and the African Diaspora*, Rosalyn Terborg-Penn, Sharon Harley, and Andrea Benton Rushing, eds. Washington: Howard University Press, 1987.

Sterling-Folker, Jennifer, "Competing Paradigms or Birds of a Feather? Constructivism and Neo-Liberalism Compared." *International Studies Quarterly*. 44, no. 1 (2000): 97–119.

Stolberg, Sherl G. "Still Crusading, but Now on the Inside." *New York Times*, March 29, 2011. Accessed November 30, 2013. www.nytimes.com/2011/03/30/world/30power.html?_r=0.

Strype, John. *Annals of the Reformation and Annals of the Reformation and Establishment of Religion and Other Various Occurrences in the Church of England*, John Wyat, 1709.

Tanner, Joseph Robson. *Tudor Constitutional Documents, A.D. 1485–1603*. CUP Archives, 1948.

Taylor, Charles. "Why We Need a Radical Redefinition of Secularism." In *Power of Religion in the Public Sphere*, edited by Eduardo Mendieta and Jonathan Van Antwerpen, 34–59. New York: Columbia University Press, 2011.

"The Academic and the Writer on Enduring Love," *Standard Media*. Sunday, November 9, 2008. Accessed December 3, 2013.

"The Rent She Paid for Her Room on Earth," *The Telegraph*. Last modified April 1, 2002. Accessed January 2, 2014. www.telegraph.co.uk/comment/telegraph-view/3574827/The-rent-she-paid-for-her-room-on-earth.html.

Thuku, Harry and Kenneth King. *Harry Thuku: A Biography*. Nairobi: Oxford University Press, 1970.

Tilly, Louise and Vivian Patraka, eds. *Feminist Revisions: What Has Been and What Might Be*. Ann Arbor: University of Michigan, 1983.

Tominey, Camilia. "The Real Value of the Royal Family: Queen's Accounts to Be Audited." *The Express*. February 17, 2013. Accessed February 23, 2014. www.expresss.co,uk./news/uk/378183/The-real-value-of-the-Royal-family-Queen-s-accounts-to-be-audited.

Toulmin, Stephen, *The Uses of Argument*. Cambridge: Cambridge University Press, 1958.

Toulmin, Stephen, Richard Rieke, and Allan Janik, *An Introduction to Reasoning*. 2nd ed. New York: Macmillan Publishing Co, 1984.

Tulis, Jeffrey. "On the Forms of Rhetorical Leadership." In *Beyond the Rhetorical Presidency*, edited by Martin J. Medhurst, 29–34. College Station: Texas A&M University Press, 2008.

———. *The Rhetorical Presidency*. Princeton: Princeton University Press, 1987.

Udvardy, Monica. "Theorizing Past and Present Women's Organization in Kenya." *World Development*, 26 (1998): 1749–61.

Ulrichsen, Kristian Coates. "The Gulf States and the Rebalance of Regional and Global Power." Working paper, James A. Baker III Institute for Public Policy, Rice University, Houston, TX, 2014. Accessed December 19, 2013. bakerinstitute.org/media/files/Research/ec7b03d8/CME-Pub-GulfStates-010813.pdf.

United Nations. "Report of the UN Secretary-General: A Life of Dignity for All." Accessed December 29, 2013. www.un.org/millenniumgoals/pdf/SG_Report_MDG_EN.pdf.

United Nations Conference on Trade and Development [UNCTAD]. *The Least Developed Countries Report: Growth with Employment for Inclusive and Sustainable Development.* New York, United Nations, 2013.

UN Dag Hammarskjöld Library. "United Nations Bibliographic Information System." Last modified November 2013. unbisnet.un.org/.

UN Department of Economic and Social Affairs. *The United Nations Development Strategy Beyond 2015.* New York: United Nations, 2012.

UN General Assembly, 55th Session. "United Nations Millennium Declaration" (A/RES/55/2). Last modified September 18, 2000. www.un.org/millennium/declaration/ares552e.htm.

———. 59th Session. "In Larger Freedom: Towards Development, Security and Human Rights for All" (A/59/2005). Last modified March 21, 2005. www.unmillenniumproject.org/documents/UNworldsummit.pdf.

———. 65th Session. "Keeping the Promise: United to Achieve the Millennium Development Goals" (A/RES/65/1). Last modified October 19, 2010. www.un.org/en/mdg/summit2010/pdf/outcome_documentN1051260.pdf.

———. 68th Session. "Outcome Document of the Special Event to Follow Up Efforts Made Towards Achieving the Millennium Development Goals" (Draft resolution A/68/L.4). Last modified October 1, 2013. www.un.org/en/ga/search/view_doc.asp?symbol=A/68/L.4.

UN News Center. "UN Chief Urges World Leaders to Answer Demands of Their People for Dignity, Development." Accessed February 22, 2014. www.un.org/apps/news/story.asp?NewsID=45950&Cr=general+debate&Cr1#.Uwimq_1dWTk.

UN Statistics Division. "Official List of MDG Indicators." Last modified January 15, 2008. mdgs.un.org/unsd/mdg/host.aspx?Content=indicators/officiallist.htm.

UN Women. "The Twenty-First Century Will Be the Century of Girls and Women." September 23, 2011. www.unwomen.org/en/news/stories/2011/9/the-21st-century-will-be-the-century-of-girls-and-women.

———. "'Taking Action Together, We Can Make the Twenty-First Century the Century of Women'—UN Women Executive Director." Accessed February 21, 2013. www.unwomen.org/ca/news/stories/2013/10/ed-addres-to-third-committee-of-the-general-assembly.

University of Nairobi. "A Brief on Founding Distinguished Chair of WMI Professor Wangari Muta Maathai," Wangari Maathai Institute for Peace and Environmental Studies, University of Nairobi. Accessed September 24, 2013. www.uonbi.ac.ke/node/3946.

Video Player, "Nobelprize.org." Nobel Media AB 2013. December 2012. Accessed December 28, 2012. nobelprize.org/mediaplayer/index.php?id=120.

Warnicke, Retha. "Why Elizabeth I Never Married." *History Review* no. 67 (September 2010).

"Wartime Broadcast." *The Official Website of the British Monarchy.* Last modified 2009. Accessed January 4, 2014. www.royal.gov.uk/ImagesandBroadcasts/Historic%20speeches%20and%20broadcasts/Wartimebroadcast1940.aspx.

Wendt, Alexander, *Social Theory of International Politics.* Cambridge: Cambridge University Press, 1999.

Williams-Black, Joy. "*The Expansion of Higher Education for Kenyans, with Special Emphasis on Women, 1959–1969.*" Ph.D. diss., University of Illinois Urbana-Champaign, 2008.

———. "Gender, (Under) Development and Globalization: A History of Development Theory and Practice in Sub-Saharan Africa." Paper presented at the Second Annual Graduate Symposium on Women's and Gender History, Champaign, Illinois, March 22–24, 2001.

Wipper, Audrey. "Kikuyu Women and the Harry Thuku Disturbances: Some Uniformities of Female Militancy," *Africa: Journal of the International African Institute,* 59 (1989): 300–37.

———. "The Maendeleo ya Wanawake Movement in the Colonial Period." *Rural Africana,* (1975–1976) 27–30.

———. "The Maendeleo ya Wanawake Organization: The Co-optation of Leadership," *African Studies Review,* 18 (December 1975): 99–120.

Wood, B. D. "Presidential Rhetoric and Economic Leadership." *Presidential Studies Quarterly* 34, no. 3 The Public Presidency (2004): 573–606.

Woodgate, Graham and Michael Redclift, "From a 'Sociology of Nature' to Environmental Sociology: Beyond Social Construction." *Environmental Values.* 7 (1998): 3–24.

Zarefsky, David. "The Presidency Has Always Been a Place for Rhetorical Leadership." In *The Presidency and Rhetorical Leadership*, edited by Leroy G. Dorsey, 20–41. College Station: Texas A&M University Press, 2008.

Zeveloff, Julie. "Dubai Sets a World Record with the World's Largest Firework Display on New Year's Eve." *Business Insider,* Dec. 31, 2013. Accessed March 1, 2014. www.businessinsider.com/dubai-record-fireworks-new-years-2013-12.

Zinn, Howard. "On Terror." *Z-Net,* August 21, 2007. Accessed September 24, 2008. www.zmag.org/Zinn.

Index

Aberfan, Wales, 26–27
Altrincham, Lord, 24–25, 27, 33
Arab Feminist Union (AFU), 148–49

"Century of Women," ix, 89
Churchill, Winston, 26–27, 112
"Citizen Journalism," 146
Clinton, Hillary, vii–viii, xiii, 89, 110, 116–18

Days of My Life. See Ogot, Grace Akinyi
Diana, Princess of Wales, ix, x, 10, 19–21, 25–35
discourse: environmental, x, 41–57, 59, 70–71, 73, 92, *95*, 128; gender, viii–ix, 3–5, 7–11, 14–16, 34–35, 56, 65, 68–69, 74, 80, 90–92, 94–*95*, 97–100, *103*, 105, 119, 127–31, 133, 137, 145–48, 152–55, 157; political, xii, 129–30, 134–35, 157; religious, 147, 155

education, xii–xiii, 47, 50–51, 53, 65–66, 69–70, 73–74, 76, 80, 92, *95*–96, 98–*102*, 104, 128–31, 133–34, 136–37, 139–40, 147–49; Africa, 41, 44–57, 59, 65–73, 77, 81, 82n14, 83n30, 84n84, *93*, *95*, 97–100, *102*, 104, 109, 115–16, 119; Education City, 130, 132, 136, 140; Education for a New Era project, 131; educational campaigns, 70; educational models, 128; educational policy, 128; educational reform, 130–31; higher education, xivn7, 66, 69, 74; primary education, 92, 96, 100; Qatar, xii, 127–132, 134, 136–40; Qatar Foundation for Science, Education and Community Development (QF), 128, 130, 132–34, 136–37, 139–40; Technology Education and Design (TED), 139; Edward VIII, 20–21, 23, 26, 36n12; Wallis Warfield Simpson, 21
Egyptian Revolution, xii, 145–47, 150, 153, 157
Elizabeth I, ix, 3–15; Mary of Hungary, 14; Mary, Queen of Scots, 14; Mary Tudor 4, 14, 16n9; Matilda, 4; "Tilbury Camp speech," 11, 15
Elizabeth II, ix–x, 19–20, 23–24, 26–28, 33–35; King George V, 20; King George VI (Prince Albert), 20–23, 26, 36n12; Prince Charles, 28, 32;

Prince Henry (Harry), 31–32; Prince Philip, 25; Prince William, x, 31–32, 35; Queen Elizabeth (mother of Elizabeth II), 22; Queen Juliana of the Netherlands, 22; Queen Victoria, 19, 34

Facebook, 34, 146, 149–50, 152, 159n45, 160n47
Feminine Rhetorical Style, 94–100, 104–105
feminine style, 94, *97*, 99–100
feminism, 84n58, 145, 147, 149; Arab, 148; colonial, 147
feminist discourse, 146, 148, 158n10

Green Belt Movement (GBM), 41, 44, 47, 49–51, 54, 57, 68, 70, 72–73
Grey, Lady Jane, 4
Gulf Cooperation Council (GCC), 127, 129–30

Kenya African National Union (KANU), 67, 75
kings of England; Henry I, 4; Henry II, 4
Knox, John, 5

leadership 3, 30, 49, 66, 69, 72, 89–92, 94, 99, 104–105, 111, 128, 130; global, xii; language, viii–xii, xiii, 5, 7, 9, 11–12, 14–15, 24, 42–43, 59, 68, 76–77, 80, 91, *93*, 117; political, 91; presidential, viii, xi, xivn7, 30, 71, 78–79, 81n2, 90–91, 110, 116–17; vice-presidential, 78
Lesbian, Gay, Bisexual, and Transgendered (LGBT), 119

Maathai, Wangari Muta, x, 41, 44–59; 63n86, 66, 68–74, 78–81; "Inaugural World Food Law Distinguished Lecture," 45, 51; "Nobel Peace Prize Acceptance Speech," 45; "Sustained Development, Democracy, and Peace in Africa," 45, 55; *Unbowed*, 68, 70–72, 80
Mahfouz, Asmaa, 146–47, 149–57, 158n10, 159n45, 160nn46–47; April 6 Youth Movement, 146–47, 149–51; April 6 YouTube video, 150, 152–56, 158n10, 159n45, 160n47; Moza, Sheikha, xi, 127–34, 136–39, 140; Education City (EC), 130, 132, 136, 140; honorary degrees, 130; Qatar Foundation for Science, Education and Community Development (QF), 130, 132–34, 136; Sheikh Hamad, 127, 130, 140

National Council of Women in Kenya (NCWK), 70
Ngilu, Charity, x, xivn7, 65–66, 68, 77–81, 81n2, 85n93
Nobel Peace Prize, x, 41, 45, 55, 56, 59, 61n13, 71–72
Non-governmental organization (NGO), vii–viii, xiiin3, 44, 151, 159n43
North Atlantic Treaty Organization (NATO), 112, 115

Obama, Barack, xi, xiii, 116–20
Ogot, Grace Akinyi, x, 65–66, 68, 74–77, 79–81, 84n84, 84n93; Bethwell Ogot, 74–75; *Days of My Life,* 74, 80

Power, Samantha, xi, 109–12, 115, 119; *A Problem from Hell: America and the Age of Genocide,* 113–15; *Chasing the Flame: Sergio Vieira de Mello and the Fight to Save the World,* 116; *Realizing Human Rights: Moving From Inspiration to Impact,* 111–12; United Nations Ambassador (UN Ambassador), 99, 119–20 rhetorical action: democratic, 49–53, 58, 63n86, 82n16; discursive constructivism, 42–43; genocide, xi, 110–17, 119; invitational, 153; legal, 14, 53, 70, 91, 119, 136, 150; masculine, 14, 67, 73, 75, 108n32, 152–153; peace, x, 10, 23, 33–34, 41, 43–46, 48–59, 70, 72–73, 92, 95, 109, 111–12, 118; religion, viii, xii, 16n3, 56, 76–77, 80, 128, 130, 132, 135, 145, 147–49, 152, 155–57; social constructivism, 41–44, 53, 59; style, 3, 11, 80, 92–93, 112, 116, 153; transnational, 129, 146

rhetorical terms; *anaphora*, 52–53, 62n83; consubstantiatial, 28, 155; *ethos,* xii, 10, 24, 26, 28, 30–32, 34, 44, 48, 54, 59, 110–11, 116, 119, 130; identification, 10, 20, 28–30, 33, 35, 129, 147–49, 152, 155–56; *logos*, 28, 44–45, 48, 52, 54–55, 57, 59; *pathos*, 28–29, 31–32, 44, 51, 55, 58–59

social media, xii, 34, 79, 146, 150

Twitter, 150–151

United Nations (UN), vii, ix, xi–xii, 44, 69, 89, 92–97, 99,100, 102, 105, 107n23, 109–13,115, 117–19, 128–29, 139; Millennium Development Goals (MDG), xi, 89, 91–92, 94–105, 107n23; United Nations Educational Scientific and Cultural Organization (UNESCO), xii, *96*, 129; United Nations General Assembly (UN GA, the General Assembly), xi, 44, 89, 90, 92–*93*, *97*, *102*, 107n23, 128; YouTube, viii, xii, 34, 66, 146–47

About the Contributors

William Carney is an Associate Professor and Director of Composition at Cameron University in Oklahoma. His research interests include public and religious rhetoric, experiential learning, and teaching English as a Second Language. He has published in various edited collections and in journals such as the *Journal of Language Teaching* and *Research and Intercultural Communication Studies*. He is presently involved in local and state-wide initiatives to provide authentic service learning and internship opportunities for undergraduate students.

Charlotte Evans is a freelance writer and editor based in the United States. She has written several articles and books on gender issues as well as branding and marketing strategies. She has also ghostwritten historical studies on the nineteenth-century transportation industry in the United States and key political figures of that period. She is currently working on a study of gender in nineteenth- and twentieth-century literature. Born in the United Kingdom, Charlotte Evans studied literature in both England and the United States. She lives in Lancaster, PA, with her two children.

Valerie M. Hennings (Ph.D., University of Wisconsin-Madison) is an assistant professor of political science in the Department of Economics, Political Science and Sociology at Morningside College in Sioux City, Iowa. Her current research examines candidate training programs and their influences on women's political participation, including their decisions to seek elected and appointed offices. In addition to publishing multiple studies focused on women, politics, and communication, she teaches courses on gender and leadership, gender and politics, political behavior, and state and local governments.

About the Contributors

Nicole Khoury holds a Ph.D. in Rhetoric, Composition, and Linguistics from Arizona State University and an MA in English Composition and Literature from California State University, San Bernardino. She is currently an assistant professor of Rhetoric and Composition at the American University of Beirut. Her research focuses on Middle Eastern women's rhetorical strategies and discourse, with particular interest on the intersections between gender and religion in the Middle Eastern context, Islamic feminist discourse, and public arguments for gender equality.

Michele Lockhart is a Senior Lecturer and teaches business communication at the University of Texas at Dallas. Her research interests include political rhetoric, women in politics, and technical and business communication. Dr. Lockhart holds degrees in broadcast journalism, political science and public administration, and rhetoric. Her previous professional experience includes serving as an analyst for the U.S. Government Accountability Office (GAO), a broadcast journalist and bureau chief, working on a gubernatorial re-election campaign, and writing speeches for an elected official.

Janet M. Martin, Professor of Government at Bowdoin College, is the author of *The Presidency and Women: Promise, Performance, and Illusion* (2003, Winner of the 2004 Richard E. Neustadt Award for the best book on the presidency); *Lessons from the Hill: The Legislative Journey of an Education Program* (1994) and co-editor of *The Other Elites: Women, Politics, and Power in the Executive Branch* (1997). She has published articles and reviews in *The Journal of Politics*, *Western Political Quarterly*, *Presidential Studies Quarterly*, and *Congress and the Presidency*. A former APSA Congressional Fellow, she worked as a legislative assistant for Senator Herb Kohl (D-WI) and Majority Leader George Mitchell (D-ME).

Kathleen Mollick is an associate professor of English at Tarleton State University, where she serves as the Director of the Writing Program. She has presented papers on topics related to composition studies, presidential discourse and twentieth-century American literature at the Conference of College Composition and Communication, the Rhetoric Society of America, and the Southwest/Texas Popular Culture Association Conference. Mollick is the co-editor, along with her colleague Michele Lockhart, of the political women's anthology *Political Women: Language and Leadership*. She has been published in *Composition Studies*, *CCTE Studies*, and she edits *The Popken Writer*, an anthology of first-year writing at Tarleton State University in Stephenville, Texas.

Catherine Waithera Mwangi is presently the Chair of the Department of Languages, Linguistics and Literature at Pwani University. She holds a BA degree in English and History from the University of Eastern Africa, Baraton, an MA degree in Communication from Daystar University, and a Ph.D. in Literature in English from the National University of Lesotho. Her research interests include African political rhetoric. Her Ph.D. thesis examines African unification oratory from a rhetorical perspective.

Oscar Gakuo Mwangi is a Senior Lecturer in the Department of Political and Administrative Studies at the National University of Lesotho. He obtained his BA and MA degrees in Political Science from the University of Nairobi and Ph.D. in Politics from Rhodes University. He has written several book chapters in the area of comparative politics, and several articles in journals such as *African Security Review, Journal of Southern African Studies, Politics, Religion & Ideology, The Journal of Modern African Studies, The Round Table: The Commonwealth Journal of International Affairs,* and *Review of African Political Economy*. His research interests focus on democratisation, governance, conflict, and environmental politics in Eastern and Southern Africa.

Mohanalakshmi Rajakumar has a Ph.D. in Literature from the University of Florida. Her academic books include *Haram in the Harem* (2009, Peter Lang), in which she examines Indian and Algerian writers' subversive use of domestic fiction to critique male privilege. *Hip Hop Dance* (Greenwood, 2012) explores the grassroots development of hip-hop dance and music before it became a commercial phenomenon. Mohana has also been recognized for her fiction: *Love Comes Later* (2012, Createspace) won the 2013 Best Indie Book Award for Romance. Her coming of age novel, *An Unlikely Goddess*, won the SheWrites New Novelist competition in 2011. You can read more about her work on her website: www.mohadoha.com.

Laura Steckman (Ph.D., University of Wisconsin-Madison) is an affiliate with the Center for Southeast Asian Studies at the University of Wisconsin-Madison. Her current research examines issues surrounding ethnicity and identity, particularly the historical and contemporary processes that lead to ethnogenesis in Southeast Asian ethnic groups.

Joy Williams-Black is the Associate Director of the Center for Black Studies at Northern Illinois University where she teaches courses in the Black Studies Minor. As a graduate student, she received a Fulbright award to complete dissertation fieldwork in Kenya and England. She earned her Ph.D. in History at the University of Illinois at Urbana-Champaign. Her research interests include African colonial history, African American social history, and women and gender history.